traditions AND visions

EDITORS
Julius M. Gribou, AIA
Robert G. Hanley, AIA
Thomas E. Robey, AIA

WRITERS OF ARCHITECTURAL TEXT
Lewis F. Fisher
Maria Watson Pfeiffer

PHOTOGRAPHY
Craig D. Blackmon, FAIA
Unless otherwise noted

MAPS
Blue Marble Maps LLC

GRAPHIC DESIGN AND ART DIRECTION
Coral Diaz

PRODUCTION AND DESIGN SUPPORT
StudioAkimbo:
Noelle Artigue
Cynthia Greenwood

STYLE EDITOR
Sarah Nawrocki

Library of Congress Catalog Number
2007923954

ISBN 978-1-4243-3424-7

11 10 09 08 07 5 4 3 2 1

WITH THE KIND SUPPORT OF

AIA San Antonio is grateful for the support of local professionals and businesses, whose generosity made this book possible.

Title Sponsor
H-E-B

Publication Sponsor
The American Institute of Architects

Section Sponsors
San Antonio Conservation Society [Central Section]
Lionforce Building Systems [South Section]
Daniel J. Sullivan Family Foundation [North Central Section]

Firm Sponsors
Benefactor
Sprinkle Robey Architects
Rehler Vaughn & Koone

Patrons
Alamo Architects
Beaty Palmer Architects
Ford Powell & Carson Architects & Planners
Insite Architects
John Grable Architect
Kell Muñoz Architects
Lake | Flato Architects
Madeline Anz Slay Architecture
Marmon Mok
Overland Partners
Pfluger Associates Architects

Contributors
Durand-Hollis Rupe Architects
Michael G. Imber Architect
Thorn + Graves Architects

Essay Sponsors
San Antonio Chapter of the AGC
The Builder's Exchange of Texas, Inc.
Galo Properties
Texas Masonry Council

As the guiding force behind this effort, AIA San Antonio's Guidebook Editors-Julius M. Gribou, AIA, Robert G. Hanley, AIA, and Thom E. Robey, AIA - have shown unending endurance in selecting projects and images, and then collecting and managing the information contained herein. It was a huge task, and we are incredibly appreciative.

We are also thankful for the professionals who provided considerable expertise in the unfamiliar territory of book publishing. Lewis F. Fisher and Maria Watson Pfeiffer developed a lively and coherent text from an uneven crop of project notes. Coral Diaz of Palo Design provided a visually distinctive graphic design for the book. The photographic talents of Craig Blackmon, FAIA add greatly to the visual presentation. And finally, the sector maps created by Baker Vail of Blue Marble Maps will enhance the book's usability immeasurably.

As with all chapter endeavors, AIA San Antonio staff provided significant leadership. We are grateful to Torrey Stanley Carleton, Hon. AIA, for her effective fundraising, and to Donna M. Rosenberg for her organizational and administrative skills.

For leading the early research efforts we thank sector chairs Suzan O'Connor, AIA (Central), Jeffery Fetzer, AIA (East), Darryl Ohlenbusch, AIA (South), Mike McGlone, AIA (West), Jonathon Card, AIA (North Central), Steve Kline (North), and BobWise, AIA (Beyond San Antonio).

Information and photographs for *Culture* and *Beyond San Antonio* were developed by a cadre of volunteers, organized by Guy Burnett, AIA; and including R. L. Cage; Alice Huston; Carr Hornbuckle, AIA; Charles John, AIA; Doug Lipscomb, AIA; Richard Mogas AIA; Georgia Moore; Kyle Odnes; Roy Pachecano; Roman Puentes; Cheryl Ragan; D.F. Russell; Ignacio Salas-Humara, AIA; Rebecca Schenker, AIA; Charles Schubert, AIA; Chris Schultz, AIA; Joe Stubblefield, AIA; Steven Thomas, AIA; and Maureen Tschirhart.

Among the many persons who helped gather information, the AIA San Antonio is particularly grateful to Beth Dodd and Nancy Sparrow at the Alexander Architectural Archives at the University of Texas at Austin, Gregory Smith at the Texas Historical Commission, Salvador Duenas at the San Antonio Independent School District, Julius Gordon at the Alamo Community College District, Antoinette Garza at Our Lady of the Lake University, Susie Salazar and Stacy Lunsford at St. Mary's University, and to Boone Powell, FAIA; Chester Slimp; Charles Hanus; Milton Babbit, AIA; John Crowley; and Killis Almond, FAIA.

The AIA San Antonio is grateful for the assistance and support provided by Erin Starry-Alsup, Matt Balsman; Ana Bolmeier; Ric Brendler, AIA; Philip Bryce; Matt Carrell; Cheryl Cole; Albert Condarco; Enrique Cortazor; Jorge Luis Cruz; Brett Davidson; Martha Durke; Dana Elder; Karen Eldridge; Sara Flowers; W. Eugene George, FAIA; Mary Carolyn Hollers George; Beto Gonzales; Kathleen Gribou; Morgan Hanley; Carisa Helton; Brantley Hightower; Lawrence Hohlaus; Randy Hohlaus, AIA; John Kell, Jr., AIA; Donna Lim Knickerbocker; Travis Lucy; Benjamin Lynn; Ben Marcotte; Alicia Marquez; Sam McGlone; Geoff Mysorski,; Debbie Ortega; Roy Pachecano; Sue Ann Pemberton-Haugh, AIA; Adela Popp; Roman Puentes; Austin Robey; Robin Robey; Amy Robles; Jeffery Rodriguez; Martin C. Rodriguez; Conor Samuels; Roy Schweers; Sally Smith; Steven Thomas, AIA; Joan Williams; Nina Wilson; and Ann Wisian.

AIA San Antonio is indebted to the diverse cultures and talents of all our inhabitants, past and present, for having contributed to our lively, varied, and architecturally rich city.

FOREWORD
BY BOONE POWELL, FAIA

Welcome to San Antonio. It's been 21 years since we hosted the annual meeting of the American Institute of Architects, and this year's convention once again provides us with the opportunity to take a snap-shot of our City's physical attributes. We are privileged to contribute to the tradition of the Guide Book which, along with those of other American cities in this series, forms a powerful record of American urbanism.

In the years since 1986 much has changed, but perhaps more importantly, much of the underlying strength of San Antonio has remained the same. The City has grown to become the 7th largest in the country with a metropolitan population of 1.8 million people. Still, the scale and sense of history make San Antonio seem a much smaller, friendlier, and intimate place where visitors feel comfortable and experience as unique.

The City's roots go back nearly 290 years to its founding as the site of Misión San Antonio de Valero and the Villa de San Antonio. Over the years it has been a mixing bowl of many ethnicities – described by poets and writers in the past as "cosmopolitan," and by others as a polyglot of humanity. The Spanish and Indians of the early years were joined by the backwash of individual European groups who came in the 19th Century to settle the surrounding areas as farmers and small town folk. Nearby towns such as Castroville, Fredericksburg, and Panna Maria still lie close to their original Alsatian, German, and Polish roots.

San Antonio is a meeting place in other important and most interesting ways. Its climate vacillates between wintry and tropical, arid and wet. The resulting environment creates conditions which permit a high proportion of those plant species which will grow in the contiguous United States to thrive here. Similarly, San Antonio is arguably the meeting point of the Latino Culture with that of the Anglo and of the old, mythic South with the legendary West. This represents a complex but not necessarily insurmountable challenge for our Regionalist Architects.

Today, San Antonio is undergoing historically-unprecedented growth, not just in numbers, but in the quality and creativity of what we are designing, producing and preserving. Invigorated by aggressive young architects of a mostly regionalist persuasion, the local architectural scene is vigorous, and increasingly recognized for its excellence and influence at local and national levels.

The City has recently embarked on a campaign to enhance its parks and open-space system. One important focus is the River. The downtown River Walk, our Paseo Del Rio, has inspired projects that are extending the beautification of the River upstream and downstream to form a linear park system through the entire City.

Finally, this publication is not just meant as a guide for Architects, but for all those who are interested in cities and architecture. May it prove helpful to San Antonians and visitors alike until we meet again here on the banks of the River!

Design award winning buildings are noted with a symbol

▲ AIASA

★ TSA

◉ AIA National winners

NR Structures listed in the National Register

MI CASA ES SU CASA

When the opportunity to publish a revised guidebook to San Antonio architecture arose in preparation of hosting the AIA 2007 Convention, we faced a number of important decisions. What objectives should a guidebook have? What type of content would best achieve those objectives? What format would be most supportive? And what title would best reflect the nature of architecture in our city? With San Antonio's rich and diverse history, visible in its built legacy, and the current trend-setting work of local architects, "Traditions and Visions" was clearly the appropriate choice.

Our primary objective has been to present a comprehensive overview of the area's significant architecture and distinctive places. It is intended as an educational tool for visitor and citizen alike. To do so effectively, we developed criteria to enable us to distill the breadth of architectural creativity in and around San Antonio. Projects exemplifying cultural, historical or technological significance, or those receiving recognition for design excellence from The American Institute of Architects, Texas Society of Architects, or the AIA San Antonio Chapter have been included. However, we've also chosen to provide a sampling of our cultural traditions and their institutions, memorable eateries, unique San Antonio establishments, and topical guest essays to provide a more complete vision of the place we call home.

This book covers all areas of San Antonio, divided into six manageable geographic sectors. In addition, the city's outlying areas, all accessible within roughly an hour's drive, are described in the Beyond San Antonio sector, itself partitioned into regional subsections.

The user is encouraged to use the book's resources to explore all sections of our city. There are some introductory comments and an overall location map to provide basic orientation. Each sector contains more detailed maps, keyed to the individual project listings. Each listing identifies the building or place name, address, date of completion, name of architect/designer (if known), a brief description, and a photograph, with a few minor exceptions. The cultural section, which follows the building list in each sector, provides a sampling of that area's cultural traditions, including many visual and culinary treats and surprises.

We suggest that the user start with a walking tour of the Central City; most areas lend themselves to easy strolls through visually stimulating and enchanting districts in and around downtown. From there, driving tours will open the treasures of the North, North Central, East, South, and West sectors. Even though a building is listed, it may not be accessible to the public; consequently, visitors should use caution and be respectful of private property. Beyond the city, explore the charm of the Hill Country or the open Texas landscape, dotted with historical towns and spectacular courthouses, and yes, more delectable food and unique shopping. Perhaps a search for the best BBQ should be added to your architectural treasure hunt.

We hope that this guidebook gives every visitor and citizen an introduction to the history and beauty of this truly unique region of Texas, and leaves them with a desire to explore each area more fully. We are proud of our place, with its rich and diverse heritage, and are pleased to share it with you. Mi casa es su casa.

Julius M. Gribou, AIA
Robert G. Hanley, AIA
Thom E. Robey, AIA

TRADITIONS AND VISIONS

OVERVIEW
BY LEWIS F. FISHER

From its beginnings, San Antonio was a place apart. First a waystation on the empty Spanish frontier between the Rio Grande and East Texas, the outpost evolved into a transportation hub for wagon trains trading with Mexico and supplying frontier forts.

San Antonio was the last major American town connected by a railroad. When rail service began in 1877, access to the rest of the nation was cut from days by lurching stagecoach or wagons from the Texas coast to hours by train. After a century and a half of relative isolation, San Antonio's appearance and customs were rather eccentric, and outsiders were drawn by curiosity. A Houston newspaper reported that many early travelers arriving by rail "came on pleasure only for a day to peep at the old town, and then go away to tell how queer it looked."

During the city's first fifty years of easy access to the world and its goods, its population increased tenfold, to more than 230,000 by 1930. For most of that time San Antonio was the largest city in the largest state. Yet its economy remained service-based, with little manufacturing and few of the fortunes that advanced the amenities and opportunities in cities elsewhere. A general ambience of fiesta and siesta was finally jolted by HemisFair '68, the world's fair that re-energized the city's business outlook and politics. Another major turning point was the opening of a Toyota manufacturing plant in 2006.

As San Antonio's population approached 1.4 million, the old town that attracted the first hordes of tourists was, by necessity, no more. Yet neither was it completely obliterated. As the city finally awoke from its Depression-era slumber, remaining landmarks were recognized as historic. Preservationists built on the halting efforts of those who had gone before and assured the possibility of viewing the mix of historic remains in downtown San Antonio through the prism of eras dating from the first Spaniards, who located the city as part of the fallout of feuding European empires.

In the seventeenth century, the Spanish crown was unable to attract settlers to the far northern vastness of its American colonial empire. Between Spain's vital silver mines in northern Mexico and the land-hungry French looming to the northeast in Louisiana lay only an empty, undefended frontier.

If Europeans themselves would not come, the grand solution was to turn native Americans into Europeans. The tribes would then be settled in new communities that would in turn attract settlers from Spain. The Texas frontier—and the silver mines—would be secure.

The work started in the 1690s directly on the Louisiana frontier, where Roman Catholic missions were built to begin the religious and cultural transformation of native tribes. They foundered. Not only did the French stir up trouble among the Indians, Spanish supply lines had to stretch across nearly six hundred inhospitable miles to the nearest Spanish settlements, along the Rio Grande.

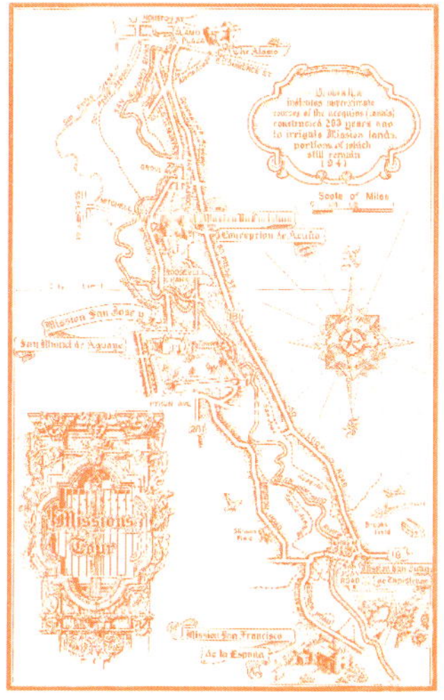

In 1691 a place named San Antonio de Padua had been identified a third of the way from the Rio Grande. There were open grasslands and a small river fed by major springs, a logical location for a much-needed waystation. In May 1718 a handful of soldiers and priests came up to establish a presidio and a mission in this spot.

The mission of San Antonio de Valero, known in its third location as the Alamo, was joined two years later by the Mission San José y San Miguel de Aguayo, likewise with an influential granddee's name astutely appended to that of a saint. In 1731 came three more missions, refugees from the still-hazardous Louisiana frontier and best known as Concepción, San Juan, and Espada. In five years a few dozen immigrants enticed from the Canary Islands qualified San Antonio's civilian community for the exalted status of villa.

So was the makeup of San Antonio shaped for the next century. Soldiers, civilians and priests endured an often fractious relationship over turf and the scarce resource of water. Cut off from the nearest city—New Orleans—by political rivalry and from larger communities in northern Mexico by distance, San Antonians struggled to survive on what they had. In the 1760s a visiting priest found San Antonio to be merely "fifty-nine houses of stone and mud and seventy-nine of wood, but all poorly built, without any preconceived plan, so that the whole resembles more a poor village than a villa."

Nevertheless, San Antonio grew into a community of 2,000 persons—the most important settlement in Texas, for there was little competition. In 1772 San Antonio was made the Spanish provincial capital.

Soon, however, the town was swept up in the ongoing political instability that caused its parent government to change five times in the next hundred years. Mexico won its independence from Spain, partly through battles fought near San Antonio, in 1820. Then came the Texas War of Independence from Mexico, with the Battle of the Alamo in 1836 and the Republic of Texas a reality a short time later. San Antonio was not free of military incursions from the south until the Mexican War settled the question in 1848 of the annexation of Texas to the United States. Then there was the matter of the secession of Texas from the United States and its reunion in 1865.

San Antonio had a dramatic revival from the largely deserted town of 800 souls at the end of the Mexican War. Europe was in turmoil, and San Antonio was getting a good share of the refugees. By the 1850s, German was the dominant language, followed by English and Spanish, with some strong doses of Czech, French, Italian and a few other tongues thrown in. Frederick Law Olmsted, traveling through in those years, found "a jumble of races, costumes, languages and buildings." Another was struck by "a condition widely different from what you are accustomed to behold in any American town—narrow streets, stout old walls which seem determined not to crumble away, dark, banditti-like figures that gaze at you from the low doorways."

Once stability returned with the end of the Civil War and the U.S. Army returned to protect the frontier from marauding Indians, a ranching industry took hold in the hinterlands. San Antonio became its trade center for South Texas. Ox-drawn wagon trains trundled down narrow Commerce Street to exchange goods on Military Plaza. Saddle makers and bootsmiths set up shop, saloons proliferated, and a red-light district sprang up west of San Pedro Creek. The likes of Wyatt Earp, Bat Masterson, and Butch Cassidy passed through town.

Rail transportation made it economical to bring in iron for bridges, steel for taller buildings, plate glass for store windows and all manner of consumer goods. The booming city outgrew a patched-up system of Spanish acequias, and modern water and sewer systems were built with underground pipes and indoor plumbing. Downtown streets were widened for automobile traffic. A streetcar system helped San Antonio spread outward in every direction.

Meanwhile, the expanded Fort Sam Houston became the largest post in the U.S. Army in the face of instability south of the border, which was also bringing fundamental changes in the city's ethnic makeup. As several hundred thousand Mexican refugees streamed into San Antonio, Fort Sam Houston supplied Gen. John J. Pershing's expedition into Mexico in search of Pancho Villa. More military bases opened, taking advantage of the region's sunny climate, so conducive to ground and flight training.

A skyscraper-building rage in the 1920s ended abruptly with the Depression. Sapped of enthusiasm, San Antonio's economy was dominated only by the five military bases until business leaders got hold of themselves and rejuvenated things with HemisFair '68, the 1968 world's fair that qualified its downtown site for urban renewal and construction of a modern convention center. The fair's Tower of the Americas became a new symbol for the city. The River Walk came to life, tourism boomed, and a shift in political control from the old guard brought political, social, and economic change that also upgraded the status of minority groups.

When Kelly Air Force Base, the city's largest employer, closed in the 1990s, San Antonio's economy was already on its way to diversity. The ever-expanding Convention Center fueled construction of ever-larger hotels. The South Texas Medical Center grew into a major complex northwest of downtown. Southwestern Bell moved its corporate headquarters to San Antonio and turned into AT&T. Toyota built its first manufacturing plant in Texas in southern San Antonio. The San Antonio Spurs, three-time National Basketball Association champions, added another dimension of excitement.

San Antonio, however, seems certain to stand apart from convention, manufacturing, and corporate headquarters cities elsewhere. Nowhere else does a River Walk have the level of visitors—five million a year—yet curl so unobtrusively through a downtown. No other city in the nation has as large a cluster of Spanish missions, four of them preserved in San Antonio Missions National Historical Park. The fifth mission, the Alamo, remains a unique monument to human courage.

Clad in the colors of Spain and Mexico, planted where the foothills of the Hill Country meet the Texas coastal plain and the fringes of the Chihuahuan Desert, where residents can enjoy Tejano music in a neighborhood bar or shop at a Neiman Marcus, San Antonio is both laid back and moving fast-forward, a city of fiestas quite at home in the modern world.

Howard Peak is a former Mayor of San Antonio and an urban planner.

ON CONSERVATION
BY HOWARD PEAK

San Antonio has long been blessed with many wonderful assets, some natural and others created by man over time. The natural features have sometimes been a challenge for us in that we have been slow to recognize their associated opportunities and, even then, to capitalize fully on them. The San Antonio River is one such example - an essential reason for our very existence here - yet it has taken many years both to appreciate fully all that it offers and act upon it.

Other examples can be found in our secondary waterways, the numerous creeks which traverse the City. The major creeks, Leon, Olmos, and Salado, run from the northern edges of San Antonio, through the city, and on beyond our southern City limits. Unfortunately, they're usually known for some kind of problem - flooding, trash and debris - and for a variety of illegal activities. Yet they are also places of historical significance and, still today, natural beauty.

Other cities across the country and around the world have long seen the value of these features and have taken the steps necessary to make the most of them by way of parks and recreation areas, often as part of a trail system accommodating hiking, biking, and more. Examples include Denver; Scottsdale; Columbia, MD; and the Town Lake trails in Austin.

San Antonio's best example of a linear park, and it's a great one, is the San Antonio River. And what a resource it has been for this area, from its utility as a source of water to its position today as an economic generator and statement for our city. While the downtown River Walk is more intensively developed than typically associated with linear parks, the principle is the same: capitalizing on a waterway (or, in some instances including the River extension into Rivercenter Mall and the Convention Center, creating one) to develop trails, parks, residences, offices, and other uses to encourage activity and create value. In fact, work to expand the success of the River in San Antonio continues today as the City, the County, and the San Antonio River Authority have combined efforts to construct improvements appropriate to the location north and south of downtown.

To help create a mental picture of what a system of linear parks would look like, think of a map of the City with the San Antonio River and Olmos Creek through the center, and Leon and Salado Creeks flowing down the west and east sides into the Medina and San Antonio Rivers respectively. Along the way are pockets of existing parks, including a few new opportunities, that can now be connected to allow people to move from park to park, neighborhood to neighborhood, and many such combinations. Taken a step further, create a system of sidewalks and bike lanes along east/west streets and we'd have a nice crisscross network which would more easily and safely facilitate, and encourage, travel throughout the city. Mobility would be improved, as would our health. In addition to the major creeks mentioned, there are many other smaller creeks and tributaries to which the linear parks concept can be applied.

Though behind other cities, San Antonio is gradually becoming more aware of the opportunities associated with our creeks and has begun a process to utilize them more fully and appropriately. The City Council adopted a Creeks Based Linear Parks Plan in the Spring of 2001 and began to identify projects and funding sources. Money was specifically identified for linear parks in the 1998 and 2003 City bond elections as well as the Proposition 3 sales tax referendum in 2000. State and federal funding has also been utilized to total some $30M to date. In addition to the plan already mentioned, along with design guidelines, most of the City's efforts to date have focused on identifying and purchasing properties, with an impressive network either already purchased or in process at this time. The result is the beginnings of a network of linear sections along Leon and Salado Creeks with more to come shortly. In addition, the Council recently established the Linear Creekways Parks Advisory Board, a citizens group that will advise the Council and staff on linear creek related programs throughout the city.

In terms of actually seeing something on the ground, a hike and bike trails project along Salado Creek is now under design, with construction anticipated to be completed in '07. This will be a substantial project running from Fort Sam Houston south to Comanche Park. A future project taking the trails south into Southside Lions Park would make an impressive impact on east and southeast San Antonio. Picture a greenway connecting a new park below Fort Sam to the County's Pletz Park, to Comanche and on to Southside Lions, with other amenities and neighborhoods in between. That's what the creeks-based linear parks concept is all about!

Obviously, this is a major undertaking, not to mention time consuming, and will require many years to realize fully. And, it's expensive too, including land, planning, design, and construction costs, with money especially tight these days. It's also been difficult to get some people to think beyond their narrow view of our creeks today, especially people who are threatened by flooding, crime, and other problems associated with them. Yet, one of the numerous attractions of the linear parks concept is that they usually solve several problems at once and, therefore, are a cost effective measure that, on top of the savings, create values defined several ways once completed.

In conclusion, our urban waterways, often thought of as problems, are in truth opportunities waiting to be developed properly. As with many such efforts, the concept requires vision and a commitment to follow through. Education is an important component so that the citizenry at large will understand the concept and support it. Architects can play a major role in this effort.

W. Eugene George, FAIA is a historic preservation expert who has authored a number of books and taught at various academic institutions.

SOUTH TEXAS AND MEXICO
BY W. EUGENE GEORGE, FAIA

That San Antonio defines the border with Mexico is an oft-stated observation. While the Rio Grande River which forms the boundary between Texas and Mexico from El Paso to the Gulf of Mexico is understood on maps and at border check-points as the firm demarcation between the United States and Mexico, this thin life-giving resource has served to unify its residents as one culture. The river exists as one clearly defined geographic entity, unifying rather than dividing, a common central stream toward which life has focused for millennia.

GEOGRAPHIC AND GEOLOGIC DIVERSITY: The South Texas Plains is an area covered with alluvial materials carried out from the erosion of the Edwards Plateau adjacent to the Balcones Escarpment. It may be separated from the rest of the state by a line drawn from Del Rio eastward to about San Antonio then sweeping southeastward to the Gulf of Mexico. The fault-line fields at this juncture of the South Texas Plains are important for the production and reserves of oil and natural gas. Between the Nueces River and the Rio Grande is a sub-humid to dry region known as the Brasada—a little red-hot coal. When an old-timer was asked whether he would prefer to live in the Brasada or hell, he replied that he would chose hell and rent out Texas.

In far South Texas, an agricultural region known as the Winter Garden is noted for its year-round production of vegetables by irrigation utilizing artesian wells and dams. Citrus fruit growing in Texas is centered in the Lower Rio Grande Valley where, beginning in the 1940s, the mild climate brought ever-increasing numbers of vacationers fleeing northern climes—"snowbirds" who make their winter homes in the environs of McAllen and Brownsville. Today, the World Birding Center near Mission at the tip of Texas is regarded as one of the richest birding areas north of the Mexican border, with birds found nowhere else in the United States but deepest Texas.

Traversing the Padre Island National Seashore along the Gulf Coast onward to Port Aransas, Rockport and Fulton are miles of public beaches which draw droves of sun worshippers and fishermen. The Gulf also forms a funnel for hurricane-force winds up to 175 miles an hour—the largest and most destructive storms affecting the Texas coast from June through October. With questionable wisdom, "palatial Mediterranean-style homes in gated seaside communities" are being built here. More about birds, the Aransas National Wildlife Refuge near Rockport is on the Central Flyway which extends from Alaska southward and is the wintering ground for the rare Whooping Cranes and 320 species of other birds.

Nineteenth century travelers and naturalists who came to Texas and recorded their impressions included John James Audubon who, with his son, made an expedition in 1837 along the Texas Coast documenting birds and animals for his Birds of America (1830 onward). Father and son returned to Texas a few years later, sailing to the mouth of the Rio Grande then heading overland collecting material for their Quadrupeds of North America (1845+). Frederick Law Olmstead described the coastal prairie towns and his travels into northern Mexico in A Journey Through Texas (1857).

HISTORIC DIVERSITY: The history of South Texas, which fills hundred of volumes, is nothing if not contentious. It was all about struggles for dominance between France and Spain—then Mexico after achieving independence from Spain in 1821—the years when Texas was a republic (1836-46) followed by the annexation of Texas by the U.S.—wars, border disputes, hostile Indians, bandidos, cattle rustling, pirates and smugglers.

Certainly the dilemmas that confronted the Catholic missionaries in their efforts to introduce Christianity and civilization to indigenous populations were epic. As ranching is one of the characteristic South Texas enterprises, it should be noted that the ranching tradition began in eighteenth century in the missions of the Spanish Colonial period. Livestock raising and exporting, the main industry of the missions, laid the foundations for such famous ranches as the King Ranch which began in 1852 with the purchase of a Spanish land grant and spans four counties with foreign outposts.

Today, precious survivals of historic and ethnic diversity are threatened. Moving southward just 25 miles from San Antonio, the Alsatian village of Castroville on the Medina River, founded in 1842, is a national and state historic district extensively documented by the Historic American Buildings Survey. But Castroville is in the path of the fast developing edge of a metropolis. What is to save it from the blight of speculative subdivisions? Panna Maria, the oldest permanent Polish settlement in America, founded in 1854, is at a safer distance 55 miles southeast of San Antonio.

In terms of ethnicity, survivals from the Spanish Colonial epoch are more numerous. Goliad, on the San Antonio River, was established in 1749 and is one of the oldest Spanish Colonial municipalities in the state. The Goliad Massacre of 1836 during the Texas War for Independence is remembered along with the Alamo. The Spanish effort to keep possession of the territory north of the Rio Grande led the royal government in 1749 to authorize José de Escandón's expedition to evaluate ways to halt French and even fears of English encroachment. The French explorer, Sieur de LaSalle , had landed colonists at Matagorda Bay on the Texas coast in 1685 and built Fort St. Louis by Garcitas Creek. His effort failed but sparked a renewal of Spanish exploration in the entire Gulf region.

Escandón founded the Province of Nuevo Santander comprising the present state of Tamaulipas and part of trans-Nueces Texas including the towns of Camargo,

Reynosa, Mier and Revilla south of the river. It was the last part of north eastern Mexico to be conquered and effectively occupied. Laredo north of the river was also founded by Escandón. The earliest mention of attempts to navigate the Rio Grande go back before 1795. The most distant place inland reached by commercial river boats was the town of Roma which is famed for its classically-inspired brick buildings built by the German-born Heinrich Portscheller in the late nineteenth century.

Finally, Texas tall tales fill scores of volumes —but one must suffice. In 1836, anticipating that Mexican troops might land on the Texas seaboard, a mounted ranger group was dispatched to patrol the coast. When suspicious vessels loaded with provisions for the Mexican army arrived in Copano Bay, the mounted troops employed decoy signals and captured the three schooners. These heroes live in fame as the Horse Marines. In spite of the seeming austerity of the landscape, South Texas has more than enough interesting facets to inspire the investigations of many lifetimes.

Vincent B. Canizaro, Ph.D. is an assistant professor at the University of Texas at San Antonio College of Architecture.

RECENT VOICES: "SAN ANTONIO'S REGIONAL TRADITION OF LIBERATION" BY VINCENT B. CANIZARO, Ph.D.

"Regionalism of Liberation. This is the manifestation of a region that is especially in tune with the emerging thought of the time. We call such a manifestation 'regional' only because it has not yet emerged elsewhere."

- Harwell Hamilton Harris

"A region is marked by what is immediate and tangible. Dealing with it frees one's mind from a mass of abstractions, generalities and unrealities. There, one finds himself thinking unique thoughts. They are unique because the forces he deals with are unique. Also, everything there is smaller than in the world outside; and the pattern is simpler there. So one dares to experiment and manipulate. If the result has significance for the world outside, it will be accepted outside. What the world could not conceive it now adopts, making it a part of itself. In time, the product will shed both the region's name and the characteristics peculiar to the region. Thus does a region outdo itself."

- Harwell Hamilton Harris

A guide, such as the one in your hands, has two goals. It seeks to document, not only the architecture of San Antonio, but also the work of San Antonio architects. In other places such a distinction would be less meaningful than it is here. For over the years these two have been uneasy bedfellows as the economy of the city has lagged behind our sister cities in the state. While San Antonio can claim to have some of the brightest architectural talent in Texas, much of their work has traditionally been constructed in places of greater prosperity such as Austin, Houston, or Dallas/Ft. Worth. In spite of and partly because of its marginal position, San Antonio has served as a distinctly fertile place for architects. As a locale somewhat remote from the rest of the state, with a rich architectural heritage, and anemic economy, architects have often found here a unique environment that has fostered pragmatism, conservation, and a respect for tradition *that virtually requires innovation.*

Further, San Antonio, the city and its architects, exhibits what Steven Fox aptly described as an "insistent notion of regionalism " and what H.H. Harris referred to as a "regionalism of liberation." There is no consistent style or even set of issues that concerns our architects, but a shared ethos – an ethos that should be seen as the legacy of O'Neil Ford. Through the mentoring of David R. Williams, Ford's mid-century appreciation and appropriation of regional building traditions led to an appreciation of local craft, traditions of building, climatic-sensitivity, and the honest expression of materials. This led to his much celebrated experimentation with materials and structure, local and global, that influenced much of his own and regional architecture in and around San Antonio. Writ through a tectonically-modern idiom, Ford established the possibility that regionally-inspired and respectful architecture need not look like architecture of the past, setting the stage for the future. He embodied what has become central to architectural practice in San Antonio that would be an enigma elsewhere – an architect sensitively engaged in the preservation of the past while also an avidly experimenting into the future. Relying on the legacy of the talented and eclectic Atlee B. Ayres and Alfred Giles, out-of-staters like Cyrus Eidlitz, and colleagues such as L. Brooks Martin, and Arch Swank, for whom San Antonio's out-of-the-way-ness was a crucible, Ford cemented a tradition of experimentation, inventiveness, and innovation in a place with a great degree of presence and history.

And it is partly due to this kind of appreciation that San Antonio still has much of its historic architecture. Besides the ever-present emotive power of our missions and buildings from the 18th and 19th Century, much of the past continues to frame the future. From remnants of our celebrated "ditches" or acequias and street plans based in the Laws of the Indies we have the relatively permanent and unique street layout of the downtown. And from Robert Hugman's visionary reclamation of the San Antonio River as a pedestrian way we have the seeds of city centered around the outdoors and in concert with the natural landscape. And from our sluggish economy we have not yet had to suffer the pains of development suffered by more prosperous locales, which have little of their built heritage left to worry over its preservation. San Antonio is a place where tradition is never dated. Where tradition is understood as context and where the root word of tradition, "tradere" which means to carry forward, is observed in a generative and non-restrictive fashion. That which is traditional is that which we carry forward, some of which is admittedly baggage, but hopefully the baggage that carries the necessities such a toothbrush and razor, and the nice clothes that give us cause to celebrate who and where we are. Such work is demonstrated through respect for the specific context of adjacent buildings and neighborhoods and for an awareness of the lessons these buildings, built before the placeless enablement of A/C. Here there is a lack of fear of holding on to excellent examples of our past creativity. "Proceed and be bold," the late Samuel Mockbee once said.

And yet, we must be cautious. As we prosper the opportunity to experience the talents of our own local architects increases, but so do the negative pressures of development. We have recently lost significant architectural places: Harding Black's self-built pottery studio, La Gloria, and Trinity University's Northrup Hall are the most prominent – evidence that our growth is pressuring architecture and our sense of place in an unprecedented way. In terms of the environment or the quality of life for all residents of the city we also still have a ways to go. Continued sprawl to our ecologically sensitive north, persistent poverty, substandard housing, constant attempts to weaken civic and tree-preservation ordinances, and the continued presence of drainage ditches and potholes rather than linear parks and bikeways are evidence of a city out of balance. Yet, there are some very bright spots amid this chaos in the form of park improvements, increased downtown re-inhabitation, a vibrant arts scene, excellent individual architectural projects, and a stronger society of conservation.

All of these, I hope are sustainable future trends. Revitalizing all of San Antonio's waterways, making the streets safer for pedestrians, and cyclists, and an economy that employs its own in the beautification of its own places are issues worth fighting for and architects have no reason not to be at the forefront of such efforts.

So in thinking about the future in terms of San Antonio's ever-present past my best hope is for the tradition of experimentation, inventiveness, and innovation to continue. It is a hope that lies in the hands of an emerging generation of architects who have demonstrated respect for this tradition such as Darryl Ohlenbusch and Candid Rogers. In an earlier incarnation of this guide (1986), the editors referred to "an exuberant new school of local architecture, one that sums up in uninhibited ways the qualities peculiar to its place." This was a lesson taken to heart by those architects who have become the established and influential practices within the city, state, and the nation. Lake/Flato's national AIA award is not only an affirmation of the talent of their own designers, but also of the approach and sensitivity of all our architects.

But what form the work of the future may take is something of an open question that need not be. A long look at San Antonio architecture reveals a tradition of buildings and strategies that are responsive to the region. Something residents here have had to do in the past and now must choose to do is make peace with the environment that sustains them. In the late 19th Century, architects responded to this concern pragmatically and stylistically. New York architect Cyrus Eidlitz's First National Bank was passively-cooled as were all buildings prior to mechanical ventilation. But as a response to culture, his bank was detailed in Moorish-Syrian motifs in reference to the architecture of a place of equally harsh climatic conditions as those of southwest Texas. It was a meaningful kind of regional analogy tied to the hot humid experiential reality we, sans air conditioning, still experience today. And although it may seem quaint or out-dated to us today, such references seem to me far more locally relevant than bold formalist expressions clad in titanium. By mid-century local responses to place were more studied, scientific, and mature. The deep overhangs and careful siting of O'Neil Ford's work at Trinity University and Milton Ryan's houses updated climatic response in a modern idiom and helped people cope with the reality of their city. Recently, however, San Antonio has lagged behind other cities in the application of sustainable principles, which are best understood as means of connecting us, experientially, climatically, and ecologically, to the place in which we live. Our architects know this and have demonstrated their abilities in other cities such as Houston and Bozeman,

Montana. But such work is an infrastructural concern that requires grass-roots and governmental leadership for implementation, and the active interest of our clients. Nevertheless, architects, who wish to carry forward Ford's unstated challenge for a sensitive and progressive architecture, should see sustainability as key to continuing tradition of experimentation, inventiveness, and innovation for which San Antonio architecture and architects have become well-known. As we grow, San Antonians can hope to be the beneficiaries of the local sensitivity and abilities of our own architects.

So I offer these thoughts in closing with regard to the architects if San Antonio. It is my hope that their work: foster connectedness to place and be a response to the need to live locally. Not in spite of global concerns and possibilities, but in order to better take advantage of them. And as such, the promise of regional architecture in San Antonio, is the promise of re-embedding ourselves within the reality and diversity of our local places – critically and comfortably. San Antonio architecture has the possibility, through thoughtful reference, to situate us within the continuity of our individual and shared human history for which style matters, but must be taken seriously. Further, there is no reason why our work should not be understood as a progressive and high performance architecture. One that is highly attuned to the constancy and change of the local environment and which opens up possibilities for understanding where and with whom one lives. It should allow awareness of local climate and the changing of seasons, Lastly it should open up the possibility of shared purpose, in which the concerns of here are understood as linked to there: ecologically, economically, and socially.

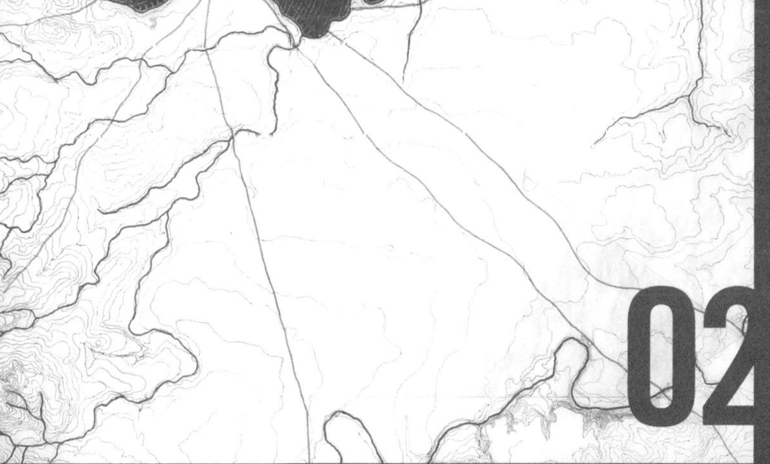

02

WITH THE KIND SUPPORT OF

CENTRAL CITY, SINCE 1720s

A few years after being set up near San Pedro Springs in 1718, San Antonio was moved two miles south to the present center of downtown. The level site was well watered by two streams—San Pedro Creek on the west and the San Antonio River on the east—and by a growing system of acequias, irrigation ditches of the type engineered in Moorish Spain and maintained in San Antonio for nearly two centuries.

According to the sixteenth-century Laws of the Indies governing Spanish town planning in the New World, San Antonio was laid out around central plazas. From them extended a grid of streets narrow enough to escape all but the noontime rays of the scorching summer sun. Much of this plan can still be identified, though it was corrupted as new streets broke from the grid to follow the winding contours of the river and the acequias.

Continuing political instability limited change in San Antonio until Texas joined the United States in 1845. European immigrants swelled the ranks of American settlers, and the town took on a polyglot appearance made more conventional in building styles only when standard construction materials could be easily brought in following arrival of the railroad in 1877. Even then, taller buildings going up in the mode of other places coexisted beside vernacular structures of earlier times. In an early-twentieth-century building boom, however, many older buildings were lost in wholesale street widenings that dealt with the Spanish legacy of narrow streets. New construction, which coincided with the regional popularity of Spanish Colonial Revival architecture, came to a sudden halt with the Depression, and did not resume for forty years.

Once HemisFair '68 re-energized the city, new skyscrapers again began going up. But what remained from four decades before was suddenly considered historic. New preservation laws and tax incentives created an often uneasy partnership between preservationists and developers that has nevertheless succeeded in documenting the passage of time in San Antonio while still allowing for new development. The city is made even more distinctive by the River Walk, a world-renowned two-mile linear park that winds through the heart of downtown.

By the beginning of the twentieth century, San Antonio's overburdened river-fed acequia system had been abandoned for a system of reservoirs and underground pipes drawing from artesian wells, which lowered the water table and caused the river to decline. In 1914 the city completed landscaping of the downtown banks as a park. Seven years later a disastrous flood led to construction of a retaining dam near the head of the river. Several bends were also straightened and floodgates constructed at the ends of both legs of a horseshoe-shaped bend in the center of town. This began a debate on whether the riverbanks should remain a park or, in the newly flood-protected Great Bend, have some level of commercial development as proposed by landscape architect Robert H. H. Hugman, whose plan prevailed. After WPA construction of the basic present-day River Walk in 1939–41, however, use of the River Walk languished. Construction of two river-front hotels for HemisFair in 1968 finally brought the level of pedestrian traffic necessary to support the commercial development Hugman had intended.

Whether commercial development was beginning to overshadow the River Walk's intended mix of small-scale businesses and park-like landscaping became a matter of debate at the beginning of the twenty-first century, even as its overwhelming success was inspiring plans to extend the River Walk several miles to the north nearly to Brackenridge Park and several miles to the south to Mission Espada, in the process linking, with hiking and bicycle trails, the four southern missions of San Antonio Missions National Historical Park.

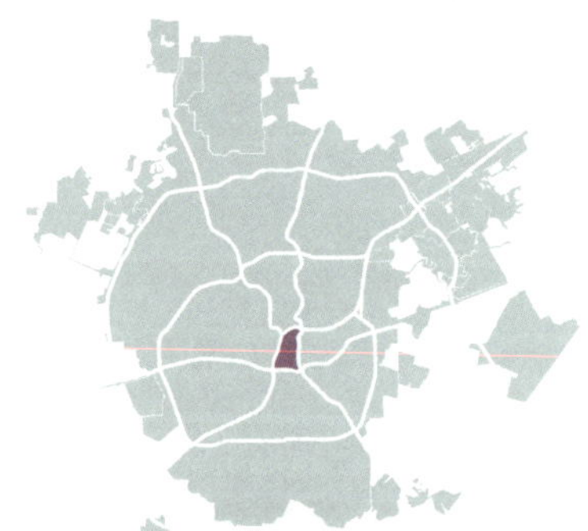

1

1 NR THE ALAMO, 1744
(MISSION SAN ANTONIO DE VALERO)

Once part of a large mission complex established in 1724, the present Alamo church was begun in 1744. Its façade was intended to reflect a common Spanish configuration with twin bell towers, but these were never finished. As heavy limestone walls made the church and its surrounding compound an ideal fortress, after the mission was secularized in 1793 the Alamo was garrisoned by Spanish and then Mexican troops. Texan settlers rebelled against Mexico in 1835 and seized the Alamo, making a heroic but fatal stand here in early 1836. When Texan independence was won later that year, little remained of the church besides its walls and the delicate stone carving of its facade. Nevertheless, the U.S. Army repaired the church and adjoining convento after Texas joined the Union in 1845. The Quartermaster Corps built the now-familiar parapet over the unfinished church's façade in 1849 with a profile designed to disguise its new gabled roof. In 1883 the state purchased the building as a symbol of the battle a half century before. In 1920 Alfred Giles's son E. Palmer Giles designed a reinforced-concrete vaulted roof for the structure similar to the intended original design. The Daughters of the Republic of Texas have served as custodians of the Alamo as a shrine since 1905. Under their care, the grounds have been enlarge, and a museum and library built.

ADDRESS
Alamo Plaza

ARCHITECTS
Antonio Tello and Hieronimo Ybarra, master masons

RENOVATED
1849, 1920
Parapet credited to John Fries

The surrounding park was completed in 1938. Ongoing restoration, cleaning and repointing under the supervision of Ford, Powell & Carson's Carolyn Peterson has revealed some original Spanish-era fresco decorations.

2 NR ALAMO PLAZA, SINCE CIRCA 1724

Much of present-day Alamo Plaza was the mission's enclosed courtyard. Archaeological digs since the 1970s have located the ancient wall perimeters. The original outlines are reflected in paving stones laid in front of the Alamo church and in excavated wall foundations on the west side. After the 1836 Texan

defeat here, the Mexican army demolished much of the enclosed compound. The U.S. Army cleared much of the rest of the area and occupied the remaining stone buildings as a quartermaster depot after 1846. This attracted trading houses and hotels, and the open plaza became one of the busiest sites in the city. Although the Army moved out of the Alamo in 1879, the location of the post office at the plaza's south end in 1887 and the Joske Brothers store next door in 1889 reinvigorated the plaza. In 1890, the city assumed landscaping responsibilities. The towering marble and granite cenotaph at the plaza's north end, designed by Adams & Adams with sculpted figures by Pompeo Coppini, was erected in 1939 by the Texas Centennial Commission to commemorate those who died in the battle of the Alamo. The plaza was renovated for the nation's sesquicentennial in 1976 and a gazebo was built to replicate an earlier structure. Since then, surrounding shops have yielded to visitor-oriented attractions.

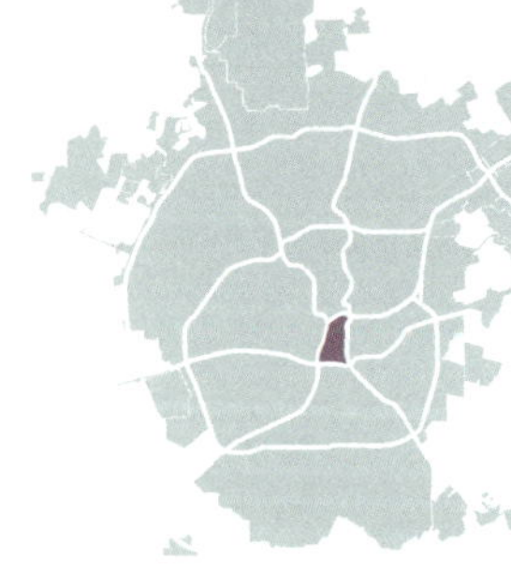

3 NR MENGER HOTEL, 1859

The Menger Hotel was built to serve the busy commercial district that grew up around the Alamo and surrounding plaza. The original Greek Revival style building was enlarged several times in the late 1800s. Alfred Giles's 1909 remodeling reflected the city's growing sophistication with an exuberance of Renaissance Revival details executed in stuccoed brick, cast iron and pressed metal. An interior rotunda provides light and a circulation hub, each level marked with Corinthian columns and filigreed balustrades. The hotel's 1887 front wing to the north was replaced in 1949 with an addition by Ayres & Ayres. That firm also completed the last major addition in 1967.

ADDRESS
204 Alamo Plaza

ARCHITECT
John Fries
J. H. Kampmann, contractor

RENOVATIONS AND ADDITIONS
1887, 1909, 1949, 1967, 1987

4 NR REUTER BUILDING, 1891

Although not quite as dramatic or inventive as Wahrenberger's superb San Antonio Turnverein of the same year, the William Reuter Building is nevertheless one of the best late nineteenth century commercial buildings in the city. Reuter's ground-floor barroom was elaborately decorated and the top floor housed spacious club rooms for the Knights of Pythias. Of special note are two projecting bays which provided second-floor offices with outstanding views of the Alamo. Wahrenberger officed here, possibly on the second floor, after the building's completion. By the 1960s the bay windows had been removed and the building painted and partially draped in metal. A full restoration,

ADDRESS
217 Alamo Plaza

ARCHITECT
James Wahrenberger

including reconstructed bay windows, was completed in 1978.

ADDRESS
300 Block, Alamo Plaza

ARCHITECTS
Ford, Powell & Carson

5 PASEO DEL ALAMO, 1981

This public pedestrian concourse connects Alamo Plaza with the River Walk, two blocks to the west. At the Alamo Plaza entrance are fragments of the west wall of Mission San Antonio de Valero. From these archeological remains to the river, the paseo steps down repeatedly, conveying pedestrians alongside—and beneath—channeled waters reminiscent of the city's historic acequias and aqueduct. On the passageway wall is a mosaic tile mural by local artist Tom Stell

depicting San Antonio scenes. The course descends 27 feet from Alamo Plaza to the river, passing through the sixteen-story lobby of the Hyatt Regency Hotel and ending near the North Presa Street bridge.

ADDRESS
317–23 Alamo Plaza

ARCHITECT
Alfred Giles

RENOVATED
1984–85

6 NR CROCKETT BLOCK, 1882–83

This row of four three-story buildings with an Italianate façade was built along the old west wall of the Alamo's courtyard by entrepreneurs William and Albert Maverick. Giles articulated the design with cast iron piers on the ground level and angular and round arches of limestone above, capped with an entablature of pressed metal. By the early 1980s the building's original windows and detailing were obscured by false fronts and awkward blinds. The Crockett Block's façade was restored during renovations supervised by Humberto Saldaña and Associates.

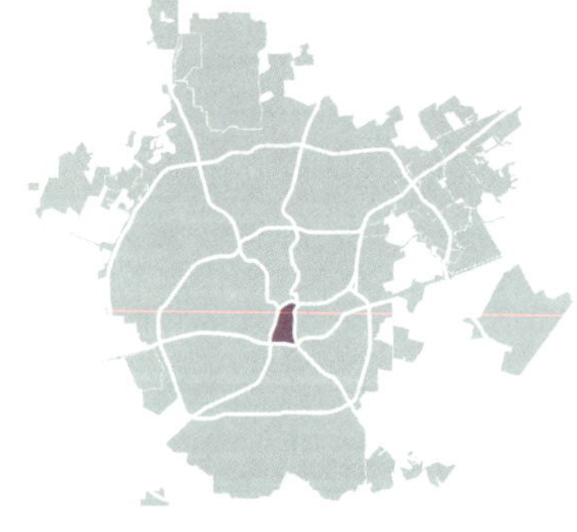

7

8

7 NR UNITED STATES POST OFFICE AND COURTHOUSE, 1937

This vast, five-story, limestone-faced federal building supplanted James Riely Gordon's 1891 castellated Romanesque post office building. It is an exemplary work of monumental urban architecture. The French-born Philadelphia architect Paul Philippe Cret, who during the 1930s executed major architectural commissions in Texas—all in a single, full-bodied classical style—deployed the beautifully modulated elevations of the new post office to define the north end of Alamo Plaza, creating a sense of bounded open space yet not competing with the Alamo. The restrained classical detailing rewards careful study of the building. The vestibule just inside the main entrance contains Howard Cook's 1939 fresco mural, "San Antonio's Importance in Texas History".

ADDRESS
615 East Houston Street

ARCHITECT
Ralph Cameron
Paul Philippe Cret, consulting architect, Philadelphia

RENOVATED
1976, 2002

8 NR MEDICAL ARTS BUILDING, 1926
(EMILY MORGAN HOTEL)

Ralph Cameron clad this V-plan structure with cut stone on the first two floors and encrusted the upper eleven floors with Gothic details in terra cotta. The building is topped with a flying buttressed corner turret and a chateauesque mansard roof. It provides a dramatic focal point for the eastern edge of downtown when seen from several blocks down Houston Street. It first housed doctors' offices and a hospital. The building's multi-paned windows were replaced with single panes

ADDRESS
705 East Houston Street

ARCHITECT
Ralph H. Cameron

when the building was renovated as an office building in 1976.

ADDRESS
411 Bonham Street

ARCHITECT
James Wahrenberger

9 TURNVEREIN BUILDING, 1891 **(BONHAM EXCHANGE)**
Located in an area that has suffered greatly from demolition, this landmark was constructed by San Antonio's Turnverein, a nineteenth century social and gymnastic club that later Anglicized its name to the Turners. The local membership included prominent German immigrants who commissioned a design that attested to their group's status. An enlarged version of the Reuter Building, also built in 1891, the Turnverein represents Wahrenberger's most sophisticated work. The complexity of the main façade is almost overworked, but the building is nevertheless an excellent example of how Renaissance elements were used before the architectural climate of the country changed with the World's Columbian Exposition of 1893. This structure would actually be more at home on the streets of Paris than in any American city of the period.

9

10

ADDRESS
301 East Crockett Street

ARCHITECTS
Phelps & Jacob

RENOVATIONS AND ADDITIONS
1927, 1968, 1983

10★ NR CROCKETT HOTEL, 1909
The Crockett Hotel was designed by Henry T. Phelps and Donald R. Jacob for San Antonio Lodge No. 11 of the Independent Order of Odd Fellows. It housed a hotel on the first four floors and the order's lodge on the top two floors above. In 1927 Phelps designed a seven-story west wing and a new seventh floor above the original building. A major renovation in 1983 was supervised by Ford, Powell & Carson as one of San Antonio's early conversions of a downtown structure to new use. The other nondescript building is on an important site just behind the Alamo but was never the equal of the more elegant downtown hotels. The transformation of the hotel's light well into a glazed-in atrium provides for some dramatic moments on the interior, although the height of the resulting space is in conflict with the hotel's otherwise domestic character. The small bar overlooking the Lady Bird Johnson Fountain is the most convivial space in the new creation, and the rooftop hot tub provides one of the most unusual means of viewing the Alamo, especially at night.

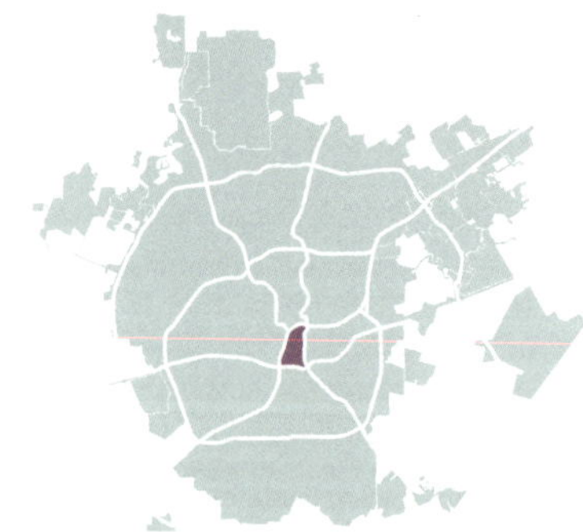

11

LADY BIRD JOHNSON FOUNTAIN, 1974 *NO PHOTO*
Modeled on the generally more ornate public fountains of Mexico, the Lady Bird Johnson Fountain's subdued presence is perhaps fitting for its site just to the rear of the Alamo near where bodies of Alamo defenders reputedly were burned. Unfortunately, the fountain is generally dry due to water restrictions, and intrusive traffic bumpers meant to protect it from converging automobiles detract from its appearance.

ADDRESS
Bonham and Crockett streets intersection

ARCHITECTS
Ford, Powell & Carson

11 RIVERCENTER MALL, 1988
Rivercenter Mall is part of a downtown redevelopment project that transformed a sprawling parking lot into a multi-level retail center overlooking the River Walk. The river channel and walkways were extended, a new lagoon was dug, streets were rerouted, bridges were built and the historic Fairmount Hotel was moved from the site. The changes were meshed with public improvements designed by Ford, Powell & Carson. On the west the mall was anchored by the four-story former Joske's department store, extending the mall's reach to Alamo Plaza. On the east it is anchored by the forty-two-story, 1,000-room Marriott Rivercenter Hotel, which surpassed the Smith-Young Tower as the city's tallest building. Plans in 2007 included additional restaurants and outdoor seating plus restoration of the early twentieth-century Joske's brick façade facing Commerce Street. A new adjoining luxury hotel was also proposed.

ADDRESS
849 East Commerce Street

ARCHITECTS
Urban Design Group, Tulsa

ADDRESS
623 East Commerce Street

ARCHITECT
Theodore E. Giraud
Spire, James Wahrenberger

RESTORED
1981

12 NR ST. JOSEPH'S CATHOLIC CHURCH, 1876–98

The city's growing German Catholic community worshipped at San Fernando Church until after the Civil War, when the congregation was ready for its own church and requested use of the old Alamo mission. When the request was denied because the Catholic archdiocese had a binding lease with the U.S. Army for use of the Alamo as a supply depot, this Gothic Revival edifice was begun in 1868. The limestone church was completed in 1898 by Wahrenberger's spire. Art glass windows made by Emil Frei in Munich, Germany, were installed in 1902. When church members refused to sell the building to be razed as part of the expansion

12

13

of the adjoining Joske's Department Store in 1939, the department store was built around three sides of the church, which then became known to locals as "St. Joske's." Restoration in 1981 was supervised by Ford, Powell & Carson.

ADDRESS
100 Alamo Plaza

ARCHITECT
Bartlett Cocke
John Graham Company, Seattle, consulting architects

RENOVATIONS AND ADDITIONS
1953

13 NR JOSKE'S DEPARTMENT STORE, 1939

Bartlett Cocke's massive five-story building for San Antonio's oldest department store incorporates the remaining structure of Alfred Giles and Henri Guindon's 1889 Joske Brothers store along the south side of Alamo Plaza and extending a block south to Commerce Street. Extensive additions were designed in 1910 by Leo M. J. Dielmann. The old west elevation was faced with smooth limestone combining modernistic massing and composition with florid Spanish Renaissance ornament, while the historic south elevation was obscured in 1967 by a molded fiberglass screen of matching design. The ground-floor shadow boxes were wreathed in miniature reproductions of Mission San José's famous sacristy window. Cocke maintained the character of his original design in the 1953 addition along Commerce Street. In 1987 Joske's was converted into Dillard's, which shrunk retail operations to the lower two stories and connected the east end of the building to the new Rivercenter Mall.

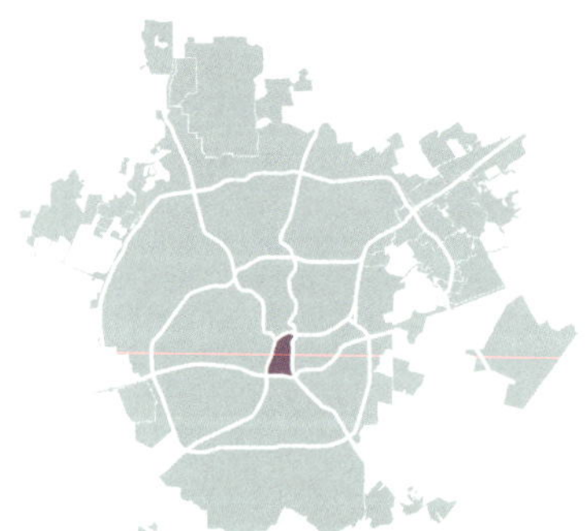

14 NR SCHROEDER–YTURRI HOUSE, CIRCA 1870

The earliest known owner of this one-story stuccoed-limestone house was George Schroeder, who lived here until 1910. Italianate details add a sophisticated note to an otherwise vernacular, symmetrical-plan residence, a good example of a typical late nineteenth century San Antonio house. E. H. Yturri owned the home from 1936 to 1965. Renovated by the City Water Board (now the San Antonio Water System) as a museum, the house later became vacant.

ADDRESS
1040 East Commerce Street

ADDRESS
Bounded by Durango Boulevard, South Alamo Street, Market Street and IH 35

HEMISFAIR PLAZA, SINCE 1968

San Antonio's business community roused itself from four decades of post-Depression lethargy to put on a world's fair, HemisFair '68. But clearing the 92-acre site where 1,600 persons had lived on two dozen streets, plus building complex new facilities and gaining international participation, left little energy or time to plan for the fairground's future. Lost in the shuffle had been three-fourths of the site's 100-plus buildings designated as historic, though the remaining historic structures, such as the [15a] Halff House, restored for use in the fair drew the most praise from visiting architectural critics. Afterward the historic buildings fared little better than most of the former fairgrounds, which drew a series of elaborate and mostly unfulfilled plans for revitalization. Patchwork redevelopment gradually emerged around the landmark Tower of the Americas, the former state and federal pavilions and the convention center complex, which spread into much of the site once its original buildings had enabled San Antonio to become a major convention destination. Although parts of the former fairgrounds even still lack effective use, the economic and political transformation unleashed by the fair has made it a watershed event for San Antonio.

15a

15

ADDRESS
HemisFair Plaza

ARCHITECTS
Ford, Powell & Carson

RENOVATED
2006

15 TOWER OF THE AMERICAS, 1968

Built as the centerpiece of HemisFair '68, San Antonio's world's fair, this 622-foot-high tower is still the tallest structure in San Antonio and has become a favorite symbol for the city. Six levels of publicly accessible restaurant and observation decks rotate at the rate of one revolution per hour atop the cylindrical, slipformed concrete spindle. HemisFair's theme was the Confluence of Civilizations in the Americas. In keeping with the theme, around the tower's base Tom Stell, a member of the Dallas Nine group of regional artists, created six glass mosaic panels depicting Indians of North and South America. Tower facilities were renovated in 2006 under Ford, Powell & Carson.

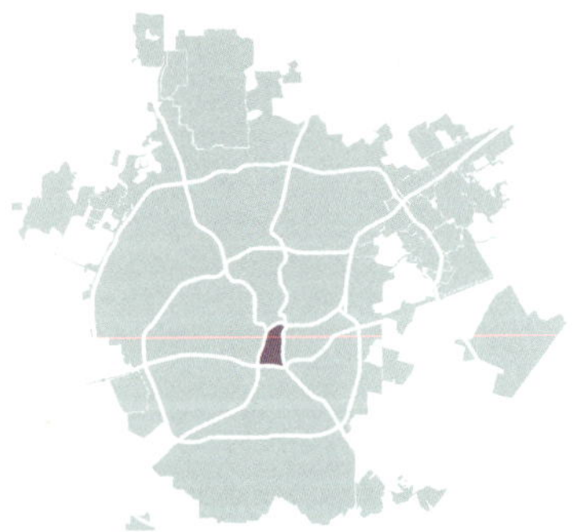

16▲ SAN ANTONIO CONVENTION CENTER, 1968

The 1.3 million-square-foot Convention Center was begun in part with federal urban renewal funds used to finance much of the world fair's construction. It was later named in honor of longtime San Antonio congressman Henry B. Gonzalez. The original complex included a domed arena and a 2,500-seat Theater for the Performing Arts, later named in honor of former Mayor Lila Cockrell. High on the theater's front elevation is a 100-foot long by 22-foot high mosaic tile mural depicting HemisFair '68's theme, the Confluence of Civilizations in the Americas, by the Mexican muralist Juan O'Gorman. A River Walk extension into the fairgrounds ended in a lagoon surrounded by the Convention Center's exhibit halls and theater. In 2001 the lagoon became no longer a terminus but part of an extended channel, as the River Walk was built onward in a significant Convention Center expansion that involved razing the arena. Interior decor recalls basic themes of local architecture, in particular of the Spanish missions. The project was overseen by Thompson, Ventulett, Stainback & Associates/Kell Muñoz Wigodsky. A 1,000-room convention center hotel and condominium tower designed by Arquitectonica is to open in 2008.

ADDRESS
Market Street at
South Alamo Street

ARCHITECTS
Noonan & Krocker and Phelps, Simmons & Associates

RENOVATED
2001

17 INSTITUTE OF TEXAN CULTURES, 1968
(TEXAS PAVILION FOR HEMISFAIR '68)

The Institute of Texan Cultures, built by the State of Texas as the Texas Pavilion for HemisFair '68, reflects

ADDRESS
801 South Bowie Street

ARCHITECTS
Caudill Rowlett Scott, Houston and Callins & Wagner

popular trends in American architecture in the late 1960s. Hallmarks of its design are heavy, sculptural massing, constructivist minimalism in exposed limestone aggregate concrete and camouflaging of the building's form with earthen berms. The institute, which opened in the building after HemisFair, is operated by the University of Texas at San Antonio to portray the state's multi-ethnic heritage. The building is entered from a broad, granite-paved causeway that spans a channeled, granite water garden, now often dry due to water restrictions. The interior is strictly functional, with artificially lit, loft-like exhibition space on the main floor plus a honey-combed dome area for multi-image media

17

18

presentations. The second floor houses the university's library archives and research center. The earthen berm in front of the building was leveled in the 1990s in an effort to make the building appear less forbidding and more open to the evolving HemisFair Plaza.

ADDRESS
655 East Durango Boulevard

ARCHITECTS
Marmon, Mok & Associates and Roberts, Allen & Helmke, with Donald Deskey Associates, New York

RENOVATED
1975

18 UNITED STATES COURTHOUSE, 1968 (UNITED STATES PAVILION FOR HEMISFAIR '68)

The main feature of HemisFair '68's United States Pavilion was the circular, 1,200-seat Confluence Theater, its concept envisioned by New York's Donald Deskey Associates and carried out by San Antonio architects Marmon, Mok & Associates. Inside, visitors viewed a sweeping documentary film celebrating America's diversity. A plaza, first known as the Migration Courtyard for the sculptural fountain that then defined its southern edge, linked the theater with an exhibit hall designed by Roberts, Allen & Helmke. The concrete-framed exhibit hall curved inward to correspond to the outward curve of the theater across the plaza. Seven years after the fair closed, the theater was converted into a United States courthouse, later named in memory of U.S. District Judge John H. Wood Jr. In addition to the theater renovation, the exhibit hall was converted into federal offices and an adjacent seven-story office building was designed in a complementing style, all by Ashley, Garza, Humphries Associates and by Cerna, Garza & Raba.

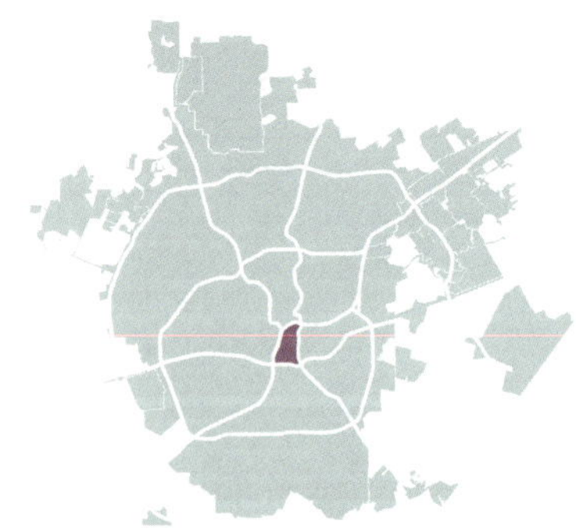

19 SCHULTZE STORE, 1890
(HUMBLE OIL COMPANY PAVILION FOR HEMISFAIR '68)

The two-story Schultze Store faces the former Goliad Street at the South Alamo Street entrance to HemisFair Plaza, and is one of twenty-two buildings preserved for reuse during the fair. Built of cut limestone blocks as a store and warehouse for the Schultze Stove and Hardware Company, it remained in the Schultze family until being acquired for the fair and converted into the modest Humble Oil Company pavilion. The finely detailed structure is one of the city's few surviving small-scale Italianate commercial buildings. It features locally manufactured cast iron work and a pressed-metal cornice reportedly made by the Schultze firm. After the fair, the building was used as a theater and later stood vacant until being renovated in 2003 as a conference center for a nearby hotel.

ADDRESS
HemisFair Plaza

RENOVATED
1968, 2003

20 NR GERMAN–ENGLISH SCHOOL, 1859–75

This grouping of one- and two-story buildings was constructed as a school for children of recent German immigrants, and is representative of the city's fine nineteenth century stone structures. The heavy limestone rubble walls and shading galleries facing a central courtyard provided insulation and protection during hot Texas summers. The two parallel pavilions are roofed in standing seam metal, a typical treatment of the times. After the school closed in 1897, the complex had a variety of tenants until being renovated under Allison B.

ADDRESS
419 South Alamo Street

ARCHITECTS
G. Friesleben, J. H. Kampmann

RENOVATED
1968, 1982

Peery as the project office for HemisFair '68. In 1982 it was again renovated, under Ford, Powell & Carson, to become a conference center for the adjacent hotel. A marker in the courtyard commemorates initialing of the North American Free Trade Agreement at an economic summit meeting here in 1992.

21

22

ADDRESS
526 East Nueva Street

RENOVATED
1982

21 NR ALDERETE HOUSES, CIRCA 1818, CIRCA 1857
These two domestic structures illustrate the evolution of local building techniques in early to mid-nineteenth century San Antonio. The rear house is presumed to be that of Dolores Alderete, given possession of the land by the Spanish government in 1812. It is of palisado construction, its walls of vertical poles laced together and plastered with a mud mixture. The front house was likely built after Englishman Robert Caile purchased the property in 1857. It is a two-room residence of stuccoed caliche blocks, with two rooms added in the late 1800s. Both houses are now roofed with standing-seam sheet metal and have been converted to residential and office use.

ADDRESS
220 Arciniega Street

RENOVATED
1979

22 NR STAFFEL/ELMENDORF/TYLER HOUSE,
CIRCA 1850 German immigrants to San Antonio combined their own building experience with details they observed on existing Texas structures. Their resulting residences were typically of one-story stuccoed stone construction, with central halls and porches patterned after those of their New World neighbors. This example was purchased after 1865 by Heino and Adeline Staffel and occupied by their descendants, the Elmendorf and Tyler families, into the twentieth century. It was restored under Ford, Powell & Carson as a meeting space for the Four Seasons Hotel.

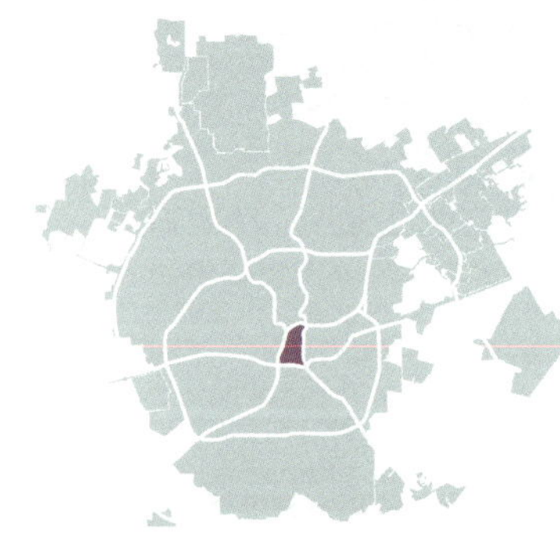

23 NR DIAZ HOUSE, CIRCA 1840

This vernacular residence of stuccoed stone exhibits a symmetrical plan, but with separate entrances and no central hall. Two inner hearths are arranged centrally and back-to-back, resulting in a "saddlebag" configuration. Few openings, small windows and thick stone walls insulated the house in both summer and winter. Porch columns are detailed with simple, Greek Revival style moldings typical of finer homes of the time. The house was restored under Ford, Powell & Carson as a meeting space for the Four Seasons Hotel.

ADDRESS
206 Arciniega Street

RENOVATED
1980

24 NR FAIRMOUNT HOTEL, 1906

This three-story brick structure with Romanesque detailing was built six blocks away in 1906 as a modest hotel and boarding house for travelers arriving and departing from the nearby Southern Pacific depot. After 1968 it was used for storage before being vacated and falling into disrepair. An agreement between the San Antonio Conservation Society and developers of Rivercenter Mall being constructed near the site led to the 3.2 million-pound Fairmount's listing in the Guinness Book of World Records as the heaviest structure moved on pneumatic tires. Once in place at its new site, Alamo Architects designed a new wing, stair-stepped downward so the building would not compete with its new neighbor, the historic German-English School. Colors were reversed on the new addition. Cream-colored brick used on the trim of the original building was the

ADDRESS
401 South Alamo Street

ARCHITECT
Leo M. J. Dielmann

MOVED AND RENOVATED
1985–86

main material for the addition, which for trim used brick in the main red color of the original structure. Iron porches reconstructed on the old building were extended across part of the new wing. Prior to the move, excavations for the new foundation revealed remains of Mexican army earthworks dating to the Battle of the Alamo and produced a rich cache of artifacts.

ADDRESS
555 South Alamo Street

ARCHITECTS
Ford, Powell & Carson

25▲ FOUR SEASONS HOTEL, 1979 *NO PHOTO*
(MARRIOTT PLAZA SAN ANTONIO HOTEL)

In advance of HemisFair '68, urban renewal laid waste to this four-and a half-acre block, sparing only four small residential structures, one of which was removed

26

later. The tract provided architects with an ideal setting for this "garden hotel" that reintroduced scale, texture and detail to the site. A four-, five- and six-story building serves as the backdrop for landscaped outdoor spaces. Shallowly pitched standing seam metal ridge roofs, tiers of metal verandahs and stucco-finished precast concrete walls suggest a relationship with La Villita to the north. The hotel's lobby and the three restored historic structures open onto lushly landscaped gardens with their fountains, terraces, pergolas and swimming pool.

ADDRESS
502 East Nueva Street

ARCHITECT
Marvin Eickenroht

26 NR ST. JOHN'S LUTHERAN CHURCH, 1932

St. John's Lutheran Church purchased this site shortly after its founding in 1857 and commissioned John Fries to build its first sanctuary. The building was substantially reconstructed in 1886 according to plans by James Wahrenberger and Albert Beckmann. C. V. Von Seutter designed the 1922 parish hall, later expanded. When the city widened the Nueva Street right-of-way in 1927, the old church was demolished. The congregation worshipped in the parish hall until the new Gothic Revival sanctuary by Marvin Eickenroht was completed in time for the church's seventy-fifth anniversary celebration in 1932. The sanctuary features impressive stained glass windows by Von Gerichten Studios of Columbus, Ohio and carvings by Alois Lang.

27

27 NR ERNST HOMESTEAD, 1890

Built on land bordering the Mission Concepción acequia, this home was purchased by Prussian immigrant William Ernst in 1896. Ernst went to Mexico during the Civil War and served as Maximilian's chef until the emperor's execution in 1867, when Ernst returned to San Antonio and operated a restaurant on Alamo Plaza. The house has been renovated for offices.

ADDRESS
411 South Presa Street

ADDRESS
Bounded by Durango Boulevard, Navarro and South Alamo streets and the San Antonio River

RENOVATED
1939–41 (O'Neil Ford), 1980

28▲ NR LA VILLITA, SINCE 1792

Although La Villita is frequently referred to as "an old Spanish town," its only structure remaining from Spanish times is the small Cos House (circa 1800), where a Mexican general and brother-in-law of Santa Anna ended the Siege of Bexar in 1835 by surrendering his army. Located two blocks south of Mission San Antonio de Valero/the Alamo, La Villita traces its history to the mid-eighteenth century, when squatters claimed mission farmland on the river's east bank, where the stream was easily forded. After the mission was secularized in 1792 and its farmlands were distributed among Indians, Spanish soldiers and civilians, La Villita,

28

28

known as Pueblo de Valero, had its own government and mayor. In 1809 it merged with surrounding settlements. Spared from the devastating 1819 flood due to its location on the river's high bank, La Villita became a desirable place to live. It thrived as a multi-cultural neighborhood through the late 1800s, when it began a decline. In the 1930s, Mayor Maury Maverick secured funding for a National Youth Administration project that restored six houses as an arts and crafts village according to plans of consulting architect O'Neil Ford, who first came to San Antonio to work on this project. Ford sought to create a mood rather than a museum-style restoration specific to a period in time. Dedicated in 1940, La Villita has grown to include some twenty-seven buildings representing continued occupation for more than two hundred years. Renovations, including removal of curbs and leveling of Villita Street, were made in 1980 under Saldaña, Williams & Schubert and Ford, Powell & Carson. With the exception of a handful of structures, La Villita is owned and managed by the City of San Antonio.

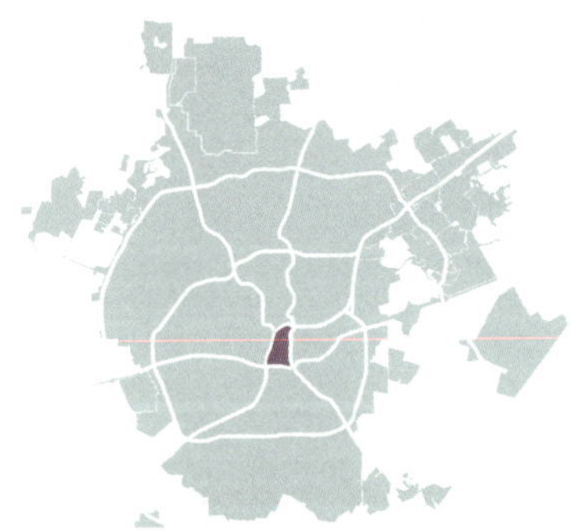

29▲★ THE PLAZAS OF LA VILLITA

Several small plazas created within La Villita since its WPA renovation lend the area a Spanish ambience. Architect O'Neil Ford had an area cleared for the first, Plaza Juarez (1941), near a group of old homes near the main entrance and named in honor of a former president of Mexico. Ford was himself honored in 1980 by the naming of a newly renovated area behind a historic church as O'Neil Ford Plaza. To its south, another small area was named [29] Plaza Nacional, opened up when five old structures incorporated into a former candy company were uncovered and restored in a 1974 project supervised by William Parrish. To the east, the area at the corner of South Alamo and Nueva streets had been cleared for storage and parking for HemisFair '68. In 1970 it was incorporated into La Villita and walled as Nueva Plaza, later renamed Maury Maverick Plaza in honor of the former mayor and congressman who had inspired the La Villita project.

ADDRESS
401 Villita Street

ARCHITECTS
O'Neil Ford & Associates

30 VILLITA ASSEMBLY HALL, 1959

This two-level, round brick building recalls the style of Edward Durrell Stone's United States Pavilion for the 1958 world's fair in Brussels. It was designed by O'Neil Ford twenty years after he served as consulting architect for La Villita's restoration. The building's clear span of 132 feet in diameter was achieved by a steel cable roof suspension system. Ford and associate N. A. Salas surfaced the concave roof and upper walls of the steel-framed assembly hall with precast panels. The lower walls and courtyard enclosures are of Mexican red brick. The central interior space opens onto a patio garden laid out by Stewart E. King with James Keeter. Lynn

30

31

Ford, O'Neil's brother, carved the wooden entry doors and handcrafted the ceramic medallions mounted on the building's exterior. The Assembly Hall's curving lines create a welcoming entry to La Villita's main section. By replacing a hulking electrical plant beside the San Antonio River, the Assembly Hall completed restoration of the scale of La Villita, and reflects Ford's belief that straightforward acknowledgment of structure and materials can be more faithful to the spirit of place than a stylistic revival.

ADDRESS
San Antonio River Walk at La Villita

ARCHITECT
Robert H. H. Hugman

31 ARNESON RIVER THEATER, 1939

On this sloping south bank of the San Antonio River, River Walk designer Robert H. H. Hugman had curved bleachers made of concrete, then had their risers stressed to appear as if they were carved from natural rock. This natural sense was augmented by sod laid inside the concrete rims of the terraced seating. Below the more vertical north bank Hugman placed the amphitheater's small stage and romantic Spanish style stage house, complete with dove cote. In 1978 the adjoining espadaña finally got its bells. Hugman did their ceremonial first striking. The river was crossed with a narrow stone bridge, highly arched so gondoliers could pass beneath. The theater is named for Edward P. Arneson, a Work Projects Administration engineer who before his untimely death had been adapting Hugman's plans for the theater.

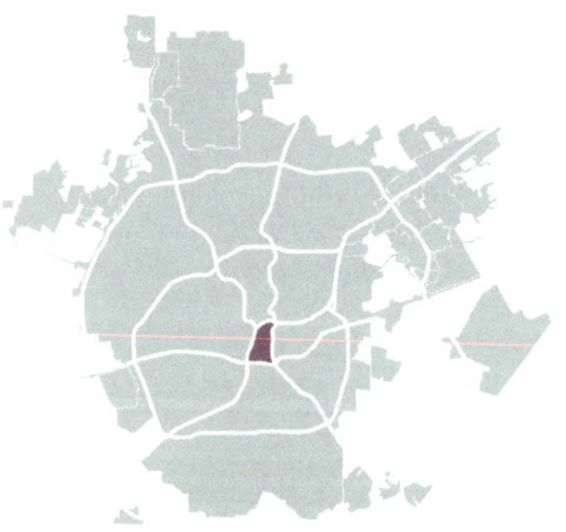

32

33

32★ HILTON PALACIO DEL RIO HOTEL, 1968

As the opening of HemisFair '68 approached, San Antonio was faced with a serious shortage of first-class hotel rooms. Local businessman and fair contractor H. B. Zachry undertook construction of this 21-story, 496-room hotel on a narrow site between Alamo Street and the river. The hotel is a notable achievement of engineering and technical deadline ingenuity. The fifth through twentieth floors consist of reinforced concrete, modular room units built, furnished and equipped off-site, trucked to the project site, and hoisted into place on either side of the slip-formed elevator core. On April 2, 1969, only 202 days after construction began, the first guests checked into the hotel, 4 days prior to the fair's opening.

ADDRESS
200 South Alamo Street

ARCHITECTS
Cerna & Garza

33 OLD SAN ANTONIO PUBLIC LIBRARY, 1930

San Antonio's second public library building, constructed on the site of the earlier Carnegie Library, is the city's finest example of Modern classicism as espoused by Berttam Grosvenor Goodhue. Herbert Green's pared-down ornamental details owe a debt to Goodhue's masterpiece, the Nebraska State Capitol. The main entrance arch is notable for the two robed figures rising from the flanking buttresses. The words of Ralph Waldo Emerson are inscribed above the front door. The building, which later housed the Hertzberg Circus Collection, was renovated in 1971 by Brooks Martin &

ADDRESS
210 West Market Street

ARCHITECT
Herbert S. Green

RENOVATED
1971

Associates. Plans being made in 2007 would convert the recently vacated building into the Dolph and Janey Briscoe Western Art Museum, designed by Lake/Flato.

ADDRESS
200 Block, South Presa Street

34 CHARLES COURT, 1981–83

This lush and cozy courtyard flanking the Old Alamo National Bank building was once a dead-end service alley for adjacent buildings facing Presa and Commerce streets, including the Batz House (circa 1850), the 1880 Pancoast Building by Alfred Giles (façade removed 1913) and the Texas Hotel (circa 1900). When they were renovated under Tuggle & Graves in the early 1980s for a new restaurant, offices,

34

35

36

shops and residences, the alley was made a principal entrance to the buildings.

ADDRESS
316 East Commerce Street

ARCHITECT
James Wahrenberger
Coughlin & Ayres, associate architects

35 NR OLD ALAMO NATIONAL BANK BUILDING, 1902

This later example of James Wahrenberger's work is best known for having been moved sixteen feet to the south in 1913 to accommodate the widening of Commerce Street. At the time, the structure was five stories tall and weighed an estimated 8,000 tons. The move was accomplished using jacks, wheels and rails while business was still being conducted inside. After the relocation, three stories were added to the building. The original cornice appears to have been placed atop the new ninth floor of what is now known as the Commerce Building.

ADDRESS
315 East Commerce Street

ARCHITECTS
Gordon & Laub

RENOVATED
1983

36 NR STEVENS BUILDING, 1891

John J. Stevens commissioned James Riely Gordon and D. E. Laub to build this Romanesque Revival edifice containing his office as well as commercial space. Eclectic façade details of round arches on columns, oriel windows and a balustraded parapet were executed in brick, limestone and granite. The depths of the Stevens Building and the adjacent Staacke Building were shortened in 1978 to provide space for a parking lot, so the back walls of both buildings are new. Five years later, Tuggle & Graves supervised restoration of the façades of the two buildings and their interiors as contemporary office space.

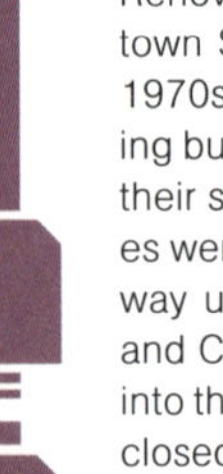

37 NR STAACKE BUILDING, 1894

The Staacke brothers—August, Rudolph, and Herman—operated their thriving carriage business from this three-story brick structure. They are also credited with bringing the first automobile to the city in 1905. James Riely Gordon utilized Texas red sandstone and red granite on the façade, detailed in Renaissance Revival motifs and complementing the adjacent Stevens Buildings designed three years earlier. The interior was adapted to contemporary office space during the 1983 Tuggle & Graves restoration of both buildings.

ADDRESS
309 East Commerce Street

ARCHITECT
James Riely Gordon

RENOVATED
1983

38★ D. HEYE SADDLERY BUILDING AND ADJOINING BUILDINGS, CIRCA 1867 **(RIO RIO RESTAURANT)**

Renovation of historic commercial buildings in downtown San Antonio grew in popularity during the early 1970s. River Walk frontage made these and neighboring buildings more valuable for their river frontage than their street-level frontage, and thus their main entrances were turned and lowered to face the bustling waterway under the supervision of Ford, Powell & Carson and Cy Wagner. These structures were first converted into the Old-West-themed Stockman Restaurant—since closed—with three-story high ceilings and an interior decorated in handcrafted rustic furnishings. The restored façade remains a Commerce Street landmark, though the distinctive interior and River Walk façade has been remodeled for successive tenants by Sprinkle Robey Architects.

ADDRESS
409 East Commerce Street

RENOVATED
1972

ADDRESS
423–431 East Commerce Street

ARCHITECT
James Riely Gordon

39 CLIFFORD BUILDING, 1891 (ROYALTY COIN)

While not quite as exuberant as the Stevens and Staacke buildings nearby, the Clifford Building exhibits James Riely Gordon's ability to work with an unusual and rather confined site. The rounded end that serves as a tower alongside the San Antonio River is a fine example of late nineteenth century brickwork, with no ornate details to detract from the smooth curving masonry walls. The cupola provides an unexpected break from the mass of the structure. The Clifford Building retains a remarkable degree of its original integrity as one of the fine nineteenth century structures remaining on Commerce Street.

ADDRESS
102 West Crockett Street

ARCHITECTS
The Kelwood Company

RENOVATED
1970s

40 NR CASINO CLUB BUILDING, 1927

This six-story flatiron-shaped building was completed in 1927 as headquarters for a local social organization, the San Antonio Casino Club. Its Meso-American Revival style is signified by the stepped pyramidal design of its entry tower and by the carved brick and cast-stone trim ornamentation of its top and ground floors. Oklahoma oilman Thomas Gilcrease acquired the building in 1940 for his corporate offices and to house his growing collection of Western art. After Gilcrease's collection moved to Tulsa, the building was largely vacant from the early 1950s until the late 1970s, when it was converted to apartments and retail space and the river-level basement was excavated for restaurant use.

ADDRESS
110 East Crockett Street

ARCHITECTS
Coughlin & Ayres

RENOVATED
1965, 1986, 2005

41▲ CHANDLER BUILDING, 1895

This small but well designed two-story office block was built for insurance mogul and investor E. B. Chandler. It is one of the few surviving works of the brief partnership of Atlee B. Ayres and Charles A. Coughlin, whose untimely death occurred in 1905. While the firm's original design is still evident, the building, one of the first along the San Antonio River Walk to be renovated, was extensively altered in 1965 under Brooks Martin. Much of the original exterior design was restored in the 2005 conversion under Humberto Saldaña & Associates from offices to a theme restaurant.

42 HYATT REGENCY HOTEL, 1981

This sixteen-story, 633-room hotel, designed in large part by Atlanta architect Raymond F. Stainback, is wrapped around a signature Hyatt atrium lobby. The lobby is made unique by the Paseo del Alamo, a public accessway leading from the Alamo to the river, which appears to flow through the atrium into the main stream; however, a clear plastic wall actually blocks the flow and allows it to be recycled to the head of the Paseo. The lobby court on the west has a glass curtain wall shielded by rows of bright red canopies, set in a delicate network of steel webbing and providing a welcome note of texture and color. Approached from Losoya Street, the Hyatt's dazzlingly white, poured-in-place concrete mass looms like an iceberg in the midst of the city. From other vantage points, however, it is surprisingly unobtrusive and does not overwhelm its surroundings. Across Losoya Street, between the Paseo and Houston Street, is the Hyatt Garage with its contextually attentive ground-floor retail arcade.

ADDRESS
123 Losoya Street

ARCHITECTS
Thompson, Ventulett, Stainback & Asscociates, Atlanta and Ford, Powell & Carson

43 NIX PROFESSIONAL BUILDING, 1929

Henry Phelps's brick and polychrome terra cotta exterior conceals a complex design incorporating a hospital, parking garage and medical offices. The building exhibits what is perhaps the city's finest collection of terra cotta ornamentation. Elaborate brass fixtures mark the entrance to the ornate lobby where, sadly, the decorative coffered ceiling has been obscured.

ADDRESS
410 Navarro Street

ARCHITECT
Henry T. Phelps

Thousands of San Antonians boast of being born here on the banks of the San Antonio River, and the Nix remains a thriving medical center.

ADDRESS
112 College Street

ARCHITECT
Francois P. Giraud

RENOVATED
1967, 1979

44 LA MANSION DEL RIO HOTEL, 1867

Built on the site of St. Mary's Institute, a Catholic school for boys opened in 1853, the hotel complex incorporates the school's early buildings, including the three-story stone building designed by Francois P. Giraud and completed in 1867. After what became St. Mary's University moved the last of its classes to the newer campus, these buildings were remodeled, expanded and converted to a hotel in Wallace B. Thomas's design

in 1967. Giraud's building was significantly altered by addition of balconies, an attic-level mansard roof and an arched entrance portal. Thomas organized the six-story, 200-room hotel around a central patio and featured inset and projecting balconies on the new River Walk elevation. Dallas architects Harwood K. Smith & Partners adopted and maintained Thomas's organization, massing and details in their 1979 remodeling. The hotel presents a romantic and somewhat eclectic architectural interpretation of San Antonio's Spanish Colonial past. The hotel is currently known as Omni La Mansion del Rio.

HOUSTON STREET

Houston Street was little more than a series of variously named muddy pathways until the mid-nineteenth century, when a bridge was built to span the river and the thoroughfare was named for the much-revered Sam Houston. Commerce Street remained the town's dominant business street, however, while Houston Street, wider and less congested, was lined with one-story frame and ironclad shacks and vacant lots. By the mid-1880s, more substantial structures, many built by the Maverick family, began to line Houston Street. Multi-story residential and commercial buildings of brick and stone dominated until the 1920s, when the downtown construction boom transformed the street with steel and reinforced concrete skyscrapers. At Alamo Plaza, the Medical Arts building's Gothic tower served as a fitting bookend for the upper end of the street. As Houston Street's vitality was sapped by the advent of suburban shopping malls in the 1960s and by subsequent business closures, the city embarked on a seventy-block, $22 million TriParty Improvement Project to rebuild downtown's aging infrastructure and provide street amenities, though the effort seemed only to hasten Houston Street's decline. In 1998, however, Federal Realty Trust announced ambitious plans to renovate a dozen key Houston Street properties. Aided by new downtown housing and a thriving convention and tourism market, life began returning to the street.

ADDRESS
208 E. Houston

ARCHITECT
John Eberson, Chicago

RENOVATED
1983, 1996

45▲★ NR MAJESTIC THEATER BUILDING, 1929

The Majestic Theater, inspired by San Antonio's Spanish and Moorish heritage, is one of the nation's grand surviving atmospheric theaters. When prolific theater designer John Eberson's Majestic opened just before the Depression, the Majestic was state-of-the-art in entertainment. Patrons were transported to another world as they sat in air-conditioned comfort under a canopy of floating clouds and twinkling stars surrounded by cleverly lit architectural vignettes. The auditorium occupies six levels of the accompanying steel frame, fifteen-story office building, which is topped by a three-story residential penthouse. The Majestic closed in

1974. It later reopened as a venue for touring Broadway shows after some renovation by Houston's Barry Moore Architects. Restoration work in 1989 by Milton Babbitt was followed in 1996 by a complete interior restoration by Battersby Ornamental under direction of 3D/International.

ADDRESS
Houston and South St. Mary's streets

ARCHITECTS
Mauran, Russell and Crowell, St. Louis

RENOVATED
1992, 1998

46 NR BRADY BUILDING/EMPIRE THEATER, 1914

Thomas Brady's classical revival style complex incorporated an office building and an ornate 1,800-seat theater for film and theatrical presentations. This structure and the Gunter Hotel directly across the street, designed by then-named Mauran, Russell and Garden, make a fine pairing of the St. Louis firm's work. The steel frame brick building features terra cotta trim and a copper canopy topped with an eagle above the Empire Theater's entrance. Spandrel panels above the second floor feature cast stone medallions with eagles. The theater closed in 1975 and the Brady Building was converted into apartments in 1992. Six years later the theater reopened as an 850-seat performing arts venue. Both renovations were by 3D/I.

47

48

47 HOTEL VALENCIA , 2002

The Hotel Valencia, a twelve-story, 213-room boutique hotel, is part of a Houston Street redevelopment project. The Italian Mediterranean style building with bright colors and simple lines features elevators and a grand staircase connecting Houston Street to the riverside restaurant and the River Walk. Of commercial structures built by George M. Maverick on the site, the most distinctive—an 1898 two-story building designed by Alfred Giles at the corner of St. Mary's Street—was incorporated into the hotel project and restored to its original appearance. Its missing upper-level bay windows were replicated.

ADDRESS
150 East Houston Street

ARCHITECTS
3D/I

48 NR BOOK BUILDING, 1906

The red brick Book Building is noted for its series of dramatic round-arched window bays on the street façades. The scale of these openings results in an unusual, almost airy, look to the outer skin. Dwight Book, a civil engineer and U.S. Army officer, is believed to have been the designer, and was probably capable of doing the work. The Coffee House, believed to have been the first business on the level of the San Antonio River, opened on the lower level about 1920. The rear patio overlooking the River Walk is a later addition.

ADDRESS
130 East Houston Street

ARCHITECT
Attributed to
Dwight Dana Book

ADDRESS
100 East Houston Street

ARCHITECTS
Sanguinet & Staats, Fort Worth and Houston

RENOVATED
1982

49▲ NR RAND BUILDING, 1913

This eight-story building, designed for Edwin Rand by Marshall R. Sanguinet and Carl G. Staats, was occupied by Wolff and Marx, a department store, from 1913 until 1965. The two early-twentieth-century skyscraper kings of Texas combined midwestern progressive composition and fenestration with New York French classical ornamentation, a rare combination for San Antonio. In 1981 the San Antonio Conservation Society saved the building from being demolished by Frost National Bank and arranged its sale to Randstone Ventures. The Marmon Mok Partnership restored the exterior and inserted a nine-story glazed court that rises through the center of the building, now owned and used for offices by Frost National Bank, which maintains its main banking center across the street.

49

50

ADDRESS
314 West Houston Street

ARCHITECT
N. Strauss Nayfach

RENOVATED
2000–

50 ALAMEDA THEATER/CASA DE MEXICO INTERNATIONAL BUILDING, 1949

The Alameda, last of the great movie palaces built in San Antonio, is said to have been the largest theater ever dedicated to Spanish-language films and performing arts. The theater and adjoining four-story Casa de Mexico International Building were designed as an entertainment and professional center catering to the heavily Mexican American clientele of the western central business district. The Alameda hosted Mexico's leading stars of music and stage and screened Spanish-language films through the 1970s. Strauss Nayfach's late Modernistic design is totally uninhibited, as orange, green and blue tile work, aluminum arabesques and the unparalleled 86-foot high illuminated sign attest. The San Antonio Conservation Society fought successfully to preserve the building in 1982. It was purchased by the City of San Antonio and leased to Centro Alameda Inc. The office building was renovated in 2000 under Burton Rose Gonzales. Theater restoration directed by Killis Almond is creating a Pan-Latino performing arts center to operate in conjunction with the Smithsonian Institution's Museo Alameda at El Mercado.

51

52

51▲★ FROST NATIONAL BANK AND MOTORBANK, 1973 Frost Bank moved in 1973 from its long-time home on Main Plaza to this nearby twenty-two-story tower, designed by Jones & Kell, in conjunction with New York architect Charles Luckman. Its strong granite frame signifies institutional strength and stability, though the slabs of gray granite seem a bit somber in a city noted for its sunshine and light. Near the motor bank across the street, low walls enclosing an open park area are of stone from remains of an early Presbyterian church, cleared with other structures from the block in the early 1980s for a high-rise office tower, which, like that planned by the onetime RepublicBank two blocks away, remains to be built.

ADDRESS
100 West Houston Street

ARCHITECTS
Jones & Kell and Charles Luckman, New York

52▲ HOUSTON STREET BRIDGE, CA. 1915
The concrete Houston Street bridge was built about 1915 to replace an iron bridge constructed in 1871. Its most notable features are the lighted obelisks with hand-painted tiles by Malou Flato depicting San Antonio's Spanish missions and put in place during a downtown revitalization project in 2001.

ADDRESS
Houston Street and San Antonio River

RENOVATED
2001

53 REPUBLICBANK PLAZA, 1985
RepublicBank Plaza mitigated the sheer scale and formal aloofness of its new plaza by aligning walls of a 13-story, 300,000-square-foot office block with Houston and St. Mary's streets, by providing sidewalk arcades and by configuring an interior link down broad

ADDRESS
175 East Houston Street

ARCHITECTS
Ford, Powell & Carson and Fisher & Spillman

steps to the River Walk for a mid-block, 36-story office tower. Over considerable public protest, all but the terra-cotta-adorned façade, marquee, entrance bay and ticket booth of the landmark 1926 Texas Theater, designed by Kansas City's Boller Brothers, was demolished to make way for the new complex. Dallas-based RepublicBank disappeared in a series of mergers that followed banking collapses in Texas in the mid-1980s. A high-rise tower is yet to be built in the plaza's still-vacant central area.

53

54

55

ADDRESS
East Houston and North St. Mary's streets

ARCHITECT
E. Howard Company, Boston

MOVED
1910

RESTORED
1990

54 HERTZBERG CLOCK, 1878

Considered by many to be the official timepiece of downtown San Antonio, the Hertzberg Clock first served as functional advertising for Hertzberg Jewelry Company in front of the firm's original location on Commerce Street. The clock was moved with Hertzberg's to this location in 1910 and here remains, donated to the San Antonio Conservation Society and restored, even though Hertzberg's is gone and its 1910 building has been razed.

ADDRESS
205 East Houston Street

ARCHITECTS
Mauran, Russell & Garden, St. Louis

RENOVATED
1927, 1980

55 GUNTER HOTEL, 1909

The Gunter is the first of several Texas hotels designed by Mauran, Russell & Garden, later Mauran, Russell & Crowell. Others include the Rice Hotel in Houston, the Galvez in Galveston and the Blackstone in Forth Worth. The Gunter's original design, with multi-story three-sided bays and terra-cotta-decorated base floors, is a good example of the Chicago-style high rise. The top three floors were added when the hotel was remodeled in 1927 by its then owner, legendary hotelier T. B. Baker, according to the design of Herbert S. Green. After declining in the 1960s and 1970s, the Gunter was renovated in 1980 in a plan by Robert V. Buck. The signature mezzanine level veranda was enclosed to permit additional seating for dining. The three-story lobby retains its 1926 appearance.

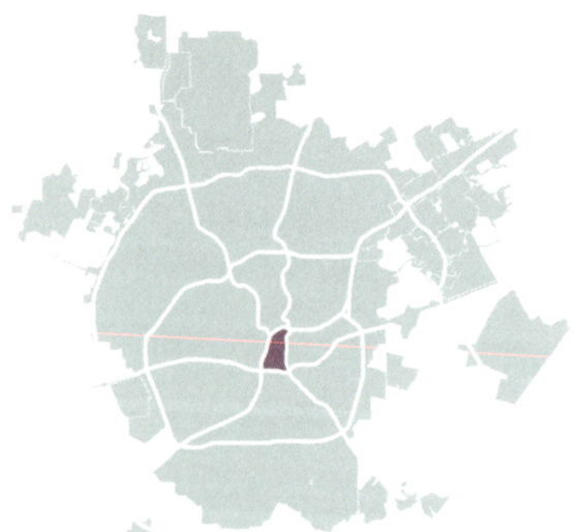

56 FROST BROTHERS BUILDING, 1911
(PRINCESS THEATER)

This four-story building was constructed as the Princess Theater. A 1930 remodeling for Blum's, a specialty store, gave the building its recessed entry and stylish show windows. It is best known for housing Frost Brothers, an elegant clothing and specialty store which moved in after Blum's failed during the Depression. Frost Brothers closed in 1986. The vacant building was purchased by Federal Realty Investment Corporation as part of its Houston Street redevelopment project and was converted to office use by 3D/I in 2002.

ADDRESS
217 East Houston Street

ARCHITECTS
Ralph Cameron and Harvey L. Page

REMODELED
1930, 2002

57 NR CENTRAL TRUST COMPANY BUILDING, 1919
(SOUTH TEXAS BUILDING)

Sanguinet and Staats, in partnership with San Antonio architect Charles T. Boelhauwe, designed this twelve-story structure for the Central Trust Company. Dubbed the "million dollar bank," the building, with its steel frame and veneers of brick, green granite and terra cotta, was the town's tallest when completed. Ayres & Ayres remodeled the lower three floors in 1947. Renamed the South Texas Building in 1932 after Central Trust failed during the Depression, the building was totally renovated in 1982 under The Benham Group. It continues to house a financial institution and offices.

ADDRESS
603 Navarro Street

ARCHITECTS
Sanguinet, Staats and Boelhauwe, Fort Worth; Atlee B. Ayres, consulting architect

RENOVATED
1947, 1982

ADDRESS
303 East Houston Street

RENOVATED
1920, 1937, 2001

58 VOGUE BUILDING, CIRCA 1895

This former L. P. Peck Furniture Store, built in the late 1890s, was redesigned for Vogue, a women's clothing store, by Herbert S. Green in 1920. Further remodeling included addition of a sixth floor. The exterior was remodeled again, under Ralph Cameron, in 1937. It is likely the tallest wood-framed building in the city. In 2001, restoration by 3D/I for office use as part of the Houston Street redevelopment project returned the building to its original red brick and terra cotta appearance.

58

59

ADDRESS
315 East Houston Street

ARCHITECT
Edward F. Sibbert, New York

59 KRESS BUILDING, 1938

Edward Sibbert, S. H. Kress and Company's chief architect, endowed the five-story San Antonio store with details common in his more than fifty Art Deco store designs from 1929 to 1944. Sibbert sought to give Kress a streamlined image, with sleek exteriors and gracious interiors that, in the drabness of the Depression, would cause customers to linger. Sibbert's San Antonio storefront is sheathed, typically, in terra cotta in shades of dull pink, yellow, green and copper. Scrolled pediments atop the corner bays and Modernistic vertical fluting between window bays are thick, heavy and flat. The signature signage is integrated with the architecture and oriented to the flow of traffic along Houston Street. Future renovation of the Kress Building is to incorporate it into an adjacent hotel and condominium tower.

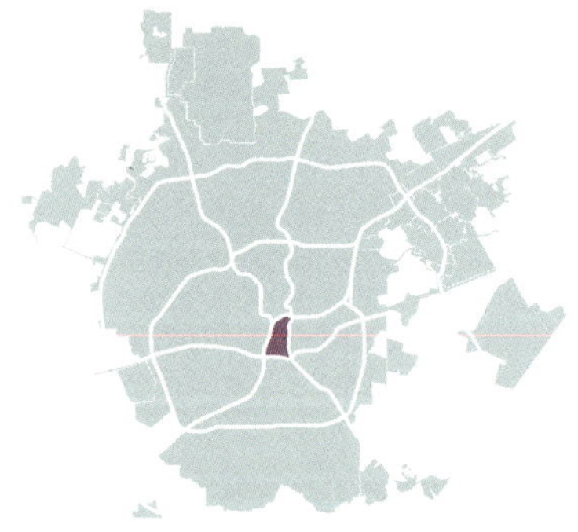

60

61

60 BENNETT BUILDING, 1917

This structure was built for J. M. Bennett in 1917 as a two-story retail building. The third floor was added in 1926. The first tenant was Frost Brothers, which later moved to larger quarters on the same block. Purchased by Federal Realty Trust, the building was renovated as part of the Houston Street redevelopment project. An adjacent small office structure was demolished to create a courtyard for adjoining buildings, and a new building was constructed at the back of the courtyard. Windows and doors of the Bennett Building's newly exposed side elevation open onto the courtyard. The 2002 renovations were by 3D/I, which offices on the upper floor.

ADDRESS
219 East Houston Street

ARCHITECTS
Alfred Giles Company

RENOVATED
1926, 2002

61 NR J. C. PENNEY COMPANY, 1918
(BURNS BUILDING)

Built as the Burns Building, this structure housed a succession of retail stores. The longest-tenured tenant was J. C. Penney, which operated within from 1941 to 1985. Reinforced concrete construction created a "daylight store" with widely spaced bays and large windows to admit generous amounts of natural light. The recessed entryway and large display windows provided the store maximum streetfront exposure. Modifications were designed by Ralph Cameron in 1921. The long vacant building was renovated for offices in 1998 under the direction of Richard Mycue.

ADDRESS
401 East Houston Street

ARCHITECTS
Sanguinet and Staats, Fort Worth and Houston, in association with Charles Boelhauwe

RENOVATED
1921, 1998

ADDRESS
110 Broadway at East Houston Street

ARCHITECTS
Coughlin & Ayres

RENOVATED
1984

62 NR G. BEDELL MOORE BUILDING, 1904

Early in his career Atlee B. Ayres and his first partner, Charles A. Coughlin, were commissioned by rancher, lumberman and real estate investor G. Bedell Moore to design this commercial building. Composition of the façade design, with round-arched window bays framing three stories, is standard for the period, but the extensive use of ornamental terra cotta represents a significant development on the local scene. A sixth floor with lighted rooftop garden was added in 1909. Ayres officed here for twenty years before moving to his later masterpiece, the Smith-Young Tower. After years of being dipped in white paint, this building's exterior was restored to its multi-colored original appearance in 1984 under the Urban Design Group of Tulsa, Oklahoma. The interior was renovated for offices and a skylit atrium was added.

62

63

ADDRESS
East Houston Street at North Presa Street

ARCHITECT
Lou Harrington

RENOVATED
1997

63 NR MAVERICK BUILDING, 1922

The Maverick Building was constructed in 1922 by members of the Maverick family on part of the site of the Maverick Hotel, a Second Empire landmark designed by Alfred Giles and demolished to make way for extension of Presa Street north across the river to Houston Street. The reinforced concrete building is faced in red brick and set on a three-story cut stone base. Ornamentation at the lower level was to be replicated at the top when the building reached its planned height of twenty-two stories, but construction halted at the ninth floor, which thus lacks ornamentation. Above storefront shops were offices leased to a variety of tenants, including architects Bartlett Cocke and Marvin Eickenroht. After the downtown office market declined in the 1970s, the building became vacant. It was renovated for apartments in 1997 by Lloyd Walker Jary and Associates.

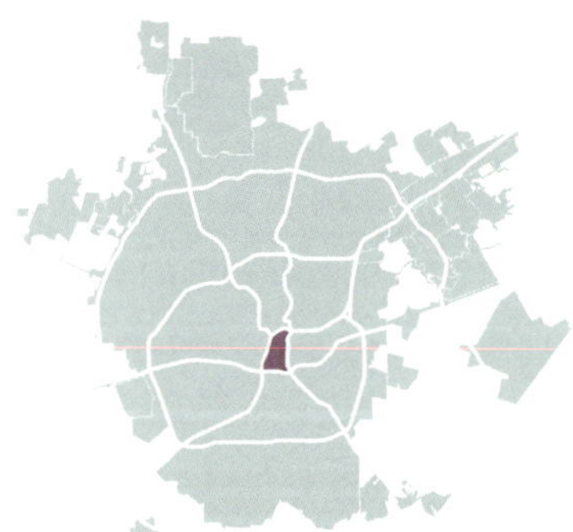

64 BUCKHORN MUSEUM AND SALOON, CIRCA 1912
(MAVERICK STORE BUILDING)

This two-story retail structure is among numerous Houston Street buildings constructed by the Maverick family. In 1921 it was substantially remodeled by its original architect, Will Noonan, when extension of Presa Street north to meet Houston Street claimed more than fifty feet of the building. The remaining structure was converted to the Buckhorn Museum and Saloon in 1999 to house the collection of trophies and western memorabilia begun by Albert Friedrich, who opened his original saloon in the late 1880s and decorated it with trophies from hunting trips and contributions from cattle drivers and trail hands who frequented the bar. The collection was acquired by the latter-day Lone Star Brewery in the 1950s and moved to its plant south of downtown, where it drew an international audience. The collection was reacquired by the Friedrich family in 1998 and moved to this building after it was remodeled by Alamo Architects.

ADDRESS
318 East Houston Street

ARCHITECT
Will N. Noonan

RENOVATED
1921, 1999

65 TRAVIS PARK METHODIST CHURCH, 1886

Travis Park Methodist Church houses the city's oldest Methodist congregation in a building that has had numerous additions and alterations over the years. The original structure, with its cylindrical tower, was constructed by builder Francis Crider, a member of the congregation. The church was enlarged in 1902 by Harvey L. Page, whose design extended the façade

ADDRESS
230 East Travis Street

ARCHITECT
Francis Crider

RENOVATED
1902, 1956

along Navarro Street and included a large auditorium. A fire in 1955 destroyed most of the original interior. Post-fire alterations and additions were designed by Ralph Cameron. While Travis Park Methodist may not be the architectural equal of St. Mark's Episcopal Church across Travis Park, it is nevertheless an important reminder of the nineteenth century scale of the park and its environs.

ADDRESS
300 East Travis Street

ARCHITECT
J. Flood Walker

REDESIGNED
1936, John M. Marriott

RENOVATED
1941, 1983

66 NR ST. ANTHONY HOTEL, 1909–10

The elegant St. Anthony Hotel was built in three sections facing Travis Park. The first portion was built in 1909 in an Alamo Revival style on the corner of Travis and Navarro streets. Its upper stories were slightly set back from the lower street level façade. The following year the St. Anthony was more than doubled in size with an annex to the east, crowned by a single Alamo Revival parapet more elaborate than the three on the original building and with upper stories flush with the street level facade. The buildings were connected by an extended lobby with large windows facing the park dubbed Peacock Alley, after the noted promenade in New York's Waldorf-Astoria Hotel. In 1936 a major redesign by John M. Marriott unified the two portions by extending the façade of the first building to make it flush with the second and then adding two stories to the original building and one to the annex. Five years later Fred S. Jones extended Marriott's elevations with an addition east to the end of the block at Jefferson Street. With the new air conditioning, the transformed hotel could bill itself as "the world's largest completely and continuously air conditioned hotel." Interior remodelings by Ayres & Ayres from the 1920s through the 1960s included dining rooms decorated by Dorothy Draper. When the 352-room St. Anthony was renovated in 1983 under Chumney, Jones & Kell, public spaces were restored to their 1936 appearance.

67

68

67 NR BARR BUILDING, 1912

The Barr Building, conspicuous on lower Broadway by virtue of its size and unusual detailing, is one of San Antonio's numerous small-scale commercial buildings designed by Leo M. J. Dielmann. It was designed to serve owner and photographer David Perry Barr, who leased out the ground level and lived and officed on the second floor, which features an inset balcony overlooking the street. A north-facing skylight provided ample natural lighting for Barr's studio. The building was renovated in 1983 under Richard Mycue.

ADDRESS
213–19 Broadway

ARCHITECT
Leo M. J. Dielmann

RENOVATED
1983

68 TRAVIS PARK, CIRCA 1870

The land for Travis Park was willed to the city by Samuel Augustus Maverick, a signer of the Texas Declaration of Independence, and his wife, Mary Adams Maverick, who had used the property as an orchard for their home on Alamo Plaza to the southeast. During the Civil War it was a campground for Confederate soldiers gathering to go to war. First named Travis Plaza, after Alamo hero William Barret Travis, the square was planted and fenced in the 1870s. A Victorian-style bandstand and game tables were later added. In 1900 the local chapter of the United Daughters of the Confederacy donated the central monument, designed by Virginia Montgomery and topped by a Confederate soldier sculpted by Frank Teich. The monument is flanked by iron cannons. In 1953–57 the San Antonio Conservation Society defeated plans for construction of a municipal

ADDRESS
Bounded by Travis, Navarro, Pecan and Jefferson streets

parking garage beneath the park. Renovations under O'Neill & Perez in 1985 included a concrete perimeter retaining wall.

ADDRESS
315 East Pecan Street

ARCHITECT
Richard Upjohn, New York

RENOVATED
1927, 1951, 2007

69 NR ST. MARK'S EPISCOPAL CHURCH, 1875
Designed by front-ranking Gothic Revival church architect Richard Upjohn, noted for designing Wall Street's Trinity Church in New York, the cornerstone of St. Mark's was laid in 1859. The building had not risen above its foundations when the Civil War broke out, however, and it was not completed until 1875. The exterior is dominated by heavy limestone walls, while timber framing in the interior conveys a much lighter feeling.

69

70

Massing at the east end includes a small bell cote. The 1927 education building and parish hall to the west were designed by the Alfred Giles Company in collaboration with Albert F. Beckmann. A major remodeling in 1949–51 under Henry Steinbomer added a bell tower at the southwest corner of the original building with an entrance leading into a new narthex, linked by a cloister to the parish hall nearby. Commercial buildings later acquired to the west were mostly replaced and incorporated into a unified façade in a project under way in 2007 and supervised by Ford, Powell & Carson.

ADDRESS
700 North St. Mary's Street

ARCHITECTS
Marmon Mok

70▲ MARMON MOK LOBBY, 1997
Marmon Mok's renovated reception area included new colors and finishes and focused on creating an open, inviting space to demonstrate the firm's design abilities and provide a display gallery for work-in-progress.

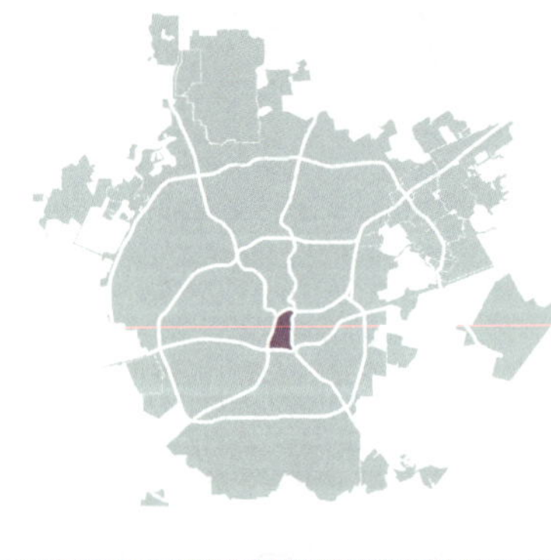

71 SOUTHWESTERN BELL TELEPHONE BUILDING, 1931

While Southwestern Bell's St. Louis–based corporate architect Irving R. Timlin was designing Tudor Revival buildings for the company in Missouri and Art Deco in Oklahoma, he chose an extreme style of Spanish Baroque for the new nine-story Southwestern Bell headquarters in San Antonio. The façade was chamfered on the northeast in deference to the nearby Municipal Auditorium, at the head of an urban plaza. Cast stone ornamentation on the face of the building's first three stories is no doubt the most lavish example of this work in a city noted for its Spanish Colonial Revival commercial and residential architecture, a style that had already peaked in San Antonio and elsewhere. The decoration was echoed in ornamentation crowning the exterior shell and in a central penthouse set back but not chamfered on the roof. The penthouse was removed in 1954 when the building was extended upward. Much of the original upper ornamentation was removed from its original location and moved upward to adorn the top of the building at its new height.

ADDRESS
105 Auditorium Circle

ARCHITECT
Irving R. Timlin, St. Louis

RENOVATED
1954

ADDRESS
100 Auditorium Circle

ARCHITECTS
Atlee B. and Robert M. Ayres, George R. Willis, Emmett T. Jackson

RENOVATED
1985

72 NR MUNICIPAL AUDITORIUM, 1926

Municipal Auditorium, one of the state's most distinguished Spanish Colonial Revival landmarks, stands at the head of what became an urban plaza. The auditorium's triangular site was newly created by elimination of a bend in the San Antonio River. A veneer of Indiana limestone covers the reinforced concrete structure. The arcaded entrance is flanked by broad, low twin towers with domes roofed with glazed ceramic tiles. Following a serious fire in 1979, Phelps/Garza/Bomberger oversaw the building's restoration, including rebuilding of the steel roof frame and the ninety-foot high flyloft.

ADDRESS
119 Taylor Street

ARCHITECT
Alfred Giles

RENOVATED
1981

73 NR MAVERICK–CARTER HOUSE, 1894

This monumental three-story Richardson Romanesque home was built for real estate investor William H. Maverick and was one of many structures designed by Alfred Giles for members of the Maverick family. It was reportedly inspired by a home Maverick had admired in Cleveland, Ohio. Its irregular outline is broken by turrets, projecting bays and mostly rectangular openings with massive stone lintels and sills. A notable exception is the round-arched quasi-Palladian window on the second floor over the main entrance. Rear galleries once caught the breeze from a now-straightened bend of the San Antonio River. Interior paneling is in maple, oak and teak. A rooftop observatory was added after the house was acquired in 1914 by H. C. Carter and his wife, Aline Badger Carter, an amateur astronomer and onetime poet laureate of Texas.

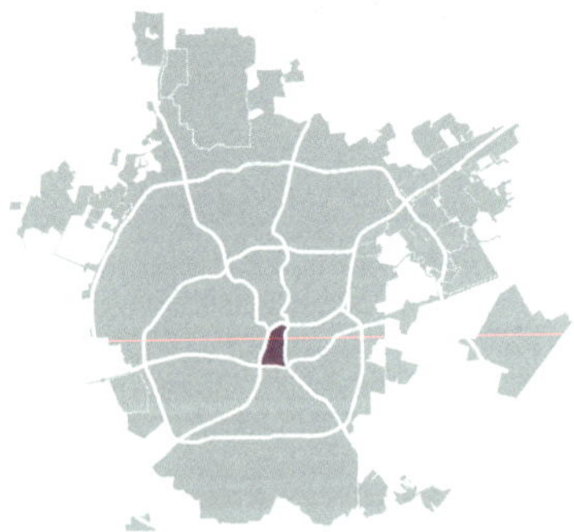

74

75

74 FIRST PRESBYTERIAN CHURCH, 1909

Atlee B. Ayres, not generally recognized as a prolific church architect, completed numerous commissions for congregations throughout Texas, though his design for First Presbyterian Church is not highly imaginative. The lack of a spire, planned but never built, makes the church seem somewhat heavier than intended. Nonetheless, the execution of Ayres's design in rusticated stone with massive corner towers has made it an enduring example of local ecclesiastical design. The interior contains monumental wood framing. The sanctuary and its related structures, with additions and remodelings by Paul J. Silber (1924), Henry Steinbomer (1952), Marvin Eickenroth (1966) and Marmon, Barclay, Souter, Foster and Hays (1988), now encompass the entire block, serving one of the nation's largest downtown Presbyterian congregations.

ADDRESS
408 North Alamo Street

ARCHITECT
Atlee B. Ayres

RENOVATED
1924, 1952, 1966, 1988

75 EXPRESS-NEWS BUILDING, 1929

The San Antonio Express-News, founded in 1865, constructed this then state-of-the-art facility in 1929. Publisher Frank Huntress was a longtime admirer of Chicago publisher Robert R. McCormick. This building's twelve-story corner tower resembles McCormick's Tribune Tower on a smaller scale. Herbert Green's reinforced concrete and limestone work features an ornate entry and decorated spandrel panels. Above the entrance is Pompeo Coppini's stone bas relief depiction of publishing, with figures representing labor, edu-

ADDRESS
301 Avenue E

ARCHITECT
Herbert S. Green

RENOVATED
1971, 1994

cation, knowledge, enlightenment, truth and justice. The vestibule and octagonal lobby are heavily decorated with marble and mosaic tile and feature ornamental bronze doors and grill work. Later additions include an adjoining production facility along Fourth Street completed in 1994 under Lance, Larcade & Bechtol.

ADDRESS
311 Third Street

76▲ 608 EAST TRAVIS, 1917

This reinforced concrete and tile building first housed an automobile dealership selling Chandlers and Hupmobiles. Its loft-style structure with steel frame awning windows is typical of utilitarian buildings of the period. The primary façade is faced in brick with arched

76

77

openings and a decorated parapet while the secondary façade on Travis Street is more plainly detailed, likely due to the building having been shortened when Travis Street was extended in the 1920s. The unfinished side walls reveal the concrete structure. The building was renovated by the architectural firm Lake/Flato for its offices.

ADDRESS
308 Avenue E

ARCHITECTS
Herbert M. Greene, Dallas
Ralph Cameron

77 NR SCOTTISH RITE TEMPLE, 1924

San Antonio's Scottish Rite Temple was designed in a manner befitting the ancient heritage of the Masonic orders and is one of the city's finest works from the 1920s. Ralph Cameron finished plans for the building begun by Herbert Greene, who also designed Scottish Rite temples in Dallas and El Paso. The Classical Revival stone structure with terra cotta and enamel decoration is notable for its eight colossal Corinthian columns and the bas relief frieze by Pompeo Coppini, who also did the monumental bronze entry doors featuring George Washington, a noted Mason. The classical theme carries into the opulent interior, which continues to serve its original function.

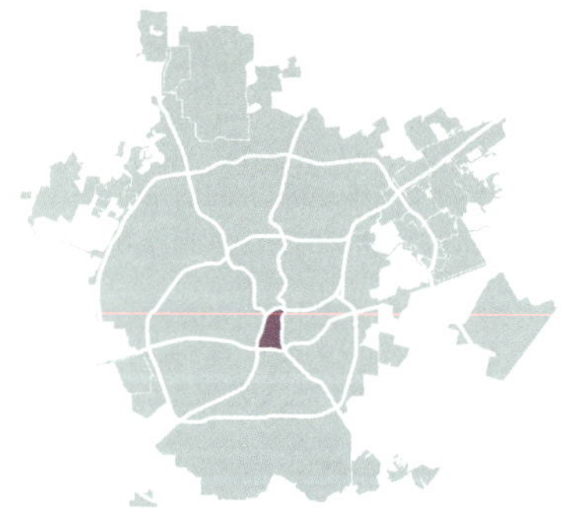

78

79

78 YWCA BUILDING, 1909
(DPT LABORATORIES)

Constructed to house the city's YWCA, Atlee B. Ayres's rather restrained Renaissance Revival design was dramatically transformed when the building was converted to office use. Though the original open entry court is now enclosed, it can still be identified through a light frame of glass and steel. The two flanking wings, supplemented by a rear addition, are now connected by pedestrian bridges that allow unobstructed views to the street and into the former courtyard. The basement swimming pool is no longer in use.

ADDRESS
318 McCullough Avenue

ARCHITECT
Atlee B. Ayres

RENOVATED
Marmon Mok 1972

79▲ DOG TEAM TOO LOFT & STUDIO, 1920s

Adaptive use of this utilitarian building on the edge of downtown created an "industrial hacienda" focused around a pool courtyard. A hodge-podge of remodeled storefronts was replaced with cement infill panels and high windows to maintain privacy and security. A new steel-framed, saw-tooth roof with north-facing clerestory windows creates a large, light-filled central living space.

ADDRESS
317 Sixth Street

ARCHITECTS
Lake/Flato

RENOVATED
2001

ADDRESS
411 Sixth Street

ARCHITECT
James Riely Gordon

RENOVATED
1978

80 NR THIELE HOUSE, 1890

James Riely Gordon, known more for his imposing mansions and public buildings, designed this modest raised cottage of buff-colored brick for a locally prominent German immigrant, August Thiele. Gordon's design is notable for the distinctive horseshoe-shaped arch that dominates the elevated porch. Together, the Thiele House and the adjacent Engleman-Muench House illustrate the evolution of vernacular architecture in San Antonio during the last half of the nineteenth century. The Thiele House was renovated for offices in 1978 by Breig and Bratton.

80

81

ADDRESS
415 Sixth Street

RENOVATED
1978

81 NR ENGLEMAN-MUENCH HOUSE, CIRCA 1860

This vernacular plastered limestone house with its low gabled roof and wide porch is typical of cottages once prevalent throughout the city and in this neighborhood, which included a wide variety of residential vernacular architecture from the last half of the nineteenth century. The neighborhood once encompassed some twenty city blocks and was known as the Irish Flat. Settled by Irish immigrants, many of whom worked for the Army, the area is often misidentified as the Irish Flats, confusing the original identification of the neighborhood's flat land with an alternate word for apartments. The Engleman-Muench House was owned by the neighboring Thiele family for many years. The two houses are jointly listed on the National Register of Historic Places as the Thiele House and Cottage. The Engleman-Muench House was renovated as offices in 1978 by Breig and Bratton.

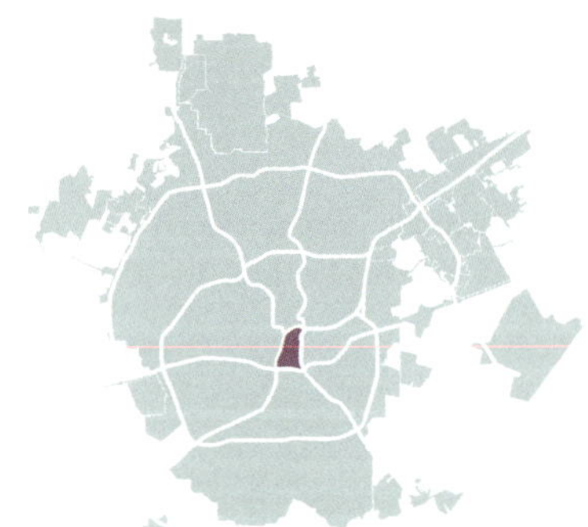

82a

82b

82c

82▲ NR OLD LONE STAR BREWERY, 1904 (SAN ANTONIO MUSEUM OF ART)

St. Louis brewer Adolphus Busch in 1892 purchased San Antonio–owned Lone Star Brewery, established on this site eight years earlier. To replace existing frame buildings with brick structures, Busch turned to the late Edmund Jungenfeld's St. Louis firm, which designed other Busch facilities. Local supervising architects were James Wahrenberger and Albert Beckmann. Beckmann also designed later buildings in the complex. The original structures, ranging in height from two to five stories, were completed in 1904 and unified by crenelated projections and other corbelled brick details. The twin towers of the main building were connected by a steel catwalk for transferring barrels. During Prohibition, the plant produced a non-alcoholic beverage. After the brewery closed and Busch sold the Lone Star name, it was used for a cotton mill and for an ice and food storage company, and fell into disrepair. In 1972 the San Antonio Museum Association optioned the buildings and began converting the decaying complex into the San Antonio Museum of Art, which opened in 1981. The museum was designed by Cambridge Seven of Cambridge, MA, and by associated architects Martin & Ortega and Chumney, Jones & Kell. The historic exterior was preserved. Glass-enclosed elevators added in each tower allowed floor-to-floor gallery previews. The former boiler and engine rooms housed Egyptian, Greek and Roman antiquities. A sky-lighted

ADDRESS
110 West Jones Avenue

ARCHITECTS
E. Jungenfeld & Co., St. Louis; Wahrenberger & Beckmann

RENOVATED
1981, 1991, 1994
Cambridge Seven

1998, 2005
Overland Partners

entrance area provides ground floor access to the towers on either side and, at the rear, into the Cowden Gallery (1991), the Luby Courtyard (1994) and the restored Beretta Hops House (1994). The steel catwalk connecting the towers at the upper level was replaced by an enclosed glass sky bridge offering expansive views of the city. Additions by Overland Partners include an eastern wing to house the [82b] Nelson Rockefeller Center for Latin American Art (1998) and the award-winning [82c] Lenora and Walter F. Brown Asian Art Wing (2005), inspired by Japanese shoji screens.

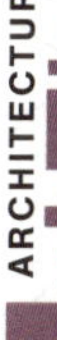

ADDRESS
819 Augusta Street

ARCHITECT
Alfred Giles

83 KING HOUSE, 1880 (BRIGHT SHAWL)

Dr. Claudius Augustus King hired fellow Englishman Alfred Giles to design this L-plan house as his office and residence. Representative of an important house type common in central Texas, this cottage is more ambitious than most in terms of its detailing, finely tooled limestone and projecting bay. It was acquired by the Junior League in 1929 for its meeting place and a tea room known as the Bright Shawl. A new wing in the 1970s added meeting and banquet facilities connected to the original house by a glass gallery. The main dining area was enlarged twenty years later in partnership with a major user, the Rotary Club of San Antonio.

ADDRESS
903 North St. Mary's Street

ARCHITECTS
Marmon & Mok Associates

84▲ CENTRAL YMCA, 1972

The Central YMCA is a one- and two-story structure of poured-in-place, warm-toned concrete construction. The building has projecting bays containing deep-set windows and planting troughs. Exterior walls are vertically scored to differentiate them from smooth-finished, horizontally articulated floor and roof slabs.

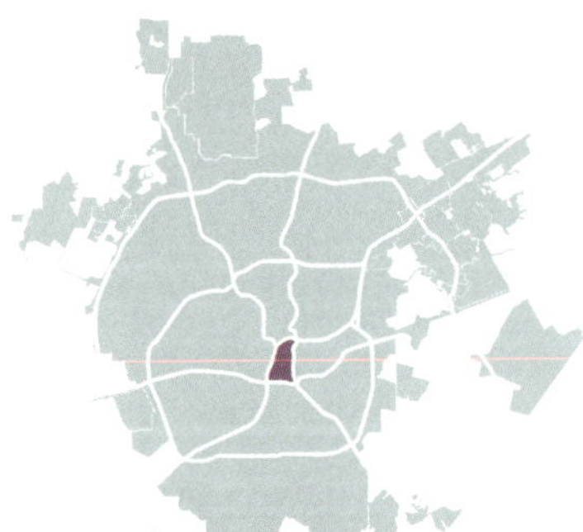

85 MADISON SQUARE PRESBYTERIAN CHURCH, 1882

Madison Square Presbyterian Church was constructed in 1882, the year after the city began to improve the adjacent public park for a new, appealing residential neighborhood now undergoing revival. Erected for the city's first Northern Presbyterian congregation, the church was built according to "Plan 16," sent by the Board of Church Erection in Philadelphia and constructed by local builder G. W. Konkle. In 1886, a tremendous storm caused the entire front of the church to collapse. The sanctuary was rebuilt in 1887, the tower added in 1895 and the adjacent assembly building completed in 1916. The church interior was remodeled by Harvey P. Smith in 1922. The education building was completed in 1957 to celebrate the church's seventy-fifth anniversary.

ADDRESS
319 Camden Street

ARCHITECT
Board of Church Erection Plan 16, Philadelphia

REBUILT
1887

RENOVATED
1895, 1916, 1957

86 CENTRAL CHRISTIAN CHURCH, 1950

Well-known church architect Henry Steinbomer was selected to design this replacement for the domed Central Christian Church building previously on the site. Steinbomer reproduced and simplified the familiar image of a neoclassical church using the characteristic San Antonio materials of tan brick and limestone. The symmetry of the church's principal elevation and the graceful row of long, arched windows along its western flank are especially effective in fixing the building to its pivotal site at the intersection of the downtown streets bordering wedge-shaped Romana Plaza.

ADDRESS
720 North Main Avenue

ARCHITECT
Henry Steinbomer

ADDRESS
1015 Navarro Street

ARCHITECT
Attributed to Arthur J. Hermann

RENOVATED
1997

87 NR THE HAVANA, 1914
(HAVANA RIVERWALK INN)

The Havana was built on land once owned by the nearby Ursuline Academy. Built by grocer Edward Melcher and his wife, Kathinka, this residential hotel's Mediterranean Revival style features twin three-story towers, broad eaves and recessed porches to provide relief from intense summer heat. In 1920 Melcher sold part of his property to the city for rerouting of the river channel, which also created land for nearby Municipal Auditorium. After standing vacant for several years, the Havana was restored in 1997 as a twenty-seven-room boutique hotel according to a design by Marmon Mok.

87

88

ADDRESS
600 Soledad Street

ARCHITECTS
Ricardo Legorreta, Mexico City; Johnson-Dempsey & Associates and Sprinkle Robey

88 SAN ANTONIO CENTRAL LIBRARY, 1995

San Antonio's Central Library mixes courtyards, shaded porticoes and strong but simple geometric forms. Mexico City architect Ricardo Legorreta, with San Antonio's Johnson-Dempsey & Associates and Sprinkle Robey Architects, was awarded the project in a city-sponsored design competition to create a library reflecting the city's rich Hispanic heritage. The library is organized around a six-story atrium that serves as the focal point for interior spaces, while the emphasis on outdoor spaces is expressed by roof terraces on various levels. Notable exterior features are the cascading fountain in the auto court and the east elevation's sculptural spheres. The exterior color was defined in a public competition as "enchilada red." Dale Chihuly's brilliantly colored "Fiesta Tower" glass sculpture was installed in the atrium in 2003 to celebrate the San Antonio Public Library's centennial.

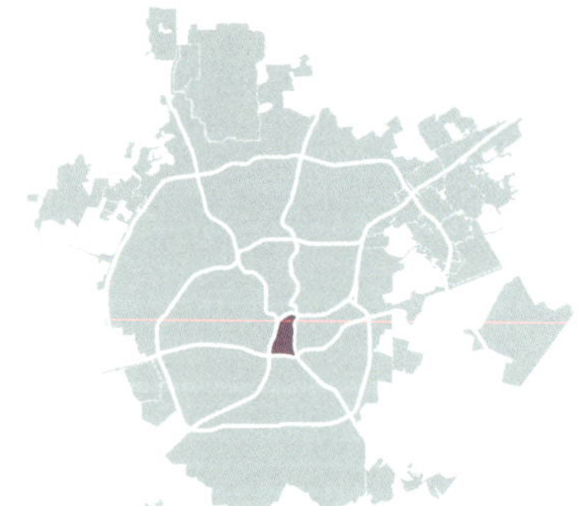

89

89

89

89★ NR OLD URSULINE ACADEMY AND CONVENT, SINCE 1851 **(SOUTHWEST SCHOOL OF ART AND CRAFT)**

Restoration of the Old Ursuline Academy and Convent is one of San Antonio's triumphs in historic preservation. The original two-story building was constructed in 1851 for Roman Catholic missionary nuns of the Ursuline Order sent to open a school for girls in frontier San Antonio. Builder/architect Jules Poinsard chose a construction method known as pise de terre, or rammed earth, which involved packing an earthen mix between wooden forms that were raised as walls grew taller. Limestone blocks were used for the five adjoining post-Civil War buildings, detailed with Gothic and Renaissance Revival elements and including a chapel attributed to Francois Giraud. In 1961 the school moved to a suburban site and the vacant, decaying downtown campus was sold. It became the target of a flurry of plans for razing and new development. A five-alarm midwinter fire in 1967 destroyed a four-story 1912 classroom wing, but all older buildings were saved. Purchase of key parcels and heroic efforts by the San Antonio Conservation Society resulted in a 1971 move by the Southwest Craft Center into some of the buildings. Renovation and restoration began in 1975 under Martin & Ortega and has continued since 1977 under Ford, Powell & Carson. Ownership of the historic campus was consolidated in 1981 by the Craft Center, which evolved into the Southwest School of Art and Craft and uses the buildings for classrooms,

ADDRESS
300 Augusta Street

ARCHITECT
Attributed to Jules Poinsard
Additions after 1866, Francois Giraud

RENOVATED
1975–86

studios and offices and for a museum, sales gallery and lunchtime restaurant. In 1998 the campus expanded into former commercial space across Navarro Street. The school's endowment is benefited by the private, independently operated Club Giraud, housed in the Ursuline's former stone stables and laundry buildings beside the San Antonio River Walk.

90

91

ADDRESS
300 Convent Street

ARCHITECTS
Skidmore, Owings & Merrill, Houston

90 INTERFIRST PLAZA, 1984
(BANK OF AMERICA BUILDING)

Built by a Texas banking conglomerate that, like the nearby RepublicBank, soon disappeared in a flurry of economically induced mergers, this distinctive landmark gains an air of drama not just from its stepped-back massing but from the pleated character of its exterior walls, which transforms the building in the light of the setting sun into a monumental sculpture. Design hints derive from San Antonio's 1920s and 30s high rises. The main lobby is an effective interior space, without the extravagance that so often accompanies bank interiors.

ADDRESS
152 East Pecan Street

ARCHITECTS
George Willis and Emmett T. Jackson

RENOVATED
1993

91▲★ NR BUILDERS EXCHANGE BUILDING, 1925

This ten-story Gothic Revival structure was built as headquarters for the Builders Exchange of San Antonio, an organization of local architects, contractors, surveyors and suppliers, who also rented individual office space. It is one of the nation's earliest buildings constructed by a National Association of Builders Exchanges member organization. After the Builders Exchange moved in 1950, the building was used for general office space. In 1993 it was converted by Lake/Flato into forty-one apartments, with restaurants on the ground floor.

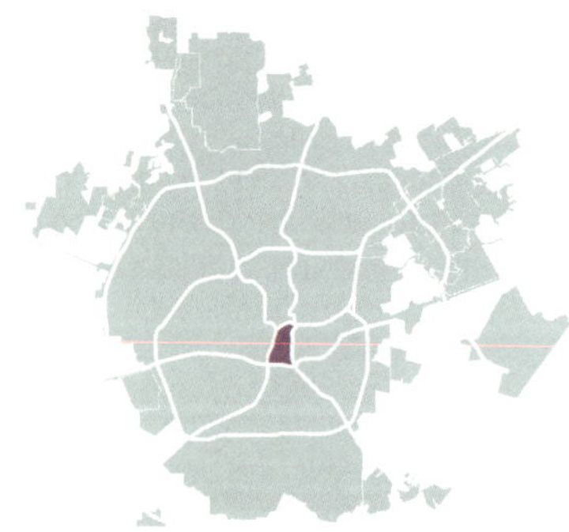

92▲ GREEN GATE BUILDING, 1927
(HARLANDALE BUILDING COMPANY)

This small office structure initially housed the Harlandale Building Company, a local real estate development firm. It is better remembered for its more colorful later tenant, the Green Gate Club, a bar and strip tease establishment. In the 1980s the deteriorated building, with its elaborately decorated cast stone façade, was adapted by Lake/Flato for a graphic design studio. The architects restored the original high-ceilinged one-story volume and courtyard while retaining such aging interior materials as the raw-concrete mezzanine and rusted columns.

ADDRESS
429 North St. Mary's Street

RENOVATED
1980s

93▲ NBC CENTER DRIVE-IN BANK, 1976 *NO PHOTO*

A ten-level parking garage, an eight-story office building, and a motor bank pavilion comprise this two-block group of structures built to complement the twenty-one-story 1957 National Bank of Commerce Building, (Kenneth Franzheim, Houston, and Ayres & Ayres), since converted to a hotel. Franzheim acknowledged San Antonio tradition by encasing his tower in tan brick and limestone, a tawny color scheme retained by Marmon Mok in this precast concrete garage and office building. The motor bank, sheltered beneath a dark, steel, space frame canopy, was treated as a sculptural element in the midst of the taller surrounding structures. The original canopy has been replaced with one retaining the original design concept.

ADDRESS
430 Soledad Street

ARCHITECTS
Marmon Mok

ADDRESS
115 East Travis Street

ARCHITECT
George Willis

94 MILAM BUILDING, 1928

The twenty-one-story Milam Building, constructed during a boom that expanded the city center north beyond Commerce and Houston streets, is cited by some as the nation's tallest brick and reinforced concrete structure at the time. It certainly carries the distinction of being the world's first high-rise structure originally designed with full mechanical air conditioning, and it is recognized as a national mechanical engineering heritage site. The decidedly blocky form of the structure, with its U-shaped central court, is most effective from a distance. Sidewalk elevations are kept plain. Spanish Revival–inspired ornament is confined to the upper floors and the top of the central tower. Once the headquarters of many leading oil and gas companies, the building continues to be used for offices.

ADDRESS
500 North Santa Rosa Street

RENOVATED
1970

95 NR MENGER SOAP WORKS, CIRCA 1873 (SAN ANTONIO SOAP WORKS)

Limestone rubble walls and rough-cut quoins and voussoirs enclose this example of early vernacular Texas industrial architecture, built by a company established in 1850 by Johann Nicholas Simon Menger, a cousin of the builder of the Menger Hotel. Located beside San Pedro Creek and its useful supply of water, the structure features tall, narrow windows for ventilating lye and chemicals during the process of making soap. In 1970 the building, nearly razed along with the rest of the neighborhood in an urban renewal project, was renovated under Robert Callaway as the office for an adjacent new complex of apartment buildings.

ADDRESS
214 West Salinas Street

RENOVATED
1981

96 NR GARCIA HOUSE, CIRCA 1856

This caliche, limestone and brick house was begun by Mariano Garcia about 1856 and enlarged about 1900, evolving as the family grew. The original front portion of the structure is representative of mid-nineteenth century vernacular design in San Antonio, while the rear two-story brick ell (circa 1900) and tower at the northwest corner (1910) typify more modern construction. Garcia's descendents lived here until the house was sold in 1981 and converted to office use.

97 NR FIRST NATIONAL BANK, 1886

Wealthy banker and philanthropist George Washington Brackenridge hired Cyrus Eidlitz to design this Moorish-inspired building for Brackenridge's First National Bank. The stepped-dome porch of the entry is supported by two polished granite Moorish columns. The adjacent Syrian-arched window has a rectangular surround carved with Moorish motifs. Brackenridge maintained a garden on the roof, where he entertained and reportedly kept a cow to provide fresh milk when he lived in his adjoining Loan and Trust building. After the bank vacated the building in 1970 it was sold for office use.

ADDRESS
213 East Commerce Street

ARCHITECT
Cyrus L. W. Eidlitz, New York

98 NR SAN ANTONIO LOAN AND TRUST BUILDING, 1903

The design of George Brackenridge's narrow Loan and Trust Company building adjacent to his First National Bank reflects the national affection for classicism, as seen in the stone detailing and pressed-metal cornice. For several years Brackenridge and his sister, Eleanor, a noted suffragette, resided on the upper three floors, using one floor for quarters, one for servants quarters and the third as a ballroom. In 2005, under the direction of Fisher Heck Architects, the exterior was restored and the basement excavated to provide access under Crockett Street to the River Walk. The building now houses offices and private apartments.

ADDRESS
235 East Commerce Street

ARCHITECT
G. Voorhees

RENOVATED
2005

ADDRESS
104 North St. Mary's Street

ARCHITECT
Robert B. Kelly

RENOVATED
2007

99 AZTEC THEATER, 1926

The Aztec Theater is one of San Antonio's fine surviving movie palaces. Set within a six-story commercial building on a prominent downtown corner, it opened in 1926. Two notable features are the 2,000-pound iron chandelier suspended over the lobby and the 1,700-pipe Wurlitzer organ. The interior riot of colored mosaic and terrazzo tile floors, simulated stone walls and Mayan friezes reminiscent of the ruins of Palenque and Mitla transported moviegoers to the world of Mesoamerica. Interior decorations are largely the work of master modeler Hannibal Pianta, with some by Henry Wedemeyer. By the 1970s the Aztec had

been divided into three theaters showing B-grade movies. Fearing the theater would be demolished, the San Antonio Conservation Society purchased the property in 1989 and sold it in 1993, with protective covenants. Nearly fifteen years later the building, including theater and offices, was at last fully restored, by Phillip B. Smith of Drury Southwest. Restoration Associates restored historic interior finishes. Tunneling from the basement beneath Crockett Street to the River Walk created a dramatic river entrance.

ADDRESS
154 East Commerce Street

ARCHITECTS
Graham, Anderson, Probst & White, Chicago

RENOVATED
1976, 2007

100 ALAMO NATIONAL BANK BUILDING, 1929 (DRURY PLAZA HOTEL)

This twenty-four-story building was erected as the new home of Alamo National Bank, first located two blocks up Commerce Street. Upper floors were leased for offices. It was designed by the Chicago firm of Graham, Anderson, Probst & White, successor to the great D. H. Burnham and among the nation's leading practitioners of classicism in the design of high-rise office buildings. In this particular work, detailing is restrained. It was converted to a Drury Plaza Hotel in 2007. At the same time the attached parking garage structure, oriented toward the adjoining flood control channel, is being incorporated into the River Walk improvements, linking the two flood gate ends of the Paeso del Rio and incorporating a new six-floor hotel addition, designed by Sprinkle Robey Architects.

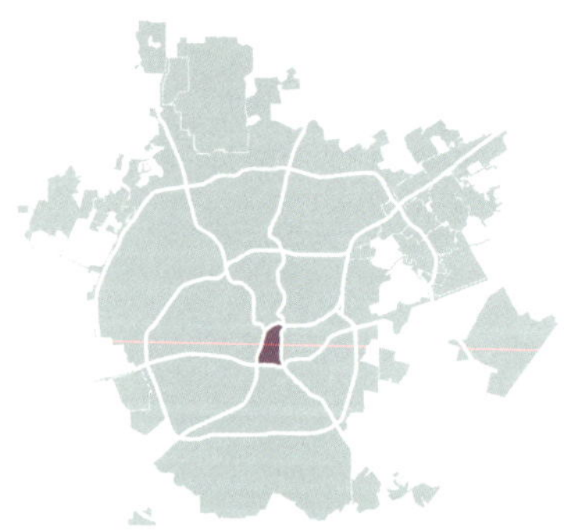

101▲ ONE ALAMO CENTER, 1981 *NO PHOTO*

This eight-story rectangular building was constructed to house additional office space and a motor bank for MBank Alamo, formerly Alamo National Bank, then located directly across South St. Mary's Street. Automobile access dominates the open, brick paved ground-floor level, with the exception of the shallow loggia facing South St. Mary's Street. Continuous spandrels of pre-cast concrete alternate with inset horizontal bands of bronze-tinted glazing. Corner bays are infilled with limestone panels.

ADDRESS
106 South St. Mary's Street

ARCHITECTS
Ford, Powell & Carson

102▲ PORTAL SAN FERNANDO, 2001

This urban park occupies one of the city's most historic corners. After the site's nineteenth century buildings facing Main Plaza were demolished in the 1970s, it languished as a parking lot until being transformed by Lake/Flato in 2001 into Portal San Fernando, as part of an effort to link Main Plaza with the River Walk below. The descending park suggests a quarry-like space, with a meandering ramped path reminiscent of a dry creek-bed. Native planting was designed by Rosa Finsley. Inscriptions designed by Celia Muñoz evoke the sweep of San Antonians' relationship with the river. At the foot of the park, a cantilevered walkway was engineered beside a flood control channel to connect with the main River Walk a block to the north.

ADDRESS
Main Plaza

ARCHITECTS
Lake/Flato

ARCHITECTS
Lake/Flato

LANDSCAPE ARCHITECTS
SWA Group

103 NR **MAIN PLAZA,** FROM 1738 **(PLAZA DE LAS ISLAS)**

Canary Island immigrants arrived in San Antonio in 1731. They began building a church facing this ground in 1738, establishing a public plaza as part of the street system grid they plotted according to the Laws of the Indies. This plaza is sometimes referred to as Plaza de las Islas, or Plaza of the Islanders. The Casas Reales, seat of municipal government, was located across from the church on the far side of the plaza, which became the setting for many of the city's early historical events. Apaches signed a peace treaty here in 1749, though they attacked citizens with a vengeance in 1789. Anglo

colonists fought Mexican forces on this plaza in the 1835 Siege of Bexar. In 1840 a peace conference with Comanche chieftains in the Casa Reales went awry, leading to a massacre and fighting that spread to the rest of the town. The U.S. Army's Department of Texas surrendered to the Confederacy in a formal ceremony here in 1861. Following the Civil War, new hotels and office buildings reinvigorated the plaza. Construction of the Bexar County Courthouse on the plaza's south side in the early 1890s gave impetus to its landscaping. Street realignments reshaped the plaza and reduced its open space in the course of the twentieth century, and the site of the Casa Reales disappeared with construction of a flood control channel just east of the plaza in 1929–30. In 2001 the city completed Portal San Fernando, a park designed by Lake/Flato that descends from Main Plaza to the flood channel, by then being incorporated into the River Walk. Closing some streets around Main Plaza was planned in 2007 to restore much of the plaza's original open space.

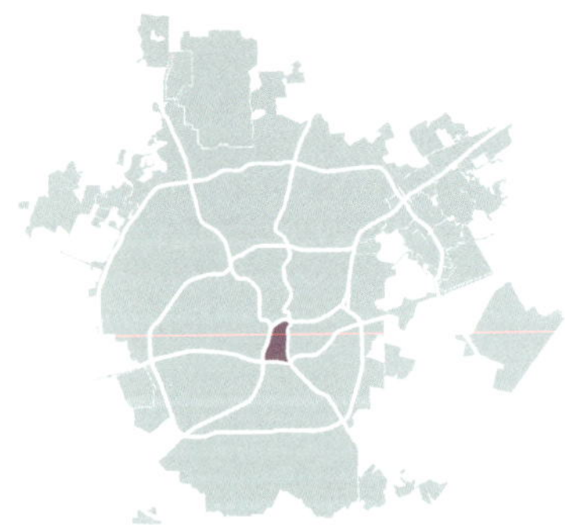

104▲★ NR SAN FERNANDO CATHEDRAL, 1755

The cornerstone of the parish church known today as San Fernando Cathedral was laid in 1738. Construction was completed with funds and materials from the Canary Island immigrants and from Mexican soldier-settlers, supplemented by a grant from the Spanish crown. Builder and stonemason Geronimo de Ibarra and stonecutter Felipe de Santiago are largely credited with completing the church in 1755. The original cruciform plan was defined by rough limestone walls and a crossing dome. This configuration and the façade with a central east entry and one bell tower are believed to have been similar to an early church at Mission San Antonio de Valero that collapsed. The original apse and a portion of the connecting walls were preserved when walls of the original nave and the tower were removed and the church was enlarged during construction of the present Gothic Revival edifice, completed in 1873. A rectory designed by Leo M. J. Dielmann was built surrounding the original apse in 1923 but removed fifty years later during restoration work under Ford, Powell & Carson, when the walls, towers and eighteenth century dome were also repaired. A total exterior and interior renovation completed in 2003 under Rafferty Rafferty Tollefson with associate architects Fisher Heck included installation of three eighteenth century style retablos. The adjacent City Centre building, also completed in 2003 under the same architects, houses a gift shop and museum, community rooms and offices.

ADDRESS
Main Plaza

ARCHITECTS
Geronimo de Ibarra, builder;
Felipe de Santiago, stonecutter
Nave and façade, Francois Giraud

RENOVATIONS AND ADDITIONS
1873, 1923, 1977, 2003

ADDRESS
Main Plaza

ARCHITECTS
Sanguinet and Staats, Fort Worth and Houston

RENOVATIONS AND ADDITIONS
1922, 1983, 1993

105▲ NR OLD FROST NATIONAL BANK BUILDING, 1922 (MUNICIPAL PLAZA BUILDING)

At twelve stories, Frost National Bank was the tallest building in San Antonio when completed in 1922. T. C. Frost had become a full partner in a mercantile store on this site in 1867, and formally established a banking function in 1880. By the 1920s the fortunes of Frost Bank and the city were growing rapidly. For the bank Sanguinet and Staats, then one of the state's leading designers of tall buildings, incorporated round bas-relief panels depicting U.S. coinage set between double-height arched window openings. The impressive banking lobby featured a marble stairway and Tiffany

105

106

electrical fixtures. A one-story annex was designed by John M. Marriott and also built in 1922. The old building, renovated in 1983, is owned by the City of San Antonio as a municipal office building. In a 1993 redesign, the upper floors were remodeled and the lobby converted to city council chambers under Beaty Saunders Architects.

ADDRESS
Main Plaza

ARCHITECTS
Gordon & Laub

RENOVATIONS AND ADDITIONS
1914, 1926, 1970, 2002

106 NR BEXAR COUNTY COURTHOUSE, 1896

James Riely Gordon and his partner D. E. Laub won the commission to design the exuberant Bexar County Courthouse shortly before ending their partnership. Gordon remained the supervising architect throughout the five-year project and went on to design a dozen other noted Texas courthouses that remain standing. The Bexar County Courthouse reflects the period's popular Romanesque style, with the addition of eclectic details in native Texas granite and sandstone. The massive segmental-arch entry is flanked by towers, one seven stories tall and topped with a beehive spire. In 1914 Leo M. J. Dielmann and Charles T. Boelhauwe designed a three-story addition to the south end. This was demolished and rebuilt in a major expansion in 1926 overseen by associated architects Raymond Phelps, Dahl Dewees, Emmett T. Jackson and George Willis. A major exterior restoration was completed under 3D/I in 2002.

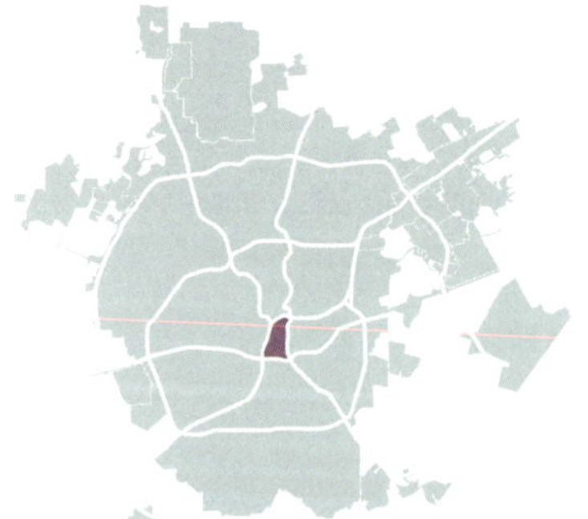

107▲ BEXAR COUNTY JUSTICE CENTER, 1990

The Bexar County Justice Center, which houses courtrooms, judges' quarters, jury rooms and related offices, incorporates native materials that complement James Riely Gordon's 1890s Richardson Romanesque courthouse across the street and other surrounding buildings. Of note is the restored portion of the Spanish Colonial era San Pedro acequia near the corner of Dolorosa Street and Main Plaza.

ADDRESS
300 Dolorosa Street

ARCHITECTS
Jones & Kell Inc., Ford Powell & Carson and Saldaña & Associates

108 NR SAN ANTONIO CITY HALL, 1891

Otto Kramer, who moved to San Antonio from Cincinnati after working in New York, Chicago and St. Louis, designed city hall with prominent Second Empire elements. Walls are of smooth-cut limestone on a rusticated base. There were turrets at each corner of the three-story building, the south turrets curving with conical roofs and the north turrets square with mansard roofs. A focal point was an ornate 135-foot clock tower. The clock tower and roofs of the turrets were removed when a fourth floor was added in 1927 and the building's design transformed in the Spanish Colonial Revival style then in vogue throughout the Southwest. The redesign by Carleton W. Adams also replaced the projecting columned central entrances on the east and west with cast stone Romanesque arches flush with the façades. Adams left some of the building's more subtle Renaissance Revival details, such as the aedicule windows, entablature courses and

ADDRESS
Military Plaza

ARCHITECT
Otto Kramer

REDESIGNED
1927, Adams & Adams

other limestone embellishments, all credited to local stonemason Frank Teich. Though city council chambers were relocated across the street to the Municipal Plaza Building in 1993, city hall still houses offices for the mayor, council and some staff. Statues and monuments commemorating historical figures and events are scattered around the surrounding greenspace.

ADDRESS
Military Plaza

RENOVATED
1930

109 NR SPANISH GOVERNOR'S PALACE, 1749 (PRESIDIO CAPTAIN'S RESIDENCE)

This one-story, flat-roofed stone structure was built as a residence and headquarters for the captain of the Presidio de Bexar. It is designated on a 1766 map as

the casa del capitán and was referred to in Spanish times by the similar term comandancia. The building was given its more glamorous but apocryphal designation as the palace of the Spanish governor himself by San Antonio's romantic pioneer preservationist Adina De Zavala. In 1915 she began an emotional campaign to save and restore the dilapidated building, extensively altered and neglected throughout the nineteenth and early twentieth centuries while used as a residence and for commercial space. De Zavala and her Texas Historical and Landmarks Association recognized the structure's significance by a front doorway's keystone date of 1749. Other groups, including the newly formed San Antonio Conservation Society, joined De Zavala's cause, and the city, aided by the popularity of the Spanish Colonial Revival movement in the Southwest, purchased the building with voter-approved bonds in 1929. In the absence of virtually any historical documentation of the building's design or of its architectural history, architect and avocational historian Harvey P. Smith traveled to Santa Fe, New Mexico to study its Governor's Palace for inspiration. He then drew reconstruction plans and supervised the San Antonio project, dedicated in 1930. Wooden entry doors were carved by the noted Austin craftsman Peter Mansbendel. What is now universally referred to as the Spanish Governor's Palace is one of San Antonio's earliest historic preservation successes. It is owned by the City of San Antonio and operated as a museum.

110

111

110 NR MILITARY PLAZA, SINCE 1720
(PLAZA DE ARMAS)
City hall is sited squarely in the center of the former drill ground of the Presidio de Bexar, a soldier-settler community founded farther to the north in 1718 and moved to this site about 1720, hence the plaza's sometime designation as Plaza de Armas. The presidio, garrisoned by mestizos from central Mexico, provided protection for the area's five outlying missions and for the adjacent Villa de San Fernando. The so-called Spanish Governor's Palace on the plaza's west side and the eighteenth century apse of San Fernando Cathedral on the east are the only remnants of Spanish colonial–era buildings that defined the plaza until after the Civil War, when most of the original one-story adobe buildings began to be replaced by two- and three-story structures of stone and brick. The plaza was the site of public executions after revolts against Spain in 1811 and 1813, of vigilante lynchings in the 1860s and of bustling market activities. Trade and the arrivals and departures of wagon trains and stagecoaches declined sharply in the 1880s, when the city's transportation hub moved to the new railroad yards on the eastern edge of downtown. As in the eighteenth century, Military Plaza remains surrounded by commercial structures, government offices and church-related buildings. Its integrity as a plaza, however, was marred less by the construction of city hall as an island in its center than by the carving up of part of the remaining western portion of

the plaza between city hall and the Spanish Governor's Palace in the 1980s for city employee parking.

ADDRESS
Military Plaza

RENOVATED
1979

111 NR MILITARY PLAZA WEST SIDE COMMERCIAL BUILDINGS, 1880–87, 1891 **(VOGEL BELT BUILDINGS)**
This group of commercial buildings is representative of San Antonio's late nineteenth century commercial development. German immigrants Edward Steves and Simon Fest built two-story retail buildings immediately south of the Spanish Governor's Palace in 1880 and 1881. These were followed in 1884 by Fest's Fashion Theater, designed by James Murphy. The remaining portion of the block was built by Fest in 1887. When a

112

fire damaged both the Fashion Theater and the Steves building in 1891, the façades were reconstructed with Italianate details. The southernmost building was made more narrow when Dolorosa Street was widened in the 1920s. Occupied for many years by the Vogel Belt Company, the buildings were renovated and their façades restored under Lance, Larcade & Bechtol in 1979 as offices for their new owner, the City of San Antonio.

ADDRESS
322–44 West Commerce Street

ARCHITECT
Attributed to Alfred Giles

RENOVATED
1986

112 NR LA CLEDE HOTEL, CIRCA 1896 **(ARCADE/CONTINENTAL HOTEL)**
This fourteen bay building was constructed as the Arcade Hotel about 1896. The design is attributed to Alfred Giles based on stylistic grounds but is otherwise not known to be documented. The building was long known as the La Clede Hotel and then as the Continental Hotel. Located adjacent to the city's old red light district, it housed a diverse clientele ranging from traveling salesmen to fugitives to refugees fleeing Mexico's 1910 revolution. Storefronts along the ground floor were altered over the years, but the upper floors survived intact. A brick parapet unites the entire composition, becoming more significant at the main entrance. In 1986 it was renovated as offices for the San Antonio Metropolitan Health District.

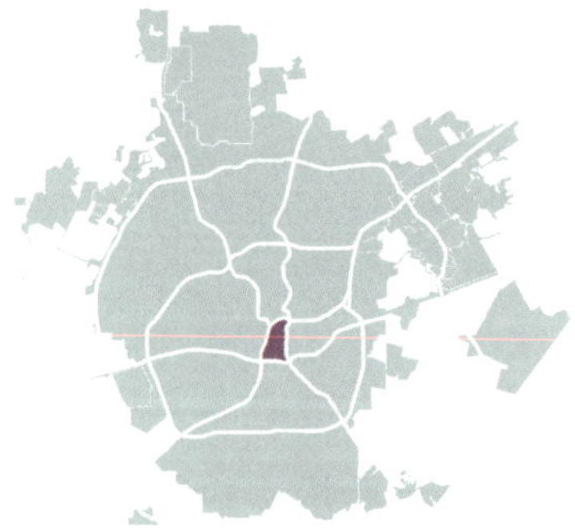

113

114

113★ NR NAVARRO HOUSE, CIRCA 1850

This three-building complex, a fine example of Texas domestic architecture, was built about 1850 as the home and office of lawyer José Antonio Navarro (1795–1871), a native-born signer of the Texas Declaration of Independence and later state senator. The vernacular design of the ell-shaped house, the detached kitchen and the two-story office represents practical construction of heavy stone walls and broad frame porches. The complex was documented by the Historic American Buildings Survey in 1936, purchased by the San Antonio Conservation Society in 1960 and restored under the direction of Brooks Martin two years later. The property was deeded to the Texas Parks and Wildlife Department in 1975, and additional restoration work was completed in 1979. It is operated by the state as a house museum.

ADDRESS
228 South Laredo Street

RENOVATED
1962, 1979

114 MILAM SQUARE, SINCE 1808

A public cemetery was established here in 1848 adjoining the old Catholic Campo Santo, where Canary Island immigrants were buried. The remains of Ben Milam, killed defending San Antonio against the Mexican army in 1835, were moved in. The cemeteries filled quickly and development encroached, causing them to be relocated. In the 1880s the vacant land was fenced, landscaped and named in honor of Milam, whose grave had been left intact. During the Texas Centennial of 1936, a monument to Milam designed by architect

ADDRESS
Bounded by Houston, Santa Rosa, Commerce and San Saba streets

RENOVATED
1976, 1993

Donald Nelson was added and soon topped by a bronze statue of Milam by sculptor Bonnie MacLeary. In 1976 landscape architect James Keeter provided a modern design for the park. This was replaced in 1993 with a design by José G. Jimenez funded by the Friends of Milam Park, spearheaded by a group of doctors from the adjoining Santa Rosa Hospital. Milam's remains were disinterred and reburied at the west end of the square. Granite markers at the east end commemorate those buried in the old Campo Santo. In the center was added a gazebo donated by the Mexican State of Jalisco. The playground, pathways, seating and tables are often used by families visiting Santa Rosa Hospital.

115

116

ADDRESS
Produce Row

RENOVATED
1976

115, 116 EL MERCADO, SINCE1890

By the 1890s, city officials had relocated San Antonio's open-air markets to the west of San Pedro Creek. A towering market house, containing an auditorium, was designed by Alfred Giles and constructed in 1900. A new market house designed by Leo M. J. Dielmann was appended to the old structure in 1922. The Giles building was demolished in 1938 to make way for a long, low arcaded structure designed by DeHaven Pitts. Along Produce Row, by the 1970s the market and two-story brick buildings from the early twentieth century had deteriorated, and the city embarked on an ambitious scheme to revive them with the entire west end of downtown. A plan by Martin & Ortega converted Produce Row [116] into a pedestrian concourse with adjoining rehabilitated storefronts. Assorted restaurants and shops, the indoor market and frequent fiestas now draw residents and visitors to El Mercado. Conversion of the 1922 market house annex into the Museo Alameda [115], a Smithsonian Institution affiliate museum designed by Houston's Jackson & Ryan and dedicated to Latino arts and culture, opened in 2007.

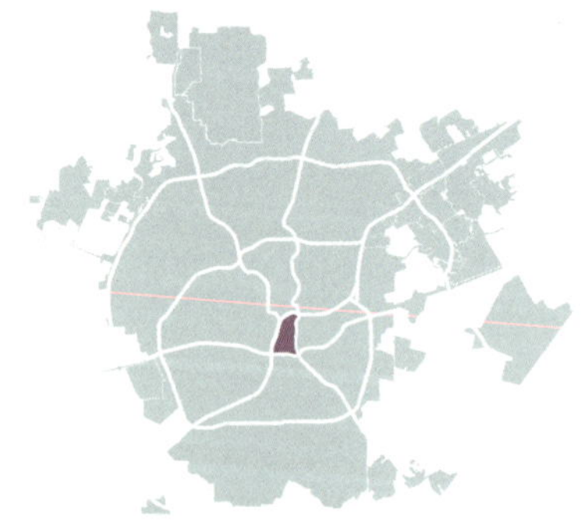

117 NR O. HENRY HOUSE, CIRCA 1870

This small vernacular house, once a common type in San Antonio, may be the city's most oft-moved historic structure. Originally built at 904 South Presa Street, it was home in the 1890s to the writer William Sydney Porter (O. Henry), who also maintained an office within for his publication *Rolling Stone*. Threatened with demolition in 1959, the house was sold for $1 to the San Antonio Conservation Society, which in turn sold it to Lone Star Brewery, which moved it to the Lone Star grounds for display. When the brewery closed, the house was relocated back near downtown to this corner, restored and reopened in 1999.

ADDRESS
North Laredo Street at Dolorosa Street

MOVED AND RENOVATED
1959, 1999

118 PLAZA HOTEL, 1927–28
(GRANADA HOMES)

A San Antonio River peninsula known as Bowen's Island was developed in the 1920s by brothers J. H. and F. A. Smith. In the area Atlee B. and Robert M. Ayres designed a cluster of buildings, including the Plaza Hotel, opened in 1927 and doubled in size the following year. The hotel reflects the Ayres firm's mastery of Spanish Colonial Revival design. While somewhat austere on the exterior, its interior contains fine detailing, including ceilings similar to fifteenth century Mudejar work in Spain.

ADDRESS
311 South St. Mary's Street

ARCHITECTS
Ayres & Ayres

ADDRESS
310 South St. Mary's Street

ARCHITECTS
Ayres & Ayres

119 NR SMITH–YOUNG TOWER, 1929
(TOWER LIFE BUILDING)

The octagonal Smith-Young Tower's exterior features mixed brick and terra-cotta detailing with Gothic-spirited ornamentation replete with gargoyles. Tiered upper floors are dramatically lighted, making the tower a highly visible nighttime beacon. The entry and lobby are richly decorated in marble and cast bronze. The landmark remained San Antonio's tallest building for six decades, until construction of the Marriott Rivercenter Hotel. Still used for offices, it now carries the name of its owner and major tenant.

ADDRESS
127 Navarro Street

ARCHITECTS
Ayres & Ayres

120 OLD FEDERAL RESERVE BANK BUILDING, 1928
(MEXICAN CONSULATE)

In 1927 the Federal Reserve Bank of Dallas opened a San Antonio branch, which moved the following year to new headquarters on the old Bowen's Island. Compared with the monumental Federal Reserve banks of the period, this moderately sized structure looks more like a local commercial bank. The institution's importance is expressed in granite, with inset Ionic columns flanking the main entrance. The interior is decorated with marble and features a decorative plaster ceiling. This sort of quiet dignity is highly appropriate for the building's present tenant, the Consulate of Mexico.

ADDRESS
225 South Presa Street

121 NR GRESSER HOUSE, CIRCA 1860

A small house was already standing on this property when it was purchased by Louis Gresser in 1861. Gresser enlarged the house to its present size and on the block-deep lot built other structures, including those that still stand on Navarro Street to the west. Detailing of the street façade is marked by particularly fine French doors and casement windows that open to the east-facing shaded porch. Few houses of this once-common type remain in the city. The Gresser house is owned by the San Antonio Conservation Society and used for offices.

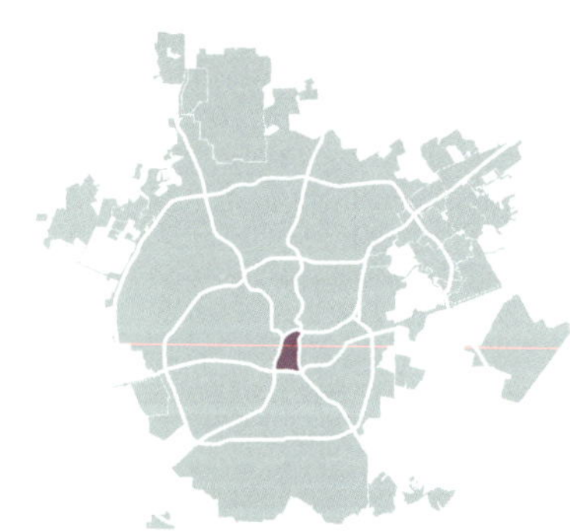

122, 123 NR & 124 UNITED STATES ARSENAL, SINCE 1860

A twelve-acre federal arsenal complex was established on the then-southern outskirts of San Antonio in 1859 to supply munitions to U.S. Army frontier forts in West Texas. Six surviving nineteenth century buildings include the [123] Magazine (1860), [123b] Stable (1874) and [124] Commander's House (circa 1883), a two-story rusticated stone building with Italianate detailing, wraparound double galleries and mansard roof, since replaced by a tile roof. The Commander's House was acquired in 1978 by the City of San Antonio for a senior citizen's community center and has since been renovated under James (Bert) Whitaker and Fisher Heck. In 1916 the southern portion of the Arsenal gained several four- and five-story warehouses, at least one of them designed by Henry T. Phelps. Two years after the Arsenal was deactivated in 1947, it was bisected by the southern extension of Main Avenue, leaving the Commander's House in the western portion but most other buildings in the eastern part. The Arsenal's subsequent use as a National Guard armory and reserve training center ended in 1976. Nearly a decade later, the ten-acre, mostly vacated eastern section was rescued by H-E-B Grocery Company as its [122] corporate headquarters complex. Hartman-Cox designed an internally focused campus unified by a central plaza. Former warehouses were accented with native limestone and finished in greenish-beige stucco and blue-gray trim. A onetime warehouse beside the

ADDRESS
South Main Avenue
at Arsenal Street

H-E-B RENOVATION
1985, Hartman-Cox,
Washington, DC

river was enhanced with gabled second-story bays and a central loggia. One new building was constructed, an office building at the north end designed in a stripped classical style to complement the monumentally scaled buildings to the south. Interiors were designed by Chumney/Urrutia and the landscaping by James E. Keeter. Consulting architects Raiford Stripling & Associates of San Augustine supervised restoration of the Arsenal and the Stable. The southernmost warehouse was renovated in 2000 under Ford, Powell & Carson.

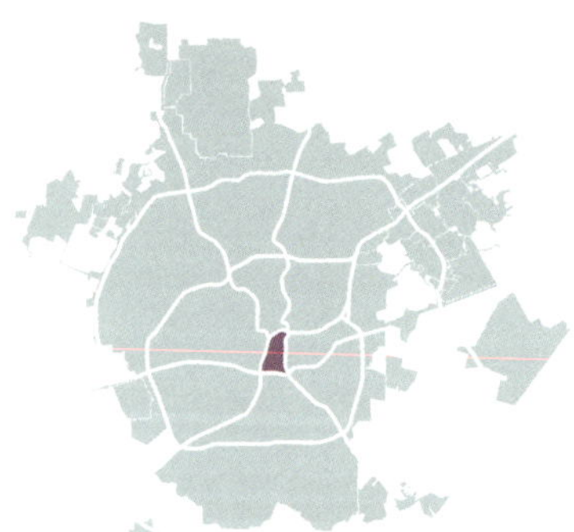

125

126

NR KING WILLIAM HISTORIC DISTRICT

The King William Street neighborhood is San Antonio's first designated historic district (1968) and the state's first National Register Historic District (1972). In the 1850s, its irrigated farmlands, which once produced crops for Mission San Antonio de Valero (the Alamo), yielded to a stylish array of limestone, brick and frame houses built by leading citizens. Its concentration of German immigrants along this curving section of the river caused this stretch to be dubbed Sauerkraut Bend. During World War I, its naming for Kaiser Wilhelm caused the main thoroughfare to be rechristened Pershing Avenue, a designation later reversed, then anglicized. A decline of several decades began to be reversed in the 1960s, as regentrification restored mansions and bungalows, converted lofts and new condominiums that blend with restaurants, shops and galleries of Southtown, along South St. Mary's and South Alamo streets, and with the Blue Star warehouse district at the area's southeastern tip.

125 WULFF HOUSE, 1870

The Anton Wulff house, which anchors the upper end of King William Street, reflects the Italianate style popularized by Andrew Jackson Downing. Ornamental frame verandahs and a half basement offered respite from the Texas heat. Wulff, who was city commissioner for parks, also landscaped the original lush surrounding gardens that extended to the nearby San Antonio River.

ADDRESS
107 King William Street

RENOVATED
1975

The house was restored as offices for the San Antonio Conservation Society in 1975. In 1982 the two-story limestone August Stuemke barn was relocated to the grounds from its downtown location at 215 North Flores Street.

ADDRESS
209 Washington Street

ARCHITECT
Alfred Giles

RENOVATED
1882

126 NR OGÉ HOUSE, 1857

Built for Newton and Catherine Mitchell, who owned a large tract of riverfront land, this was the first substantial structure in the King William neighborhood. It was originally a two-story raised cottage with half basement, much like the neighboring Blersch House. Its imposing, Charleston-like appearance is the product of a whole-

sale remodeling assigned to Alfred Giles by Louis Ogé in 1882. Giles's design added a third story, an expansive columned verandah and, on the second floor, a nicely detailed entrance and exceptional Palladian opening. The house was converted to apartments in the 1940s and is now a bed and breakfast.

ADDRESS
213 Washington Street

127 NR BLERSCH HOUSE, 1860

The Gustav Blersch house, built for the city's leading book and stationery dealer, was completed in 1860. The modified Greek Revival raised cottage has a half basement and deep front verandah. Apart from addition of a bay window (circa 1872) and sleeping porch (circa 1921), the front elevation retains its original appearance. A two-story back wing enlarged the house in 1872. The grounds, more expansive prior to river rechannelization in the 1920s, form a terrace to the River Walk, extended south from downtown in the 1980s.

ADDRESS
217 King William Street

ARCHITECT
Alfred Giles

128 NR SARTOR HOUSE, 1881

Though best known for his larger commissions, Alfred Giles created some delightful small-scale works, including this house for prominent jeweler Alexander Sartor. Street-front detailing includes five large windows opening onto a handsome deep frame verandah. The soft caliche block walls are stucooed to imitate ashlar masonry with protruding mortar joints.

129 NR ALTGELT HOUSE, 1878

ADDRESS
226 King William Street

This simple two-story limestone residence was built in 1878 for Ernst Altgelt, who moved here in 1866 from the Hill Country town of Comfort, which he helped establish. Altgelt's earlier house, a modest structure immediately to the south, is said to have been the first house on the street, affording him the honor of naming the thoroughfare; he christened it in honor of Kaiser Wilhelm I of Prussia. The street elevation is undecorated except for the arched entry, while the side is dominated by a two-story gallery with outside stairway. It is the only remaining neighborhood example of this once common feature. The tall limestone wall separating the house is a mid-twentieth century addition.

130 NR STEVENS HOUSE, 1881

ADDRESS
303 King William Street

This house, constructed for onetime postmaster John James Stevens, provides another localized example of Italianate design. Despite the imported style from the Northeast, finely crafted limestone walls label this a product of central Texas. Its narrowness gives it an almost rowhouse appearance. The asymmetrical main façade is accented by a polygonal bay on the first floor. The deep side garden is enclosed by a tall stuccoed wall, a later addition.

ADDRESS
309 King William Street

ARCHITECTS
Wahrenberger & Beckmann

131 NR HUMMEL HOUSE, 1884

This ell-plan, two-story Italianate house was constructed for sporting goods merchant and gunsmith Charles Hummel. Executed in superb limestone masonry, it is a good example of this significant nineteenth century Texas house type. The use of two varieties of verandah brackets illustrates the style's tendency toward multiple decorative forms.

ADDRESS
316 King William Street

132 NR OPPENHEIMER HOUSE, 1901

This home of banker M. L. Oppenheimer is a late example of Romanesque Revival. It is built of brick with carved stone detailing, the opposite of what would have

been the case a decade earlier, and has a deep front porch and rear second-story porch to provide shelter from the summer sun. The interior is finely detailed with oak paneling, parquet floors and art glass windows.

ADDRESS
335 King William Street

ARCHITECT
Alfred Giles

RENOVATED
1984

133 NR GROOS HOUSE, 1880

Commissioned by banker Carl Groos, this substantial limestone house backing to the San Antonio River is embellished with wide cast-iron verandahs that shade the main elevation. The polygonal bay on the south side and the somewhat undersized cupola atop the roof give the house a picturesque appearance. The cast-iron and stone front wall and fountain are both original to the property. After it was sold by the family in 1948, the house served as the local Girl Scouts headquarters until 1984, when it was remodeled by Ford, Powell & Carson as River Place, a single family residence.

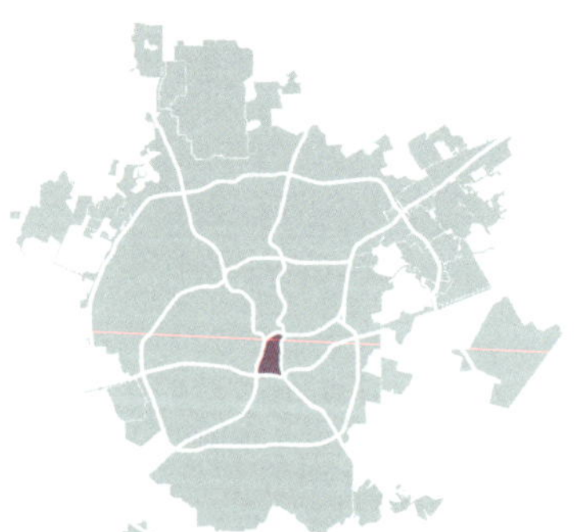

134

135

134 NR CHABOT HOUSE, 1876

ADDRESS
403 Madison Street

This simple masonry house with elaborate frame verandahs was built for English cotton merchant George Chabot. It is the most elegant structure on Madison Street. The three-bay main block has fine stonework with narrow mortar joints, while masonry is less carefully worked on the recessed southern wing. Millwork detailing is similarly handled, with paired columns on the main block and single columns on the wing. The change in baluster designs on the two lesser verandahs suggests that the jigsaw-cut flat balusters may represent a later addition. A two-story limestone ancillary building is at the rear of the property. This house is one of fourteen purchased and renovated by Walter Mathis, who is largely credited with reviving the neighborhood in the 1970s.

135 NR NORTON-POLK-MATHIS HOUSE, 1876

ADDRESS
401 King William Street

ARCHITECT
Francis Crider

ENLARGED
circa 1881, 1900

Built as a one-story structure in 1876 for hardware merchant Russel Norton, this house was enlarged and elaborated by successive owners into one of the most monumental in the King William area. A second story and rear ell were built about 1881. The ell was raised and a three-story corner tower added after 1896. Though the architect for the additions has not been identified, their craftsmanship suggests a professional designer or master builder. The late nineteenth century ornamental fence surrounding the property combines limestone with cast and wrought iron. Like many houses in the area, by the 1960s this one was subdivided and in poor repair. It was purchased and restored in 1967 as Villa Finale by Walter Mathis, who went on to renovate thirteen other neighborhood houses while living here and showcasing his fine furniture and decorative arts collections. After his death in 2006, the house passed under his will to the National Trust for Historic Preservation to become a house museum, the National Trust's first property in Texas.

ADDRESS
422 King William Street

136 NR IKE WEST HOUSE, 1888 **(ELLIS HOUSE)**
This three-story residence eclectically combines Queen Anne, Romantic Revival, Italianate and Second Empire

136

137

details. Built for stockman Smith Ellis, the house is better known for its later owner, cattleman Sol (Ike) West. Its simplified mansard roof and crested tower and portico emphasize the massing. Central focus of the design is the elaborately detailed entrance bay, its cylindrical two-story porch richly embellished with turned woodwork. The house bears a strong resemblance to Isaac Hobb's Design Number 84, published in Hobb's Architecture in 1873. The house was donated by the West family to the San Antonio Conservation Society in 1965 and resold with protective covenants. A major wing was seamlessly later added to the rear.

ADDRESS
425 King William Street

ARCHITECT
James Riely Gordon

137 NR KALTEYER HOUSE, 1892
James Riely Gordon, one of the state's most celebrated nineteenth century architects, designed this Romanesque Revival house for George Kalteyer, owner of major drug and cement companies and one of the city's wealthiest residents. It is one of the most architecturally significant structures on this noted street. Gordon was best known as a superb courthouse designer, but he was an excellent residential designer as well. This house, with its abundance of polychromed arches, reflects the architect's mastery of the Romanesque Revival of the 1880s. The fine interior finishes have been fully restored. The majority of Gordon's domestic work has unfortunately long since been demolished, making this specimen all the more important.

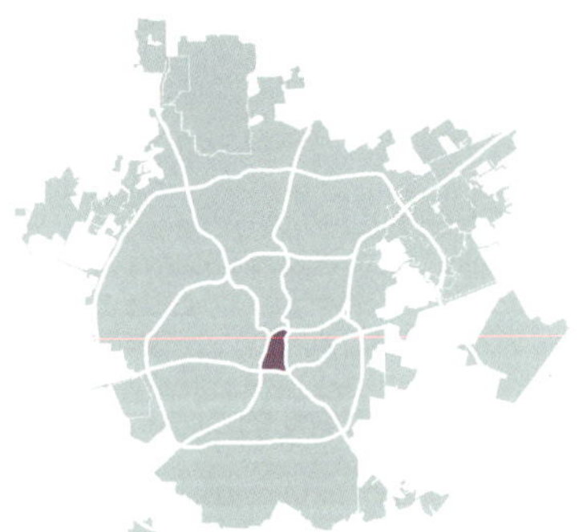

138

139

138 NR STEVES HOMESTEAD, 1875

The Steves Homestead depicts the lifestyle of wealthy San Antonio families in the 1870s. It is one of the early works of the English-born architect Alfred Giles, whose career had a profound influence on architecture in San Antonio. Lumber merchant Edward Steves retained Giles to design this limestone house, which exhibits elements of the Second Empire style. The elegance of the front elevation contrasts with the simpler rear service wing with frame verandahs. In 1952 the house was donated by a Steves granddaughter to the San Antonio Conservation Society; the interior was restored according to historic photographs, and two years later it was opened as a house museum. The stables and washhouse were also restored, and the servants quarters converted to a visitors' center. The artesian-well-fed pool in the circa 1900 brick natatorium has been floored over for the building's use as a meeting room. The doweled fence along King William Street is original to the property.

ADDRESS
509 King William Street

ARCHITECT
Alfred Giles

RENOVATED
1954, 1995

139▲ NR GUENTHER HOUSE, 1860

This was a traditional raised stone cottage when built in 1860 by German immigrant Carl Hilmar Guenther. Facing his new flour mill, the home was built beside a millrace dug between the legs of a sharp bend in the San Antonio River. A half century later, Guenther's son Erhard greatly enlarged the home, remodeling it and reorienting it away from the looming new indus-

ADDRESS
205 East Guenther Street

RENOVATED
1915

trial buildings of Pioneer Flour Mills. The only part of the original home recognizable from the outside became the one-story section projecting toward the river. Notable new features were the green tile roof and side verandah. The site changed dramatically in 1968, when the sharp bend to the south was cut off by a straight concrete channel dug past the house on the north. The milling company, now a national food conglomerate known as C. H. Guenther & Son Inc., operates the Guenther House as museum, restaurant and gift shop, using Erhard Guenther's sunroom on the ground floor and the ballroom on the third as part of the dining and banquet facilities.

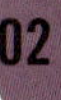

140

141

ADDRESS
155 Crofton Avenue

ARCHITECT
M. T. Eckels

140 NR BROOKS HOUSE, 1890
(HERTZBERG HOUSE)

Built for San Antonio's German-language newspaper publisher Theodore Hertzberg, this two-story beige brick house with red brick and stone accents backs on the San Antonio River at the lower end of the King William neighborhood. An expansive porch wraps around the first floor, while second-floor rooms open onto smaller upper porches. The house is best known as the home of Sidney J. Brooks Jr., one of the first U.S. Army pilots killed while training for World War I and for whom San Antonio's Brooks Air Force Base, now Brooks City Base, was named.

ADDRESS
221 Adams Street

ARCHITECTS
Otto and Carl Schulze

RENOVATED
1910

141 NR SCHULZE-SCHILO HOUSE, 1891

German immigrant building contractors and cabinet-maker brothers Otto and Carl Schulze purchased this property in 1891 and built two adjoining cottages. Carl lived in this one for several years. Subsequent owner Fritz Schilo is noted for the delicatessen that still bears his name. Though the cottage, typical of the period, was modified about 1910, it retains eclectic detailing, including Eastlake decoration on the front gable.

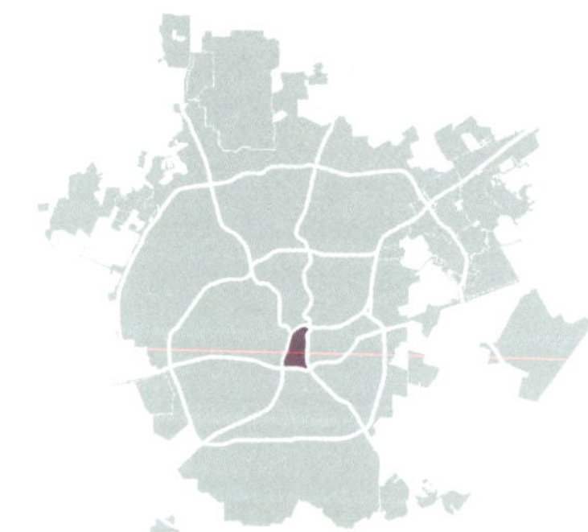

BLUE STAR ARTS COMPLEX, SINCE 1917–34
142▲ JUMP START PERFORMANCE COMPANY
143▲ BLUE STAR LOFTS

This renovated industrial warehouse district on the southeastern edge of the King William neighborhood includes museums, galleries, shops and loft residences. Prominent among them is the renovated building of the [142] Jump Start Performance Company, by Sprinkle Robey Architects, created by a volunteer team with a bare-bones budget. It includes a 150-seat performance theater, gallery, classroom and offices. Stained concrete floors, steel stairs and exposed walls and ceilings recreate the raw and industrial character. The ticket counter uses four types of granite that fit together along the ten-foot opening. The newest addition to the complex is [143] Blue Star Lofts, designed by Sprinkle Robey in 2006 with two commercial and two apartment levels. Its finishes and massing complement surrounding industrial structures by utilizing corrugated metal, expansive window fenestration and exposed structural elements. The public patios and basement integrate the structure into the existing streetscape.

ADDRESS
South Alamo and Probandt streets

ARCHITECTS
Sprinkle Robey

ADDRESS
410 East Arsenal Street

ARCHITECTS
Lake/Flato

144▲ ARSENAL HOUSE, 1989

A small lot, wonderful river views and a tight budget led to an efficient "tower" design for this 2,400-square-foot, one-room wide home. For privacy and to take advantage of the view, the main living area was located on the second floor. The third-floor master bedroom opens to two decks for upriver/downriver viewing. The stairway, the only circulation area in the house, doubles as an entry hall on the first level and as a library at intermediate levels.

144

145

146

ADDRESS
1443 South St. Mary's Street

ARCHITECT
Henry Steinbomer

145 NR WESTMINSTER PRESBYTERIAN CHURCH, 1948

Henry Steinbomer, among the first architects to study historic Texas buildings, was an early practitioner of Texas regional design. In this example, the sanctuary's stuccoed stone walls manipulate sunlight with projecting entry-bay masses, deep-set fenestration and textured surfaces. The massive campanile rises high above the roofline. The utilitarian education wing is distinguished by its six-over-one windows with sidelights and by its entry bays. The far entry is deeply set beneath a scalloped arch, with a baroque espadaña above. The building is now used as a Mennonite church.

ADDRESS
716 South Presa Street

RENOVATED
1999

146▲ CASA LAVACA, CIRCA 1920

Originally home to a chiropractic clinic, this housing complex renovated under Greg Papay consists of five structures that capture the eclectic character of the neighborhood. The project incorporates vibrant colors and native landscaping. Local artisans and members of the community helped shape the project.

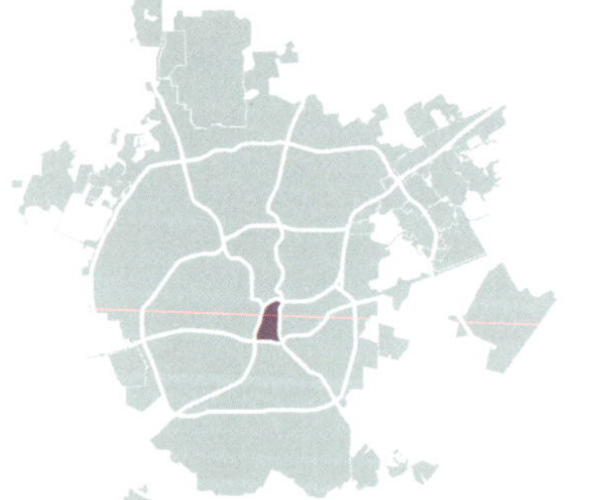

147 NR WRIGHT HOUSE, 1917

Contractor L. T. Wright, associated with the construction of many of San Antonio's major buildings, retained George Willis to design his home on a prominent corner south of downtown. Due to Willis's four years as a draftsman in the studio of Frank Lloyd Wright, the house reflects Wright's midwestern residential style. The low roof and wide eaves of the Prairie School are supported by tile-block walls finished with stucco. Decorative painter Fred Donecker added a folk art touch to the interior with stenciling and murals depicting local scenes, accenting typical Craftsman-era interior woodwork. The house and decorative interior were restored by DeLara-Almond in the 1980s for the firm's offices.

ADDRESS
342 Wilkins Avenue

ARCHITECT
George Willis

RENOVATED
1981

148 NR YTURRI-EDMUNDS COMPOUND, 1840–60

This small oasis on Mission Road beside the San Antonio River was originally part of the lands of nearby Mission Concepción. The house is a rare survivor of the type of small farmstead once common along the river. Near his mill, Manuel Yturri Castillo built this house, one of the few documented specimens of adobe construction in San Antonio. Yturri's granddaughter willed the property to the San Antonio Conservation Society in 1961. Under Marvin Eickenroht, the society reconstructed the mill and later added two historic structures to the site, the wood frame Ogé carriage house (1875), relocated from the King William area, and the caliche

ADDRESS
257 Yellowstone Street

RENOVATED
1961–70

block and stone rubble Postert house (circa 1855). The property is operated as a house museum.

ADDRESS
218 Lavaca Street

RENOVATED
2006

149▲ CASA 218, 1873

Casa 218 is a two-room limestone residence built with little more than 500 square feet. In a restoration under Candid Rogers, regional materials were used in a 960 square-foot addition set unobtrusively in back of the existing residence, with a kitchen, two bathrooms and two bedrooms.

149

150

151

ADDRESS
215 Groveton Street

ARCHITECT
Candid Rogers

150▲ GROVETON STREET STUDIOS, 2004

Located on a small urban lot adjacent to a railroad line, Groveton Street Studios is sited to maximize breezes and north lighting. The exterior is entered through eight-foot coiling doors that open to a working/parking courtyard. A smaller, more private rear courtyard is used for gathering. Native xeriscape landscaping is used throughout.

ADDRESS
923 South Alamo Street

RENOVATED
2000

151▲ KING WILLIAM LOFTS, CIRCA 1925–35

After having a succession of commercial tenants, these concrete and tile office and warehouse buildings were converted under Poteet Architects—in one of the first projects of its kind in San Antonio—to eleven loft-style condominiums. The design retained the raw feel of the original buildings and added steel windows, doors, porches and fencing. Units were marketed as unfinished shells to be customized by each buyer. A landscaped common area separates the complex from its more traditional neighbors. On the back side of the building, at 212 Madison Street, design of the multilevel Capps Loft, by Poteet Architects in association with Fab Architecture of Austin, demonstrates how industrial interiors lend themselves to minimalist modernism. Smooth new walls, glossy cabinetry and steel handrails contrast with the texture of the building's trusses and rough masonry.

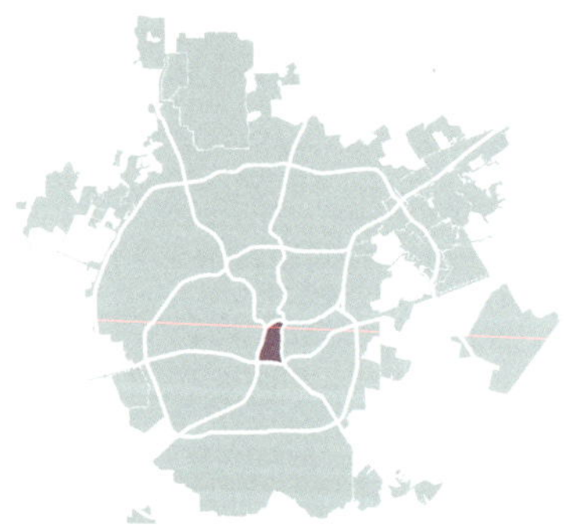

152

153

154

152▲ INTERNATIONAL CENTER, 1968

Built on the River Walk as an opaque brick box to serve as the San Antonio Central Library, this building was redesigned for city offices and international trade, finance and tourism offices after the library moved to new quarters in 1995. Lake/Flato's new design removed half the brick, added large expanses of glass and introduced a new pedestrian street through the building.

ADDRESS
203 South St. Mary's Street

ARCHITECTS
Phil Carrington and Ben Wyatt

RENOVATED
1998, Lake/Flato

153▲ PRESIDIO PLAZA, 1996

This five-story, mixed-use complex is stylistically eclectic, combining Mission, Spanish Colonial, Mediterranean and Beaux Arts traditions. Backing on Commerce Street and fronting on the River Walk, it contains two restaurants, retail spaces, banquet facilities on three floors and a penthouse apartment. The central river-level courtyard acts as an organizing device for circulation and orientation.

ADDRESS
245 East Commerce Street

ARCHITECTS
Sprinkle Robey

154▲ ST. MARY'S STREET PARKING GARAGE, 2003

The six-level, 700-car parking garage incorporates ground-floor retail and commercial space to maintain a traditional street-level character. Strong horizontal elements, including first-floor canopies, help break down the six levels of the building. Vertical elements establish a bay system as well as a hierarchy along the façade. Public art is included in the lobby areas at the ground floor and adjacent to the elevator at each floor level.

ADDRESS
400 North St. Mary's Street

ARCHITECTS
Alamo Architects

The lobby's overscaled shoe images are of pre-cast terrazzo set in a larger terrazzo field.

ADDRESS
403 Urban Loop

ARCHITECTS
Kell Muñoz Wigodsky, Inc.

155▲ PARAGON CABLE HEADQUARTERS, 1995 (TIME WARNER CABLE HEADQUARTERS)

For its local corporate offices, Time Warner Cable used vibrant colors, interior windows and walls and special lighting effects to transform standard building finishes. Uplink/downlink computer facilities and fiber optic telecommunications facilities were also incorporated into the design.

155

156

157

ADDRESS
146 East Houston Street

ARCHITECTS
Kell Muñoz Architects

156▲ ACENAR RESTAURANT, 2002

This restaurant's design incorporates sweeping curved walls, wood finishes, vibrant Saltillo tiles and dynamic colors to create an exuberant interior, inspired by the folkloric traditions of San Antonio's mestizo culture. To overlook the river, the restaurant spills from the Valencia Hotel onto an outdoor terrrace, its wall studded with a grid of molcajetes lit from below to cast striking shadows at the restaurant entrance. Acenar is on the site of a commercial structure built by George M. Maverick that once housed a restaurant, which in 1918 added a Craftsman-influenced balcony, designed by Will Noonan. The tile-roofed balcony was salvaged and repositioned as a stand-alone feature on Acenar's terrace.

ADDRESS
114 Camp Street

ARCHITECTS
Herff & Jones

RENOVATED
2005,
Poteet Architects

157 DUERLER CANDY COMPANY, 1926 (CAMP STREET RESIDENCES)

This six-story industrial building built by Duerler Candy Company was used for many years by Tobin Aerial Surveys. It was converted by Poteet Architects into twenty residential lofts known as CAMPstreet Residences. The original fabric of the exterior was preserved along with the landmark water tower. Steel and concrete porches, steel parking structures and a landscaped rooftop deck were added. The complex includes CHRISpark, a public art park designed by Rosa Finsley with trellises, fencing, signage and outbuildings by Poteet Architects.

EVENTS

FIESTA

Fiesta is San Antonio's party of the year. It is a celebration extraordinaire that each April takes the city by storm. A list of every event would be too numerous to include, but a few important highlights follow:

NIOSA Night in Old San Antonio is a shoulder-to-shoulder weeklong party on the grounds of the venerated, historic la Villita. A great cross section of cultures, foods and music unites San Antonians and visitors alike. Arrive early to avoid the crush.

PARADES A variety of parades including the Battle of Flowers, the Fiesta Flambeau (the largest night parade in the United States), the River Parade and the King William Parade, each with its own unique assembly of revelry, music, pomp and circumstance, are spaced throughout the Fiesta celebration. Even if parades aren't your thing, you are in for a special treat with any one of these choices.

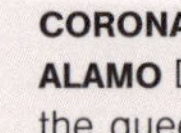

CORONATION OF THE QUEEN OF THE ORDER OF THE ALAMO During this event, which reveals the identity of the queen, the public has the opportunity to see the elaborate, long-trained gowns worn by the members of her court. It is the highlight of Fiesta for San Antonio society.

ADDRESS
Municipal Auditorium

CORNYATION A raucous, bawdy parody of local and national news-making events with no stones left unturned. No sacred cows here, just wild, quick-paced action. Leave the kids at home.

ADDRESS
Various sites;
check the listings

ADDRESS
San Antonio River

CHRISTMAS RIVER PARADE AND TREE LIGHTING
During the Christmas season, a visit to the Paseo del Rio, will find the River Walk's cypress trees drenched with 125,000 colorful lights mirrored in the surface of the river. For three weekends before Christmas, the River Walk is also illuminated with luminarios. Over 185 caroling groups take turns in nightly caroling and sing-alongs as they wind their way along the River Walk. Be sure to catch the annual holiday River Parade, held the night after Thanksgiving.

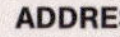

ADDRESS
South Alamo Street
(King William area)

FIRST FRIDAY On First Friday of each month this is the place to join a crowd of happy art lovers for an evening of fun. Wander up an down the street, stop in to have a drink and look at art in the galleries. The galleries and the street will be open late.

ADDRESS
111 Travis Street
San Antonio, Texas 78205

ROBERT JOHNSON'S SAN ANTONIO RECORDINGS In 1936, in the Robert Lee Hotel building, the soon-to-be nationally recognized blues musician and singer Robert Johnson recorded a series of sixteen songs that would become a cherished collectable among American blues aficionados around the world. Check out www.RobertJohnsonfilm.com for more.

ADDRESS
Travis Park
300 Travis Street
San Antonio, Texas 78205
(210) 212-8423

JAZZ'S ALIVE In September, for two days and nights, Jazz's Alive brings the best of local and regional jazz performers to beautiful, shaded Travis Park in the heart of San Antonio. Admission is free; stake out a grassy spot and enjoy the many foods and beverages. Special events are provided for children.

RETAIL/GALLERIES

PENNERS Established in 1916 by Morris Penner, the Penner family store continues the tradition of selling top quality men's clothing. Specializing in the Guayabera shirt, they sell these uniquely designed shirts throughout the world.

ADDRESS
311 West Commerce Street
San Antonio, Texas 78205
(210) 226-2487

PARIS HATTERS Since 1917, this family-owned business has been topping off the likes of Hollywood celebrities, country crooners, rock stars, presidents, ranchers and royal families with an incredible inventory of some of the best hats money can buy. Everyone needs to take a hat home from Texas, and you could not ask for a better place to shop.

ADDRESS
119 North Broadway
San Antonio, Texas 78205
(210) 223-3453

GINNY GARCIA GLASS WORKS A "hot glass" design and fabrication center specializing in the creation of one-of-a-kind blown glass lighting and sculpture, including table scapes and wall art. Creations range from the functional to the whimsical and have found their way into notable collections throughout the country. A fascinating working studio where the art of glass making can be observed firsthand.

ADDRESS
715 South Alamo Street
San Antonio, Texas 78205
(210) 354-4681

BLUE STAR Located among an assortment of wonderfully transformed warehouse spaces, this nationally recognized contemporary art space serves as a catalyst for showcasing cutting-edge art and sculpture. Call for gallery hours and exhibits.

ADDRESS
116 Blue Star
San Antonio, Texas 78204
(210) 227-6960

ARTPACE Respected both locally and around the world, ArtPace serves as a laboratory for the creation and advancement of international contemporary art. Located in an 18,000-square-foot former Hudson automobile showroom, this venue supports a wide ranging artist-in-residence program that annually brings to San

ADDRESS
445 North Main Avenue
San Antonio, Texas 78205
(210) 212-4900

Antonio the best of what the art world has to offer. With an emphasis on installation art, this galley is not to be missed.

ADDRESS
600 Hemisphere Plaza
San Antonio, Texas 78205
(210) 227-0123

INSTITUTO DE MEXICO AT SAN ANTONIO The institute houses a gallery with support spaces that facilitate a permanent presence for Mexico in San Antonio, offering a forum for dialogue and cultural discussion. It promotes Mexico's cultural heritage and assists in establishing and expanding alliances and collaborations.

ADDRESS
107 East Martin Street
San Antonio, Texas 78205
(210) 223-6292

RUTA MAYA From a tiny beginning to a well-established and highly respected business, this unique establishment represents not only great coffees grown in the highlands of Chiapas, Mexico, but an amazing collection of Central and South American objects. In a gesture of giving back and to help unite the Americas, the profits of sales are shared with the producers of the work in the country of origin. Stop in for coffee and more.

FOOD/ENTERTAINMENT

ACENAR A vibrant and fresh one-of-a-kind architectural and artistic dining and bar establishment that has a wonderful balcony overlooking the San Antonio River. Featuring Mexican cuisine with a contemporary flair. A fabulous celebration of space and a feast for the eyes and stomach.

ADDRESS
146 East Houston Street
San Antonio, Texas 78205
(210) 222-2362

AZUCA The first "Nuevo Latino" restaurant in San Antonio. Inspired by a desire to unite great cuisine, service and atmosphere of the Caribbean, Central and Latin America. Call for listings of great music and evenings with spontaneous Flamenco dancing.

ADDRESS
713 South Alamo Street
San Antonio, Texas 78205
(210) 225-5550

BEETHOVEN HALL A great indoor/outdoor German music, food and beer tradition since 1885—and it embodies the history of every year of its existence. Young and old alike will enjoy this historical setting and family atmosphere.

ADDRESS
422 Pereida Street
San Antonio, Texas 78210
(210) 222-1521

BIGA ON THE BANKS Internationally acclaimed chef Bruce Auden's menu and presentations are absolutely succulent works of art. Overlooking the San Antonio River, the restaurant offers a variety of bold and unforgettable culinary delights that have won the chef numerous and repeated awards. Leave room for dessert.

ADDRESS
203 S. St. Mary's Street #100
San Antonio, Texas 78205
(210) 225-0722

BLUE STAR BREWING COMPANY This is San Antonio's first full-scale brewpub and has a wide selection of handcrafted beers. Located on the edge of King William and on the grounds of the Blue Star Art Complex, it serves great food in a casual atmosphere. There is always interesting art on display as well as an open look at the brewing process.

ADDRESS
1414 South Alamo Street
San Antonio, Texas 78210
(210) 212-5506

LITTLE RHEIN STEAK HOUSE A sister restaurant to the Fig Tree, and located in historic La Villita, it is known for its outstanding beef menu, extensive wine list and rustic ambience. Frequented by locals, tourists and the famous alike.

ADDRESS
231 South Alamo Street
San Antonio, Texas 78205
(210) 225-2111

MADHATTER'S TEA HOUSE & CAFÉ Located in the heart of King William neighborhood, Madhatter's Tea House & Café serves an eclectic breakfast, lunch and dinner. You can choose from over fifty teas by the pot or a glass

of beer or wine. Enjoy an incredible fresh and unique entree with your friends.

ADDRESS
320 Beauregard
San Antonio, Texas 78204
(210) 212-4832

MENGER BAR Teddy Roosevelt once recruited Rough Riders in this place, which is lined with dark cherrywood walls. The long bar has ornate woodwork and glass cabinets. A lot of history is associated with this setting, so do not be surprised if you see a ghost, as many inhabit the hotel where this bar is located. Or was it the strong drink that was poured for you in this replica of the House of Lords Pub in London?

ADDRESS
204 Alamo Plaza
San Antonio, Texas 78205
(210) 223-4361

MEXICAN MANHATTAN Both the place and the servings are huge, so come hungry and ready to explore the various settings of this eatery, which has a loyal local following. Make sure that you make it to the bar with its high ceiling, exposed brick walls, great patios with a view of the River Walk and probably the best Bloody Mary in town.

ADDRESS
110 Soledad Street
San Antonio, Texas 78205
(210) 223-3913

MI TIERRA CAFÉ & PANADERÍA Opened in 1941 by Pete and Cruz Cortez in the middle of San Antonio's El Mercado, sixty years later Mi Tierra Café is a world-famous landmark known for authentic Mexican food and a warm Texas welcome. The bakery has been in operation since 1957, providing Mexican pan dulce made fresh from the oven every day. Never closes (open 24 hours, 365 days).

ADDRESS
218 Produce Row
San Antonio, Texas 78207
(210) 225-1262

more. The club is located on the San Antonio River in the Hyatt Regency Hotel.

ADDRESS
112 College Street
San Antonio, Texas 78205
(210) 518-1000

LAS CANARIAS Built on three levels that descend to the San Antonio River, this romantic restaurant is infused with Spanish Colonial charm and the nightly sounds of a Spanish classical guitar. In addition to his daily exotic creations, on Sundays chef Scott Cohen offers one of the finest brunch menus in the Alamo City.

ADDRESS
728 South Alamo Street
San Antonio, Texas 78205
(210) 224-7555

LA FRITE BELGIAN BISTRO A Belgian bistro, located in a Southtown storefront and with chef Damien Vatel at the helm, attracts neighbors from King William, Southtown, the LaVaca neighborhoods and locals from across the city.

ADDRESS
120 Produce Road
San Antonio, Texas 78207
(210) 227-7140

LA MARGARITA Sister restaurant to Mi Tierra, and located in El Mercado; at La Margarita one can indulge in great Mexican food, listen to mariachi musicians and watch life go by. This tourist and local favorite is known for its killer margaritas.

ADDRESS
152 East Pecan Street
San Antonio, Texas 78205
(210) 212-2221

LA REVE Since its opening, this fabulous French restaurant has received continuous praise for cuisine by chef Andrew Weissman, whose culinary credentials are second to none. Rated as the best restaurant in Texas and one of the top ten in the country. Expect dining precision and intimacy, from the menu and the space.

ADDRESS
306 West Market Street
San Antonio, Texas 78205
(210) 229-9222

LAS RAMBLAS Located at the River Walk level, this restaurant has a decor reminiscent of Barcelona. The menu makes an expected connection to Spanish cuisine, with a selection of tapas and a paella. Both the churros and chocolate will leave you with a memorable experience.

ADDRESS
111 West Crockett Street
San Antonio, Texas 78205
(210) 227-2782

PAESANOS Explore modern Mediterranean cuisine at Paesanos. Enjoy the legendary Shrimp Paesano or the oven-baked pizzas piled high with grilled chicken and artichokes, or the venture forth to lemon peppered salmon or tempting daily specials. Choose from the inside or terrace seating and enjoy the views of the River Walk.

ADDRESS
212 West Crockett Street
San Antonio, Texas 78205
(210) 396-5817

PESCA ON THE RIVER This addition to the River Walk features the freshest seafood flown daily from distant locations. Chef Scott Cohen has added his creative

touch, as seen in the expanded and unique menu. The seafood bar has a wide variety of oysters and clams from both coasts. When at the bar, make sure to ask about the tequila list, which is second to none in town, or perhaps the state.

ADDRESS
421 East Commerce Street
San Antonio, Texas 78205
(210) 226-8462

RIO RIO CANTINA With two River Walk patios, a bar and indoor dining rooms, Rio Rio is one of the most popular tourist eateries. The vegetarian burrito is recommended, as is the fajitas al carbon, and if you can't decide go for the botana grande or the queso flameado, Rio Rio rice and beans and a fresh salad with Rio Rio signature comino dressing. Platters of food, cold Corona, top shelf margaritas and a lively atmosphere with views of river barges make this a "don't miss."

ADDRESS
910 South Alamo Street
San Antonio, Texas 78205
(210) 223-1806

ROSARIO'S MEXICAN CAFÉ & CANTINA A perfectly crafted frozen margarita and great enchilada plate are the signature items of Rosario's. Carne guisada, porktips, fish tacos and so much more are on the menu. Enjoy the Friday night entertainment show with some of the best bands in South Texas, and prepare to dance.

ADDRESS
152 East Pecan Street
San Antonio, Texas 78205
(210) 222-2426

THE SANDBAR FISH HOUSE & MARKET Looking as much as possible like a pristine fish market, the Sandbar, an Andrew Weissman venture, has assembled a menu that reads part sushi, part oyster bar, part lobster palace—and has managed to convey the best of them.

SCHILO'S DELI A great variety of German food and the deli atmosphere make Schilo charming at an affordable price. At a convenient distance from the River Walk, Schilo offers lunch plate specials with traditional German fare. Don't forget the trademark split-pea soup and the homemade root beer with a slice of signature cherry cheesecake.

ADDRESS
424 East Commerce Street
San Antonio, Texas 78205
(210) 223-6692

SIP COFFEE & ESPRESSO BAR A quiet place to enjoy a double iced lemon pound cake accompanied with a coffee drink. Treat yourself to a macchiato and a slice of fudge, and if you come for lunch try a panini or the lobster salad sandwich.

ADDRESS
160 East Houston Street
San Antonio, Texas 78205
(210) 222-0149

TORRES TACO HAVEN This great family-owned hangout, has evolved from being a neighborhood favorite for decades to a place that attracts people throughout San Antonio. Reliable and inexpensive home cooking served in a friendly and colorful setting is worth the wait.

ADDRESS
1032 South Presa Street
San Antonio, Texas 78210
(210) 533-2444

ZINC BAR Located in the heart of historic downtown San Antonio and close to the River Walk, Zinc offers a variety of wines from all corners of the globe with emphasis on champagne and domestic varieties. Zinc Bar has an extensive menu offering fine import cigars, vintage ports, specialty cocktails and wine-friendly cuisine.

ADDRESS
207 North Presa Street
San Antonio, Texas 78205
(210) 224-2900

ZUNI GRILL The Zuni Grill is located at the foot of the historic Hugman bridge. Inspired by the flavors of the American Southwest, the menu offers a variety of plates for breakfast, lunch and dinner. Specialties are the scorpion shrimp stuffed red chiles or the blue corn chicken enchiladas; try a pear cactus margarita.

ADDRESS
223 Losoya Street
San Antonio, Texas 78205
(210) 227-0864

EL MIRADOR Long a meeting place for politicos, artists, architects and locals from the King William neighborhood, at El Mirador the Treviño family serves award-winning Mexican cuisine using the freshest ingredients. Family favorite specialty dishes, great margaritas and sopa azteca (soup) on Saturdays.

ADDRESS
722 South St. Mary's Street
San Antonio, Texas 78205
(210) 225-9444

THE FIG TREE RESTAURANT Located in the last of the family dwellings in La Villita, the warm setting of the Phelps's historical home is a wonderful backdrop for a great menu of continental cuisine. Take a break from your tour of historical La Villita and the River Walk, and treat yourself to an unforgettable meal with linens, china, sparkling silver and flowers in a home you wish was yours.

ADDRESS
515 Villita
San Antonio, Texas 78205
(210) 224-1976

THE GUENTHER HOUSE Located on a bend of the San Antonio River and on the edge of the historic King William neighborhood, the elegantly restored 1860 home includes a restaurant, museum and retail store. After breakfast or lunch, plan to spend time wandering the halls and landscaped grounds of this magnificent home.

ADDRESS
205 East Guenther Street
San Antonio, Texas 78204
(210) 227-1061

HAVANA RIVERWALK INN A State and National Historic Landmark, the Havana has been carefully restored to its original detailing in each of its 27 rooms. It is full of impressive antiques and historical photographs, and the lobby transcends the hustle and bustle of today's pressures. Club Cohiba offers premier cocktails, wines and cigars; the restaurant specializes in Cuban, Caribbean, Spanish and South American cuisine.

ADDRESS
1015 Navarro Street
San Antonio, Texas 78205
(210) 222-2008

JIM CULLUM'S LANDING Jim Cullum's Jazz Band, America's premier seven-piece classic jazz ensemble, plays Monday through Saturday with Small World taking over on Sunday nights. Seating is at tables so patrons can enjoy the fine cuisine, liquors, wines, domestic and imported beers, gourmet coffees and

ADDRESS
123 Losoya Street
San Antonio, Texas 78205
(210) 223-7266

ADDRESS
219 East Houston Street
San Antonio, Texas 78205
(210) 472-2600

BOHANAN'S PRIME STEAKS AND SEAFOOD Chef and owner Mark Bohanan offers a diverse menu built on flavor and freshness. Here diners can enjoy a delicious steak and creatively prepared seafood. The formal setting provides a nice venue for a romantic dinner. Save room for some of the signature deserts, such as the cherries jubilee.

ADDRESS
421 East Commerce Street
San Antonio, Texas 78205
(210) 224-8484

BOUDRO'S Long favored for its wonderful and unique seafood menu, this restaurant has a history of consistently serving some of the best food on the river. You can dine in the cool interior or be served at a table along the river's edge.

ADDRESS
318 East Houston Street
San Antonio, Texas 78205
(210) 247-4000

THE BUCKHORN SALOON AND MUSEUM In continuous operation since 1881, the Buckhorn has the distinguished legacy of being the place where Teddy Roosevelt recruited Rough Riders and where Pancho Villa is rumored to have started the Mexican Revolution. Amid the undisputed world's largest collection of horns and antlers, the beer is cold, the food is a cattleman's delight and the furnishings are authentic. Visit the award-winning museum, old-fashioned arcade and curio store.

ADDRESS
430 East Commerce Street
San Antonio, Texas 78205
(210) 225-6718

CASA RIO Casa Rio Mexican Food Restaurant is the patron of businesses on the river's edge. Founded in 1946, it was the first business to open its doors to the San Antonio River. The paddleboats and dinner barges had their beginnings here and helped create what the River Walk is today. Architectural detailing and ambience embody its historical setting.

The City of San Antonio can be summarized as a transcultural polymorphic urban form: a complex mosaic of urban patterns originating in the natural realm and reshaped by agricultural practice, technology and governance through multiple historical episodes.

—STEVEN LAND TILLOTSON

Urban Form and Cultural Landscape

by STEVEN LAND TILLOTSON

Steven Land Tillotson is an architect with Kell Muñoz who is highly involved in the San Antonio urban issues.
November 2006

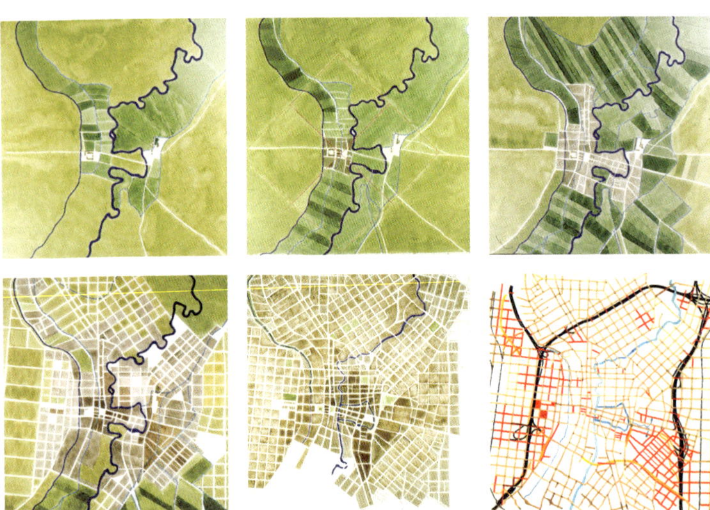

The Presidio de Bejar was established in a defendable narrow of land between the San Antonio River and San Pedro Creek, with Mission San Antonio de Valero on the east bank of the river. The presidio was a strategic hub in the regional road network; caminos reales radiated to the further frontier and to the interior of Mexico (1). The civil settlement of Villa de San Fernando followed the Leyes de las Indies, the town planning guidelines for Spanish colonization, with a central plaza mayor and street grid that aligns with the parallel coincidence of the river and creek (2). The Concepción, San José, San Juan and Espada missions were established along the river downstream. Each settlement was sustained by a system of irrigation canals called acequias that followed the terrain and created a geomorphic field pattern of labores and desagues, or fields and laterals (4). Subsequent urban expansion reflects these antecedent patterns of agricultural form and account for San Antonio's meandering street quality and irregular block geometry. Eighteenth century suburbs, or barrios, accommodated the growing population (3).

In the nineteenth century the eight leagues, approximately 25,000 acres, of surrounding municipal land were subdivided into a grid of rectangular parcels, auctioned to private ownership and established a cardinal grid for future streets. Railroads spurred urban growth and expansion (5), and by the early twentieth century the San Antonio River's course was engineered for flood control and the downtown entirely urbanized. The advent of interstate highways and rapid suburbanization greatly impacted San Antonio's development. Successors to the caminos reales, interstate highways increased regional transportation access and are connected with a series of concentric loops. The downtown expressways largely exploited the previous acequia courses for their routes, yet severed nearly two-thirds of the surface streets that connected the urban core with its adjacent neighborhoods.

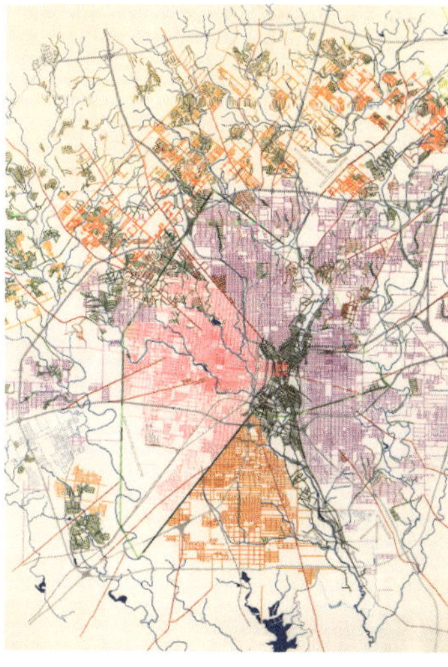

The City of San Antonio can be summarized as a transcultural polymorphic urban form: a complex mosaic of urban patterns originating in the natural realm and reshaped by agricultural practice, technology and governance through multiple historical episodes. The imprint of Spanish colonization beginning in the eighteenth century brought classical ideals of city planning and engineering pragmatism that extended well into the nineteenth century until overwhelmed by American institutions, culture and a late-arriving industrial revolution. Even with its hefty modern infrastructure and ever-expanding periphery, the consequent cultural landscape remains influenced by a persistent formative urban foundation.

ARCHITECTURE

1. The Alamo
2. Alamo Plaza
3. Menger Hotel
4. Reuter Building
5. Paseo Del Alamo
6. Crockett Block
7. United States Post Office & Courthouse
8. Medical Arts Building
9. Turnverein Building
10. Crockett Hotel
11. Rivercenter Mall
12. St. Joseph's Catholic Church
13. Joske's Department Store
14. Schroeder-Yturri House
15. Tower of the Americas
16. San Antonio Convention Center
17. Institute of Texan Cultures
18. United States Courthouse
19. Schultze Store
20. German-English School
21. Alderete Houses
22. Staffel/Elmendorf/Tyler House
23. Diaz House
24. Fairmount Hotel
25. Four Seasons Hotel
26. St. John's Lutheran Church
27. Ernst Homestead
28. La Villita Complex
29. Plazas of La Villita
30. Villita Assembly Hall
31. Arneson River Theater
32. Hilton Palacio Del Rio Hotel
33. Old San Antonio Public Library
34. Charles Court
35. Old Alamo National Bank Building
36. Stevens Building
37. Staacke Bros. Building
38. D Heye Saddlery Building
39. Clifford Building
40. Casino Club Building
41. Chandler Building
42. Hyatt Regency Hotel
43. Nix Professional Building
44. Omni La Mansion Del Rio Hotel
45. Majestic Theater Building
46. Brady Building/Empire Theater
47. Hotel Valencia
48. Book Building
49. Rand Building
50. Alameda Theater/Casa de Mexico International Building
51. Frost Motor Bank and Plaza
52. Houston Street Bridge
53. Republic Bank Plaza
54. Hertzeberg Clock
55. Gunter Hotel
56. Frost Brothers Buildings
57. Central Trust Company Building
58. Vogue Building
59. Kress Building
60. Bennet Building
61. J.C. Penney Company
62. G. Bedell Moore Building
63. Maverick Building
64. Buckhorn Museum and Saloon
65. Travis Park United Methodist Church
66. St. Anthony Hotel
67. Barr Building
68. Travis Park
69. St. Mark's Episcopal Church
70. Marmon Mok Lobby
71. Southwestern Bell Telephone Building
72. Municipal Auditorium
73. Maverick-Carter House
74. First Presbyterian Church
75. Express-News Building
76. 608 East Travis
77. Scottish Rite Temple
78. YWCA Building
79. Dog Team Too Loft & Studio
80. Thiele House
81. Engleman-Muench House
82. Old Lone Star Brewery
83. King House
84. Central YMCA
85. Madison Square Presbyterian Church
86. Central Christian Church
87. The Havana
88. San Antonio Central Library
89. Old Ursuline Academy and Convent
90. Interfirst Plaza
91. Builders Exchange Building
92. Green Gate Building
93. NBC Center Drive-In Bank
94. Milam Building
95. Menger Soap Works
96. Garcia House
97. First National Bank
98. San Antonio Loan & Trust Building
99. Aztec Theater
100. Alamo National Bank Building
101. One Alamo Center
102. Portal San Fernando
103. Main Plaza
104. San Fernando Cathedral
105. Old Frost National Bank Building
106. Bexar County Courthouse
107. Bexar County Justice Center
108. San Antonio City Hall
109. Spanish Governor's Palace
110. Military Plaza
111. Military Plaza West Side Commercial Buildings
112. La Clede Hotel
113. Navarro House
114. Milam Square
115. Museo Alameda
116. El Mercado
117. O. Henry House
118. Plaza Hotel
119. Smith-Young Tower
120. Old Federal Reserve Bank Building
121. Gresser House
122. United States Arsenal
123. Magazine Building

123b. Stable Building

124. Commander's House
125. Wulff House
126. Oge House
127. Blersch House
128. Sartor House
129. Altgelt House
130. Stevens House
131. Hummel House
132. Oppenheimer House
133. Groos House
134. Chabot House
135. Norton-Polk-Mathis House
136. Ike West House
137. Kalteyer House
138. Steves Homestead
139. Guenther House
140. Brooks House
141. Schulze-Schilo House
142. Jump Start Performance Company
143. Blue Star Lofts
144. Arsenal House
145. Westminster Presbyterian Church
146. Casa Lavaca
147. Wright House
148. Yturri-Edmunds Compound
149. Casa 218
150. Groverton Street Studios
151. King William Lofts
152. International Center
153. Presidio Plaza
154. St. Mary's Street Parking Garage
155. Paragon Cable Headquarters
156. Acenar Restaurant
157. Duerler Candy Company

ARCHITECTURE

1. Church of Mission Concepcion
2. Mission San Jose
3. Mission Espada Acequia Dam and Aqueduct
4. Chapel of Mission San Juan
5. Chapel of Mission Espada
6. Stinson Municipal Airport
7. Willow Way
8. Castillo Home
9. Voss Metal Works
10. Brooks Field Hangar 9
11. Palo Alto College

11b. Learning Resources and Academic Computing Center

12. Gonzaba Medical Group Building

03

WITH THE KIND SUPPORT OF

ARCHITECTURE

SOUTH

03

SOUTH

The South Texas Brush Country fades through southern San Antonio to reach the foothills of the Texas Hill Country in the northern part of the city. Lacking the northern sector's varied terrain and more dynamic development, southern San Antonio grew slowly in the latter half of the twentieth century. Its reputation hinged on the heritage of the four Spanish missions along the southern section of the San Antonio River, on the brief presence of early-twentieth-century resort hotels around clusters of hot springs. After the development of Kelly Airforce Base in the West Sector, Brooks Field/Airforce Base was constructed, since privatized as Brooks City Base. Mission Trail development is being enhanced by San Antonio Missions National Historical Park and river redevelopment is constructing hike-and-bike trails linked with the River Walk. But all were overshadowed by the opening in 2006 of a sprawling Toyota manufacturing plant and selection the next year of a Southside site for a 550-acre satellite campus and irrigation technology center of Texas A&M University. The resulting explosive residential, commercial and industrial growth expected over a 64-square-mile area is to be managed by the city under its ambitious City South Community Plan.

THE SPANISH MISSIONS

San Antonio's five Spanish missions form the largest such cluster in the United States. Four comprise San Antonio Missions National Historical Park. The fifth is preserved as the Alamo.

In the absence of colonists to help defend the border with French Louisiana, the missions were to Europeanize the Native Americans, who would then settle in new towns throughout Texas. Converting Native Americans into Roman Catholics was only part of the process. Also of great importance was teaching the wandering tribes to live in one place as Europeans did and to learn European-style farming and crafts. This education required buildings and plazas surrounding the missions' houses of worship. At least such construction as the domed churches at Concepción and San José would have required the presence of professional builders sent up from missionary bases in Mexico.

"Constructing pendentives requires great architectural skills," noted Robert J. Mullen of the structural support arches for domes. "It is extraordinary that on this distant northern Spanish frontier two cruciform churches have their crossings closed with domes set on pendentives."

San Antonio's first mission, San Antonio de Valero, later known as the Alamo, originated on the Río Grande and was moved north for the founding of San Antonio in 1718. San José was established two years later. The last three—San Juan, Concepcíon and Espada—were moved near San Antonio in 1731 after difficult years on the Louisiana border.

By the close of the eighteenth century, most Native Americans who survived the sweeping epidemics had been assimilated into Spanish culture, and the French were no longer a threat. The missions were all closed by 1824. Mission churches and chapels were used intermittently through the end of the century. Their rescue and preservation in the first third of the twentieth century was followed by reestablishment of Roman Catholic congregations at the four southern missions and the restoration and/or interpretation of those mission compounds, since 1983 under the auspices of the National Park Service. The church buildings remain owned by the Catholic Archdiocese of San Antonio.

1

1 NR CHURCH OF MISSION CONCEPCIÓN, 1755

The beautifully proportioned church of Mission Concepción—fully named Mission Nuestra Señora de la Purísima Concepción de Acuña—is believed to be the oldest unreconstructed Spanish Colonial–era church in the United States. It was built of a porous limestone from a nearby quarry that also supplied limestone for other missions. Its twin bell towers and crossing dome have never collapsed, and its nave vault remains known for excellent acoustics. Parapets above the nave's exterior walls conceal the ceiling's vaulting. Franciscan symbols around the main portal—topped by a nearly equilateral stone triangle—and other detailing around windows and towers are characteristic of the sparse but expressive ornamentation the Spanish friars drew upon to provide cultural and spiritual enrichment in an otherwise primitive setting. Faint traces of once brilliant quatrefoils and squares of red, blue, orange and yellow remain on the stuccoed façade. Since restoration work under Ford, Powell & Carson began in 1981, local and international conservators have uncovered sections of original wall frescoes in the tower chapel, tower baptistry, sacristy and, in particular, on a vaulted ceiling of remains of the adjoining convento (1745), where a round mestizo face combines features of European and Native American artistic traditions.

ADDRESS
807 Mission Road at Mitchell Street

RENOVATED
1861, 1887, 1913, 1981

ADDRESS
6539 San Jose Drive at Roosevelt Avenue

MASON
Antonio Salazar, probable master mason

RENOVATED
1928–37

2 NR MISSION SAN JOSÉ, SINCE 1754
(MISSION SAN JOSÉ Y SAN MIGUEL DE AGUAYO)

The vast space enclosed by Mission San José's perimeter walls, rebuilt as a Depression-era WPA project, conveys a sense of the original scale of mission life. Lining the walls' inner sides are rooms reconstructed to reflect those originally inhabited by mission Indians after San José moved to this site in 1754. Beyond the north wall, the compact acequia-powered mission grist mill (circa 1790) has been reconstructed (1938, 2001) as a working mill of the period. The 1933 rebuilding of the crumbling barrel-vaulted granary (circa 1755) restored one of the great interior spaces of early Texas.

2

The heroic reconstruction effort by the San Antonio Conservation Society that began in 1926 was supervised by Harvey P. Smith.

Churrigueresque Spanish Baroque carving makes San José's mission church (1782) a familiar landmark of the Spanish period in Texas. The detailing is especially elaborate on the two-story frontispiece of the main portal and the choir window above. Floral designs in high relief support a statue of Our Lady of Guadalupe over the entrance and, atop the choir window, a statue of the mission's patron saint, St. Joseph. On the south wall, other distinctive carving surrounds the sacristy window, known as the Rose Window.

The church's roof and dome collapsed in the 1870s. The church remained unroofed for sixty years, though its single tower was rebuilt under the supervision of Fred B. Gaenslen and Atlee B. Ayres soon after it collapsed in 1928. The main portal's original massive wooden doors disappeared in the 1890s and were replaced in 1937 by similar doors carved by Austin artisan Peter Mansbendel. The three small domes forming the roof of the adjoining sacristy (1777) have, however, remained intact. Ongoing restorations of the church were undertaken by Ford, Powell & Carson in 1984 and continue.

3

3

4

3 NR MISSION ESPADA ACEQUIA DAM AND AQUEDUCT, CIRCA 1745

A Spanish-built acequia system still irrigates fields near Mission Espada. It begins just upstream from a wing-shaped diversion dam that raises the level of the San Antonio River high enough for the water to enter the start of the ditch. After meandering slightly downward for a half mile, the acequia reaches a creek, which it crosses on a 120-foot-long, double-arched stone aqueduct, the only original Spanish Colonial aqueduct still functioning within the United States. The acequia continues on for a mile past the western wall of the mission to the surrounding fields, where gates control lateral extensions. The main acequia channel—the acequia madre—then returns to the river. Functioning sluice gates and/or their foundations can be seen at the aqueduct and near the mission wall.

ADDRESS
9044 Espada Road

4 NR CHAPEL OF MISSION SAN JUAN, CIRCA 1755

Small chapels served San Antonio's missions until large churches could be constructed. Such churches were completed at missions Concepción and San José and partly finished at San Antonio de Valero (the Alamo). At Mission San Juan Capistrano, work began about 1760 on a large church with an octagonal sacristy, but it was not finished. Some low, partially completed walls and foundations survive. Worship continued instead across the mission plaza in a narrow, wooden-roofed chapel with five recessed arches facing the plaza. At

ADDRESS
9101 Graf Road at Ashley Road

RENOVATED
1877, 1909, 1934, 1970, 1980

the north end of that façade is an espadaña for hanging three bells. Ongoing restoration of the church and surrounding compound was first undertaken by a lay priest—Francois Bouchu—in 1877, then supervised by Leo M. J. Dielmann in 1909, Harvey P. Smith in 1934 and, since 1970, by Ford, Powell & Carson.

ADDRESS
10040 Espada Road

REBUILT
1887

RENOVATED
1935, 1961, 1984, 1998

5 NR CHAPEL OF MISSION ESPADA, CIRCA 1756

The signature elements of Mission San Francisco de la Espada are its chapel's three-bell espadaña and the chapel doorway with an irregular Mudéjar arch. The arch remains a source of speculation that its stones were improperly placed by builders who may have

5

6

misunderstood their instructions. Unlike the "temporary" chapel at Mission San Juan, this chapel was actually replaced by a large church nearby, in 1762. That building, however, was determined to be structurally unsound and was torn down fifteen years later. Its foundations can still be seen. Services reverted to the chapel. By 1887, little was left but its crumbling rubble limestone façade when Father Francois Bouchu reestablished a congregation and improvised the chapel's reconstruction. Later restoration was at first supervised by Harvey P. Smith and then, since 1984, by Ford, Powell & Carson.

ADDRESS
8535 Mission Road

6 STINSON MUNICIPAL AIRPORT, 1915

Pioneer aviators Marjorie, Katherine and Eddie Stinson established the Stinson School of Flying on this site, renting the land from the City of San Antonio until World War I. It was used primarily by barnstormers and experimental pilots until the 1930s, when American, Braniff and Eastern airlines began using Stinson as the city's airport. In 1936 a 7,000-square-foot Art Deco passenger terminal designed by Henry T. Phelps was built by the WPA. Within a few years terminals and more than one hundred buildings were added by the U.S. Army Air Corps, which established Stinson Field for flight training, and commercial aviation moved to the present site of International Airport. After World War II private use gradually expanded to include flight schools, an air cargo operator, private flight services and an aviation museum.

7 WILLOW WAY, CIRCA 1930

Elizabeth Graham drew a stick along the ground to outline the ten-room masonry house she built in a pecan grove of the San Antonio River flood plain near Mission San José. She replicated mission doorways and the staircase and fireplaces of the Spanish Governor's Palace, which she operated for the city for many years. The unpretentious, spontaneous style of the home, built by craftsmen from Mexico, later charmed Mrs. Graham's new son-in-law, O'Neil Ford. The young architect set up his early office in the informally created surroundings and credited them with inspiring his commitment to the informal, vernacular architecture styles for which he became internationally known.

ADDRESS
7 Willow Way

DESIGNER/BUILDER
Elizabeth Orynski Graham

8 CASTILLO HOME, 1923

This distinctive adobe house was built by refugees from the Mexican Revolution on a foundation of thick limestone perimeter beams. A turreted, two-story octagonal tower rises at the northwest corner of the deep, broadly arched, columned porch. Rooms twelve feet high are floored in differing patterns of decorative tile imported from Spain and Mexico. Recent restoration has stabilized the tower with two-stepped flying buttresses.

ADDRESS
302 Stratford Court

ADDRESS
214 Glenn Street

9 VOSS METAL WORKS, CIRCA 1885

This three-story brick former warehouse features fifteen-foot-high ceilings and longleaf pine floors, some of them charred by the forge of its previous occupant. Conversion to residential use included creating a large plaza with a reflecting pool and use of bright colors.

ADDRESS
8061 Inner Circle Road
(Building 671)
Brooks City Base

ARCHITECT
Albert Kahn, Detroit

10 NR BROOKS FIELD HANGAR 9, 1918 **(EDWARD H. WHITE II MUSEUM OF AEROSPACE MEDICINE)**

Hangar 9, one of twelve wooden and four steel World War I hangars built on a curved line beside the then-dirt runway at Brooks Field, is the nation's oldest surviving wooden military hangar. The hangars, and Brooks Field itself, were designed by Detroit industrial architect Albert Kahn, whose other standardized plans for the U.S. Army Air Corps included Langley Field in Virginia and Arcadia Field in California. Kahn's designs are characterized by use of complex truss systems that span vast spaces. Two years after pilot training and aviation ended at the then-named Brooks Air Force Base in 1960, the burning of Hangar 14 led the base commander to call for demolition of all remaining wooden hangars on base. Only sustained pressure from aviation and historical groups led the Secretary of the Air Force to spare Hangar 9, preserved as a museum on the now privatized base.

9

10

11▲ PALO ALTO COLLEGE, 1987

Palo Alto College is the first expansion campus for the Alamo Community College District's San Antonio College north of downtown. Its original 100-acre campus contains 150,000 square feet of administrative, classroom and support space, the design of which was inspired by the Spanish missions some four miles away. The master plan featured intimate courtyards and prominent buildings placed just inside the walls surrounding a main compound. Earth tones of the missions' walls are reflected in campus units of concrete masonry with rough mortar, with bright colors and glazed tiles mixed in. Extensive use of natural light includes strategic placement of windows of various shapes to create differing qualities of light. Also inspired by the missions' architecture is the use of such spatial forms as barrel vault domes and intersections of major paths of circulation. Later additions to the Palo Alto College campus include the [11b] Learning Resources and Academic Computing Center (in 1999) by Alamo Architects in partnership with RBAI. The new additions include use of rusticated masonry, stucco walls and metal roofs used on existing campus, with contrasting elements, including glazed masonry for color and use of extensive glass.

ADDRESS
1400 West Villaret Boulevard

ARCHITECTS
DeLara Almond and Jones / Kell

ADDRESS
720 Pleasanton Road

ARCHITECTS
Ayres & Ayres

RENOVATED
1990

12▲ GONZABA MEDICAL GROUP BUILDING, 1986 (PAN AMERICAN RESTAURANT)

This building represents the unlikely transformation of a landmark Mexican restaurant, the Pan American, into a multi-specialty medical clinic. The building was renovated by Marmon Barclay Souter Foster Hays for the Gonzaba Group. Existing details and finishes were integrated with the new design to retain the spirit of the original architecture, enhanced by new landscaping and lighting.

11b

12

HOT WELLS BALLROOM Built in the early 1900s, this ballroom held many memorable dance gatherings. Currently under a private ownership, it is available for rent for special occasions.

ADDRESS
5000 South Presa
San Antonio, Texas 78205
(210) 531-9553

RANCHO DEL CHARRO This is a place where Mexican charros (expert horsemen) have the opportunity to display a tradition that goes back to sixteenth century Spain. It is an amazing display of art, horsemanship and competition and is much more romantic than a typical

western rodeo. This arena and the San Antonio Charro Association (SACA) preserve the charreria (the Mexican sport for charros). Practices are often held on Saturday and Sunday afternoons. Call for event schedule.

ADDRESS
6126 Padre Drive
San Antonio, Texas 78200
(210) 532-0693

MISSION DRIVE-IN This is the last of San Antonio's drive-ins and one of a few still active outdoor movie theatres in the country. It re-opened in 2001, and it allows you to recall the days when you piled into a car with a bunch of your friends and sat under the stars, watching the movie and everyone around you.

ADDRESS
South Cross & Roosevelt
San Antonio, Texas 78200
(210) 533-2265

MISSION OPEN AIR MARKET Every city has its flea market, and this one truly serves its community. Shop for fun or adventure, in search of the rare garage sale heirloom or household items at a reasonable price. This family-owned and -operated Southside establishment, open for more than twenty years, claims to offer "a little taste of Mexico without crossing the border." From used cars to building materials, tools, musical instruments, fresh fruit, plants and clothing, it's hard to leave without something you've convinced yourself you need.

ADDRESS
707 Moursund Boulevard
(210) 921-1569
6 a.m.–4 p.m. Wednesday and Saturday, 6 a.m.–5 p.m. Sunday

ADDRESS
1115 Roosevelt
San Antonio, Texas 78210
(210) 532-0271

KIKE'S ICE HOUSE Ice houses are the neighborhood corner stores that were once part of the everyday culture. Their name originates from the fact that they were iceboxes that stored and distributed blocks of ice before refrigeration. They evolved into part neighborhood centers, part local taverns where a favorite iced-down beer could be purchased along with groceries. A cool spot where families and friends can sit to have light dinner, listen to the juke box and play a game of dominos or checkers, Kike's is now an endangered species.

ADDRESS
2900 South Flores Street
San Antonio, Texas 78204
(210) 533-5112

BOLNER'S MARKET Serving San Antonio since 1914, this family-owned traditional meat market offers the highest quality meats done any way that you want. You can find specialties that are not available elsewhere. Not only will they cut you the best steak, their deli will custom make a great sandwich.

ADDRESS
1440 Southwest Military
San Antonio, Texas 78221
(210) 977-9161

BUD JONES MEAL-A-MINUTE RESTAURANT An iconic eatery on the Southside, this place is a long established and very popular family-style restaurant. Its all-you-can-eat fish and giant chicken fried steak will take care of your appetite. Each meal can be a great deal.

ADDRESS
1113 Pleasanton Road
San Antonio, Texas 78214
(210) 928-2829

CAMARON PELADO This Mexican seafood place offers tasty and very reasonably priced seafood. Whether you order a fish soup or a fried fish dinner, you will have an enjoyable experience eating seafood cooked in the style of the Mexican coast.

WPA BRIDGES These bridges were built over the San Antonio River at several street crossings. They were designed and built by the Works Progress Administration in the 1930s.

ADDRESS
Roosevelt Avenue
San Antonio, Texas 78200

SUSPENSION BRIDGES They span several creek and gully crossings. Built by the City of San Antonio as part of a park system along the San Antonio River connecting several missions. For hike-and-bike use only.

ADDRESS
Hike and Bike Mission Trail

MISSION BIKE TRAIL Starting in downtown San Antonio, this bike trail connects the missions and parallels the San Antonio River for miles. This leisurely ride takes you through diverse neighborhoods and open countryside; add to the experience by stopping to explore each of the missions.

City South represents a bold vision, unusual for a Texas city: planning and designing a world-class community of approximately sixty square miles cultivated by the history, traditions, culture, lessons and dreams of a collective city.

—ED GARZA

City South San Antonio
A World-Class Community

The Land of Dreams...
A Landmark of the Future

by ED GARZA

Senior Associate & Texas Practice Leader, EDAW AECOM
Former Mayor of San Antonio 2001–2005

The year is 2020 and Isidro Gonzalez, vice-president of academic affairs at the local university in City South, reflects on his community: "I never knew what it meant to live in a 'planned' community designed to celebrate history, health, culture, diversity, education and the environment—living in a 'sustainable, traditional neighborhood with conservation easements.' To be able to walk, ride a bike or jump on the VIA rail to frequent stores and restaurants was unimaginable.

"I never believed my children would be able to walk to school safely on tree-lined sidewalks passing soccer fields and cornfields. On Sundays, we attend church service down the street, but it's gratifying to see so many other architecturally rich church buildings of different denominations and faith scattered throughout City South. The benefit of diversity is highlighted with the sights, sounds and smells of the various festivals, art exhibits and concerts, which all share the same town center plaza.

"It means a lot for my wife and I to have our children grow up in a setting where they feel a part of San Antonio. To live in a place that respects the contributions of our historic missions and rivers while preserving the natural beauty of Mitchell Lake and open space from the surrounding farmland. Our home is our own and we can touch anywhere in the world with the built-in Zenex wireless technology. Having my parents live down the street in a smaller, affordable, easier-to-maintain home makes it convenient for them to see my kids every day and pass on traditions and stories. And to top it off, when Abuelita and Abuelito need a break, the neighbors step up and volunteer. I was worried when we first moved here to know first-time homebuyers and renters lived within a stone's throw of my upper-middle-class home, but later I realized that everybody aspires for advancement and a quality safe environment to live.

"I have to admit, I thought this kind of place didn't exist but in a dream. But now I'm living it, in City South San Antonio."

City South began as a policy initiative (Southside Initiative) in 2001 as a response to unbalanced growth northward breeding traffic congestion, crowded schools and conflicts regarding development over the environmentally sensitive Edwards Aquifer Recharge zone. City South represents a bold vision, unusual for a Texas city: planning and designing a world-class community of approximately sixty square miles cultivated by the history, traditions, culture, lessons and dreams of a collective city.

It would be easy to label City South as another trendy planning initiative under a "new urbanism" or "traditional neighborhood design" concept. However, more than just urban design common sense, what makes the City South vision unique and challenging is its "Texas size" scale; the way its perceived location hurdles the "wrong side of the tracks"; unique historical, environmental and cultural assets; and the unconventional multi-jurisdiction approach toward implementation. One could say the scale of City South is of Texas proportions, making it the largest single public master-planned community in the United States.

Will the dream of City South become a reality? Only time will tell.

04

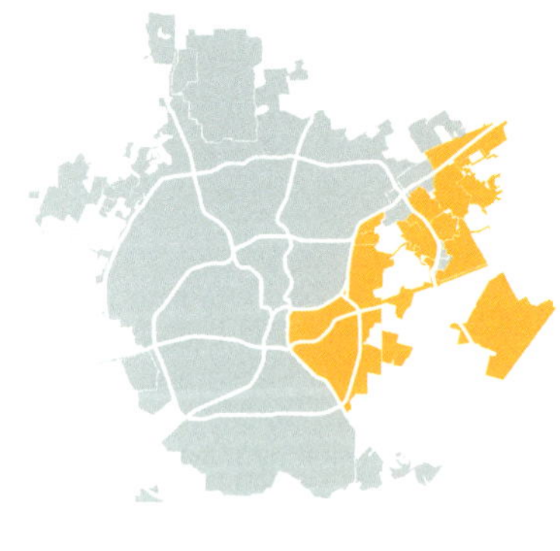

EAST

San Antonio's East Side is among the city's most interesting yet least understood areas. Separated from downtown by expressways and railroads and defined by floodplains, hills and industrial parks, its neighborhoods date from the late nineteenth century. They include the city's most historic African American churches, schools, social and cultural institutions, plus a state-of-the-art sports arena.

Irrigated farmlands just east of downtown were subdivided after the Civil War. Working-class citizens—some of them freed slaves—built small homes there. Overlooking the city, Powderhouse Hill, a Mexican Army outpost during the Texas Revolution, provided the location for a sprawling cemetery complex that today, provides glimpses into the early history of San Antonio.

Once the railroad arrived in 1877 and the municipal depot opened on the city's eastern edge, nearby residential development boomed. Such new neighborhoods as Dignowity Hill and Denver Heights attracted middle- and upper-class homeowners, who built both cottages and mansions. A thriving commercial—and later red-light—district known today as St. Paul Square developed around the Southern Pacific Railroad depot, built on East Commerce Street in 1904. San Antonians found employment at warehouses and manufacturing plants adjacent to the tracks. The area was the center of African American economic and social life, anchored by churches, the Colored Library and Auditorium, parks and after-hours music clubs catering to patrons regardless of color.

The near East Side remained stable and largely middle class until the 1950s, when, with desegregation, many younger residents began moving to outlying suburbs. Access to the East Side, already a challenge due to at-grade railroad crossings, was complicated further by construction of Interstate 37. Nevertheless, the area's religious and cultural institutions remain strong. Encouraging signs for ongoing revitalization are active neighborhood associations, continuing economic development programs, new park projects, housing and rehabilitation initiatives and rediscovery of the area's historic architecture.

ADDRESS
East Commerce Street, 1100 block

RENOVATED
1979, 1982

1▲ NR ST. PAUL SQUARE, CIRCA 1905

St. Paul Square, named for the African Methodist Episcopal church established nearby in 1868, is bisected by Commerce Street, one of the city's oldest thoroughfares. The area was sparsely developed until the railroad's arrival in 1877, when houses, lumberyards and industrial facilities filled the neighborhood. Construction of the Southern Pacific Depot on Commerce Street in 1903 spurred a second wave of development. The resulting commercial district of two- and three-story brick buildings provided lodging, cafes and stores for travelers and nearby residents. Visiting African American entertainers, who included Louis

Armstrong, Ella Fitzgerald and Count Basie, performed for mixed audiences in neighborhood clubs. In the post-war years, the area deteriorated. Its decline was exacerbated in 1960 when it was isolated from downtown by expressway construction. An urban renewal plan adopted in 1976 led to redevelopment of buildings on both sides of this section of Commerce Street. The master plan was completed by Haywood, Jordan & McCowan and Ford, Powell & Carson, with the latter's office (1979) in the notable grouping of buildings on the south side of the street. The project included façade restoration, a sky bridge and covered rear walkways that created a cohesive complex enhanced by street furniture and outdoor courts. Architects for the renovation were Larry O'Neill and Andrew Perez with Joe Stubblefield. More recently, construction of the Alamodome (1993), redevelopment of Sunset Station (1997), a thirteen-story hotel (2007) and substantial investment and renovation by local investors have focused new attention on the area. North of Commerce Street, little remains of the residential neighborhood settled by freed slaves after the Civil War, though several houses, St. Paul Church and Beacon Light Lodge are being redeveloped as offices and meeting space. Two twenty-story condominium towers with adjoining town homes are also planned.

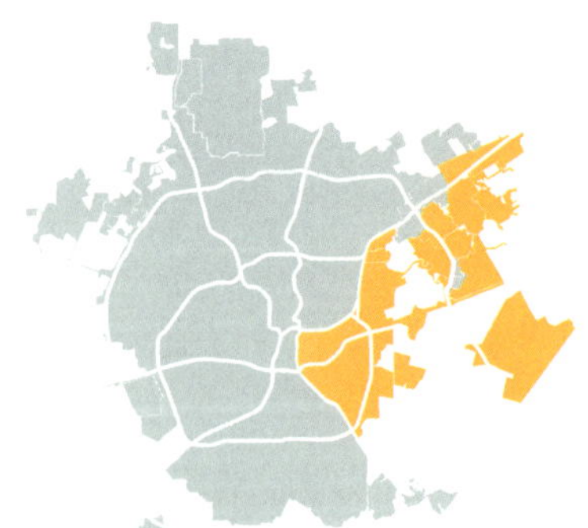

2▲ SOUTHERN PACIFIC RAILROAD DEPOT, 1903

The Mission Revival style developed in California in the 1890s, just as transcontinental railroads were expanding their presence in Texas and building magnificent depots in the style newly popular on the West Coast. San Antonio gained one of the state's finest Mission Revival stations with the Southern Pacific depot designed by the railroad's in-house engineer John D. Isaacs, assisted by architect D. J. Patterson and by W. E. Milwain. The stuccoed brick exterior is decorated with cast stone and brick detailing. The Commerce Street elevation is flanked by twin tile roofed towers and a grand curved parapet in the style of the Alamo's, making the depot a leading example of the Alamo Revival substyle of Mission Revival. The depot's interior is strictly Beaux-Arts, with cast plaster garlands and a sweeping barrel vault illuminated by two circular art-glass windows, featuring the medallion of the Sunset Route at the north end and the seal of Texas at the south end. The gilt ceiling with its enormous skylight was first adorned by "a thousand lights," all electric. The building was restored after a devastating fire in 1907. It was renovated in 1982 and remained an active AMTRAK depot until 1996, when Ford, Powell & Carson and Kell, Muñoz Wigodsky designed its restoration as part of a public/private venture's entertainment and retail complex with restaurants, music venues and shops. The outdoor plaza has a covered pavilion for large events.

ADDRESS
1174 East Commerce Street

ARCHITECTS
John D. Isaacs,
D. J. Patterson and
W.E. Milwain, San Francisco

RENOVATED
1907, 1981–84, 1998

ADDRESS
122 Heimann Street

ARCHITECT
Attributed to Atlee B. Ayres

RENOVATED
1985

3 HEIMANN BUILDING, CIRCA 1905

This is one of several hotels built to serve travelers shortly after the nearby Southern Pacific was completed. Designed to complement the depot, the Mission Revival style building features a corner tower with open belvedere roofed in pressed tin. The stucco finish is highlighted by exposed brick structural elements. Used as a hotel until 1968, the building fell into disrepair and burned in 1982. It was restored as offices during the revitalization of St. Paul Square.

3

4

5

ADDRESS
100 Montana Street

ARCHITECTS
Marmon Mok with HOK Sport+Venture+Event

4 ALAMODOME, 1993

Construction of this multi-use sport and exhibition facility was San Antonio's largest urban development project since HemisFair '68. Built on a former industrial site sandwiched between an interstate highway and a main rail line, the Alamodome was connected to the nearby convention center by newly constructed walkways and streets. Its 9.5-acre roof is suspended by cables between the four concrete towers, which rise 300 feet above pedestrian plazas. The curved side walls allow light into the concourses and provide spectacular views of the San Antonio skyline.

ADDRESS
321 North Center Street

RENOVATED
1982

5 SAMSCO BUILDING, 1912
(G. J. SUTTON STATE OFFICE BUILDING)

This sprawling industrial complex was built for the San Antonio Machine and Supply Company (SAMSCO), one of the state's largest manufacturers of windmills and equipment for the cattle industry. The westernmost building dates to 1912, while the distinctive brick archway and attached three-bay corner building were completed by the late 1920s. The rear six-story addition of concrete frame and brick curtain wall was built in 1952, by which time the plant covered an entire city block. Much of the plant was demolished after SAMSCO sold the property in 1965. Ford, Powell & Carson adapted the buildings to office use after they were acquired by the State of Texas in 1975.

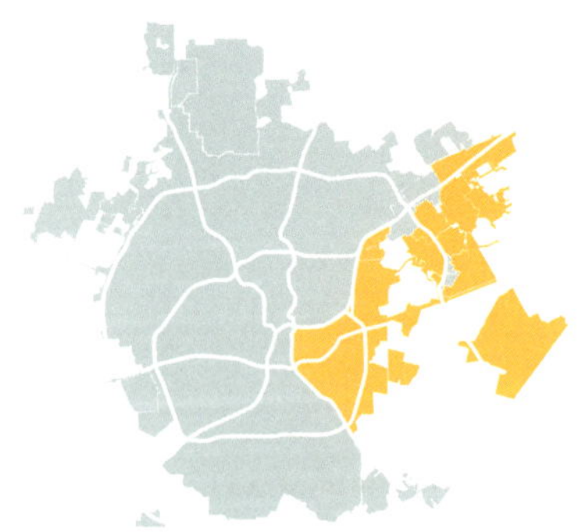

6 CARVER ACADEMY, 2001

This innovative inner-city private school consists of a series of four brick-clad classroom clusters, each connected by a covered outdoor walk that rings a cloister-like quadrangle. The library, on an axis with the entrance to the complex, is the focal point of the campus. The glass pavilion, shaded by a broad roof, is flanked by the more solid science laboratory, technology center and cafeteria.

ADDRESS
217 Robinson Place

ARCHITECTS
Lake/Flato and Kell Muñoz

7 ST. PHILIP'S COLLEGE, SINCE 1917

Since its founding in 1898, St. Philip's College has evolved from a girls' sewing class begun by the Episcopal Church into a two-year, multi-disciplinary public college. Established in La Villita, the school grew into an industrial trades school before moving to its present campus in 1917. St. Philip's became a public institution when it affiliated with San Antonio College in 1942. Original buildings on the present St. Philip's campus are no longer standing, and the oldest structures, dating from to 1949 and 1953, have been remodeled. The technical building and the learning resource center were designed by Haywood, Jordan & McCowan and Phelps, Simmons & Garza. A capital campaign reshaped the campus in the mid-1990s, when the campus's signature arches, theater and fine arts center and science building were designed by Ford, Powell & Carson, which also renovated the student center building.

ADDRESS
1801 Martin Luther King Drive

ADDRESS
One AT&T Center Parkway

ARCHITECTS
Ellerbe Becket, Lake/Flato and Kell Muñoz

8 AT&T CENTER, 2002

This 725,000-square-foot sports arena is recessed into the ground to make it appear less overwhelming. A series of shady porches, generous loggias and perforated silos ring the perimeter to further reduce the building's scale and to mitigate the harsh sunlight. A sombrilla of cables holding sheet-metal panels is strung between the arena and adjacent coliseum to shade the rear plaza. The arena's concrete frame, corrugated metal siding and terra cotta infill recall the neighborhood's industrial background. Seating capacity is 19,000. The arena's lead tenant is the San Antonio Spurs, three-time NBA champions.

8

9

ADDRESS
3302 South W.W. White Road

ARCHITECTS
Lake/Flato

9 ▲ ★ HOLT CORPORATE HEADQUARTERS, 1994

The headquarters for this heavy equipment company is on a wooded fifteen-acre site. The plan preserved existing oak trees and is organized around two courtyards, one displaying antique tractors and the other sculpture. Due to budget and scheduling issues, the building was designed with a prefabricated steel frame and simple detailing. The basic, metal barn-like design draws from the general elements of the machine shed.

ADDRESS
8047 Midcrown Drive

ARCHITECTS
Chumney, Jones & Kell

10 ▲ GECU PROTOTYPE, 1980 *NO PHOTO*

This sleek, elegantly detailed pavilion of bronze-tinted glass walls is poised beneath a hovering roof plan of white concrete and is strategically located at a bend in a busy suburban commercial thoroughfare. The structure, sunk behind grass berms, stands in marked contrast to its cluttered surroundings. Behind the minimalist pavilion, drive-in stations are grouped under a steel space-frame canopy.

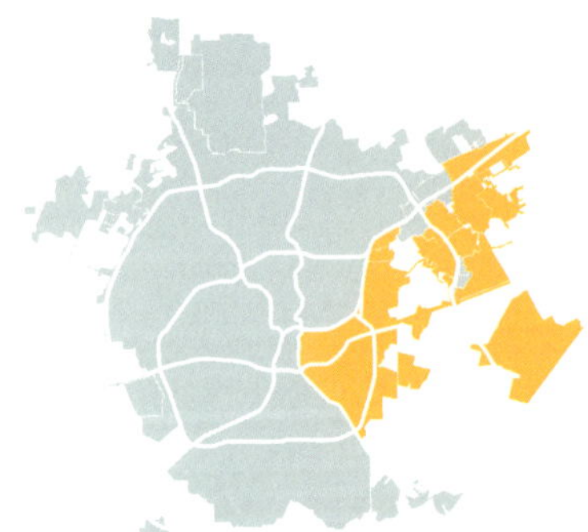

11

12a

11 NR RANDOLPH AIR FORCE BASE ADMINISTRATIVE BUILDING, 1931 This shining-white 147-foot tall structure, better known as the "Taj Mahal," is the iconic landmark of Randolph Air Force Base, which comprises the largest planned grouping of buildings of Spanish Colonial Revival architecture in the state. The mult-purpose structure includes a 1,200-seat theater in its rear wing. Its octagonal tower, capped by a chevron-patterned roof of blue and yellow glazed tiles, masks a 500,000-gallon water tank. The tower's walls are of precast concrete decorated with ornamental grille work, reflecting a Moorish influence. The Ayres & Ayres construction drawings fit into the conceptual design of Lt. Harold L. Clark, a trained architect who drew the distinctive symmetrical plan for the base and who was named architect-in-charge of the base project.

ADDRESS
Randolph Air Force Base

ARCHITECTS
Ayres & Ayres

DIGNOWITY HILL

Czech-born physician Dr. Anthony Michael Dignowity came to San Antonio in 1846, purchased and subdivided extensive acreage on the East Side. In 1854 he built his home on this 80-foot hill overlooking the city. A year after Dignowity's death in 1875, more residents arrived with the opening of Fort Sam Houston to the north. A year after that the city's first rail lines were laid at the base of the hill. More development followed laying out of streets in 1894 and extension of streetcar service and water and sewer lines by 1903. The neighborhood began to change in the 1920s as the more affluent families moved to newer areas and large homes were demolished or fell into disrepair. The Dignowity house and the adjacent Lockwood house were demolished for a park that bears both families' names. The area is a designated city historic district and is receiving renewed attention from residents and investors.

12a&b 700 BLOCK OF NORTH OLIVE STREET, SINCE 1876
This block exhibits the most complete and well maintained collection of vintage architecture remaining in Dignowity Hill. Its residences overlooking Lockwood-Dignowity Park enjoy one of the city's best skyline views. The [12b] 1886 Victorian house on the corner

12b

12c

at 805 Nolan Street was built for Ed Friedrich, who manufactured iceboxes before pioneering refrigerated storage cases and, later, room air conditioners. Next door, at 710 North Olive Street, Friedrich's daughter and son-in-law, Emmy and William Morrison Jr., built their Classical Revival cottage in 1912. The brick [12a] Dignowity House (1876, 732 North Olive Street), the oldest on the block, was built for H. L. Dignowity, son of the neighborhood's pioneer resident. It contains four fireplaces and a full basement.

ADDRESS
509 Burleson Street

ARCHITECT
Alfred Giles

12c NR EMIL ELMENDORF HOUSE, CIRCA 1884
This raised cottage reflects a plan typical of Louisiana plantation architecture. It incorporates random-coursed ashlar and standing seam metal roofing, both locally common building materials. The lower level, four feet below grade, contains a kitchen, pantry and dining and storage rooms. A long flight of stairs leads to the raised main floor, which includes the parlor, living room and three bedrooms. At the rear, the asymmetrical plan extends into an ell-shape bounded by a spacious two-story veranda.

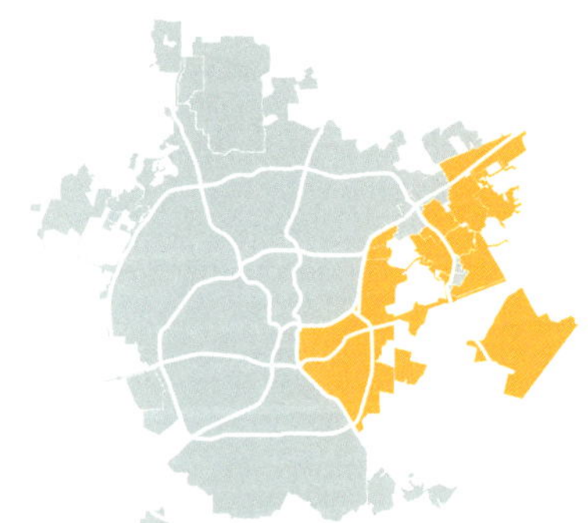

13 BRACKENRIDGE COLORED SCHOOL ANNEX NO. 2, 1907 **(LOWE WOODS EDUCATIONAL AND COMMUNITY COMPLEX)**

ADDRESS
532 Center Street

ARCHITECT
Attributed to Alfred Giles

This building is all that remains of Brackenridge Colored School, a multi-structure elementary school complex named for its donor, local philanthropist George W. Brackenridge. The original school, designed by James Wahrenberger, was finished in 1901. The first annex opened in 1904 and this classroom facility was completed in 1907. The school closed in 1936. The original building and Annex No.1 were demolished in the mid-1970s. Annex No. 2, which had deteriorated and stood vacant for several years, was renovated and expanded in 2007 by Nored Architecture for the Alamo Community College District and neighboring St. Paul United Methodist Church as an educational and community center.

14 JOHN W. AND ERASTUS SMITH ELEMENTARY SCHOOL, 1903 **(PUBLIC SCHOOL NO. 15)**

ADDRESS
823 South Gevers Street

Smith Elementary School is one of San Antonio's four surviving turn-of-the-century schools designed in the Neoclassical style. The original red brick structure features arched windows and doorways topped by prominent cast stone keystones. Changes include work by Fred B. Gaenslen (1930), additions by Gilbert Garza (1964), renovations by Norcell D. Haywood (1977 and 1995) and additions and renovations by Humberto Saldaña (1999).

ADDRESS
1615–19 Iowa Street

ARCHITECT
Fred B. Gaenslen

15 ST. GERARD'S PARISH COMPLEX, 1912–22

This represents one of the city's few intact groupings of historic Catholic institutional architecture. The beige brick school, rectory and church built by the Redemptorist order are all the work of F. B. Gaenslen, a prolific local designer of religious structures. On its upper floor the school (1912) incorporated a chapel that was converted to classrooms after the church was completed in 1922. The design of the [15b] school, since closed, features an arched portico and central projecting bay with dormered roof. The adjacent rectory (1912) also has an arched entryway, plus a tall stepped parapet topped by a cross. Expansive porches have been enclosed. The red clay tile-roofed church's central bay is decorated with elaborate cast stone detailing and flanked by tall domed corner towers, and reflects the influence of San Antonio's Spanish missions.

15

15b

16

ADDRESS
1933 East Houston Street

16 JAMES W. FANNIN ELEMENTARY SCHOOL, 1906 (PUBLIC SCHOOL NO. 12; DOROTHY PICKETT ACADEMY)

The appearance of this Neoclassical style red brick school belies its construction in several phases. Stylistic features include the columned entrance portico and second-floor elliptical arch with colonettes, prominent keystones over windows, an oculus above the entrance arch and modillions beneath the roof cornice. The building has evolved with additions by Charles T. Boelhauwe (1929) and Leo M. J. Dielmann (1959) and renovations and additions by Richard G. Morales (1977). It now serves the San Antonio Independent School District as a special, nontraditional academy.

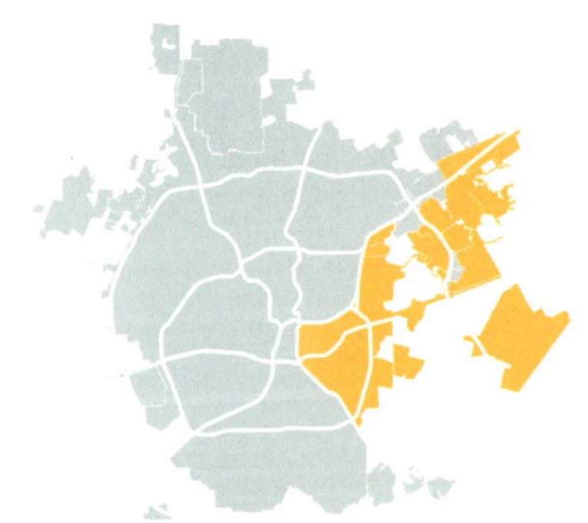

17

18

17 ST. PAUL METHODIST EPISCOPAL CHURCH, 1884 **(THE SPIRE)** Members of St. Paul Methodist Episcopal Church, founded in 1866, worshipped in two other nearby locations before completing this stone structure in 1884. The building's overall design and simple detailing offer a regional interpretation of Gothic Revival. The church anchored the surrounding African American community until the congregation moved to a larger building several blocks east in 1922. It was a funeral home and then a law office until being renovated in 2007 under Ford, Powell & Carson as a special events venue taking its name from the building's signature silver-painted pressed tin spire.

ADDRESS
230 North Center Street

ARCHITECT
Oliver W. Edwards

18▲ PACE FOODS, 1983
(LUCIFER LIGHTING COMPANY)
This building was designed as the plant and offices for Pace Foods, the then locally based manufacturer of hot sauce. The modest, economical and carefully composed structure utilizes stuccoed concrete tilt-wall panels with metal frame windows. The glazed administrative area, facing the expressway, is set behind a walled garden forecourt. The production zone is skylit and naturally ventilated. The building now serves as a manufacturing and distribution center for a lighting company.

ADDRESS
3750 North Pan Am Expressway

ARCHITECTS
Ford, Powell & Carson

ADDRESS
226 North Hackberry
San Antonio, TX 78202
(210) 207-7211

CARVER CULTURAL CENTER Created at the turn of the century as a facility to provide library services for the East Side African American community, the Carver has grown into a cultural center with a noteworthy schedule of performing arts and related educational programs, focusing primarily on the artistic achievements of African Americans.

ADDRESS
Martin Luther King Boulevard

MLK MARCH Celebrated as the one of the nation's largest Martin Luther King Day gatherings, weaving its way through the East Side, San Antonio's MLK March is estimated to gather as many as 100,000 people to commemorate Dr. Martin Luther King's legacy.

ADDRESS
100 Hoefgen Avenue
San Antonio, TX 78205
(210) 222-0561

ALDACOS In Sunset Station, just north of the Alamodome and just east of downtown, Blanca Aldaco provides authentic homemade Mexican cuisine, many of the dishes originating from her hometown roots near Gudalajara. The first-rate margaritas and a large patio are perfect for meeting convention-goers and other visitors from out of town. Make sure to leave room for the fabulous tres leches cake.

ADDRESS
1836 South Hackberry
San Antonio, TX 78210
(210) 532-4235

LITTLE RED BARN Serving satisfied customers for over forty years, this Texas tradition dishes out good steaks that are priced right. In a western setting that tells a story of Texas cattle ranches, you can choose from freshly prepared cuts of porterhouses, sirloins, T-bones and more. There are other choices beyond the steaks. The sides will more than complete the meal.

THE SMOKEHOUSE This is the successor to the legendary Bob's Smokehouse. Even though the original owner is gone, the place seems to retain his extraordinary barbecue-pit touch. The ribs, lamb, chicken and sausages, and their mesquite infused flavor, are so satisfying that the barbecue sauce is almost unnecessary. Make sure to enrich your experience with their equally tasty sides.

ADDRESS
3306 Roland Road (Rigsby Street)
San Antonio, Texas 78210
(210) 333-9548

RED BERRY MANSION Overlooking a lake that he built on his estate, alleged gambler and politician "Red" Berry built a rather unique, three-story, 12,000-square-foot mansion. This "chateau" was a home to many elaborate gambling parties that continued into the early 1960s. Recently the mansion was refurbished, by the new owner, to its original splendor and is available as a facility for hosting special events.

ADDRESS
856 Gembler Road
San Antonio, Texas 78219

SAN ANTONIO SPURS Every home game is a sellout, as San Antonio is wild about the San Antonio Spurs, three-time winners of the NBA championship and holders of the second highest winning percentage in NBA history. Perhaps, when visiting, you will be lucky to find a ticket to a game and join the thousands of loyal fans for a few hours of family-oriented fun.

ADDRESS
AT&T Center
One AT&T Center Parkway
San Antonio, Texas 78219
(210) 444-5000

SAN ANTONIO STOCK SHOW AND RODEO Each year, for two and half weeks in February, the AT&T Center is devoted to rodeo season and the Spurs hit the road. More than a million human visitors come to see cows, poultry, horses, pigs, goats, sheep and sheep dogs; marvel at bull riding, bronco busting and barrel riding; cheer at the youngsters' calf scramble; and watch one of over twenty shows by the biggest names in country and popular music.

ADDRESS
AT&T Center
One AT&T Center Parkway
San Antonio, Texas 78219
(210) 444-5000

EAST SIDE CEMETERIES

A complex of thirty-one cemeteries dating from 1853 is on a rise a half mile east of downtown. The 103-acre area reflects a century of San Antonio's social history.

These cemeteries replaced the public and Catholic burial grounds on the city's near west side, now the site of Milam Park and Santa Rosa Hospital. Consistent with the rural cemetery movement of the early 1800s, the

new burial ground was located away from the congested city in a remote location, this one once a vantage point for Spanish soldiers whose storing of ammunition here gave it the name Powderhouse Hill. Soon after the first lots were sold, the city began donating tracts to fraternal and religious organizations for their own burial grounds. The last cemetery was created in 1904.

While burials in twenty-four of the cemeteries are predominantly Anglo, seven cemeteries are solely or largely African American. There are scattered Hispanic burials, though the majority of Hispanics in the nineteenth century were interred in San Fernando Cemetery, established in about 1855 on San Antonio's west side. Public and private funds and volunteer and restitution labor have brought recent improvements, including new fencing and gravesite restoration.

ARCHITECTURE

1. St. Paul's Square
2. Southern Pacific Railroad Depot
3. Heimann Building
4. Alamodome
5. Samsco Building
6. Carver Academy
7. St. Phillip's College
8. AT&T Center
9. Holt Corporate Headquarters
10. GECU Prototype
11. Randolph AFB Administrative Building
12. Dignowity Hill

12a. 700 Block of North Olive Street
12b. 700 Block of North Olive Street
12c. Emil Elmendorf House

13. Brackenridge Colored School Annex No. 2
14. John W. and Erastus Smith Elementary School
15. St. Gerard's Parish Complex
16. James W. Fannin Elementary School
17. St. Paul Methodist Episcopal Church
18. Pace Foods

ARCHITECTURE

1. University of Texas at San Antonio Downtown Campus
2. Jose Antonio Navarro Elementary School
3. Heimann Building
4. International & Great Northern Railroad Depot
5. Ximenes Chapel
6. Prospect Hill Baptist Church
7. Mexican American Unity Council
8. Guadalupe Theater
9. Plaza Guadalupe
10. Our Lady of the Lake University
11. Ricardo G. Salinas Health Clinic
12. Raymundo Rangel Housing
13. Gardendale Elementary School
14. Nelson W. Wolff Municipal Stadium
15. Triple-S Steel supply Company
16. Kel-Lac Transit Center
17. Henry Guerra Branch Library
18. St. Mary's University
19. Sarita Kenedy East Law Library
20. National Shrine of the Little Flower
21. Thomas Jefferson High School
22. Former Balcones Heights City Hall
23. Humane Society Animal Shelter
24. Registry Building
25. One Forum Office Building
26. Medical Center Tower
27. Methodist Healthcare Ministries Corporate Headquarters
28. Canavan Center
29. United Services Automobile Associations
30. University Business Park
31. Harris Corporate Employee Breakroom
32. The University of Texas at San Antonio

32b. UTSA Biotechnology, Science and Engineering Building

33. Security Service Federal Credit Union Corporate Headquarters
34. Great Northwest Library
35. Alice P. McDermott Building, Cancer Therapy and Research Institute of Drug Development
36. Institute of Biotechnology, Univ. of Texas Health Science Center at San Antonio
37. Guadalupe Homes
38. Maury Maverick Jr. Branch Library and Fire Station No. 49

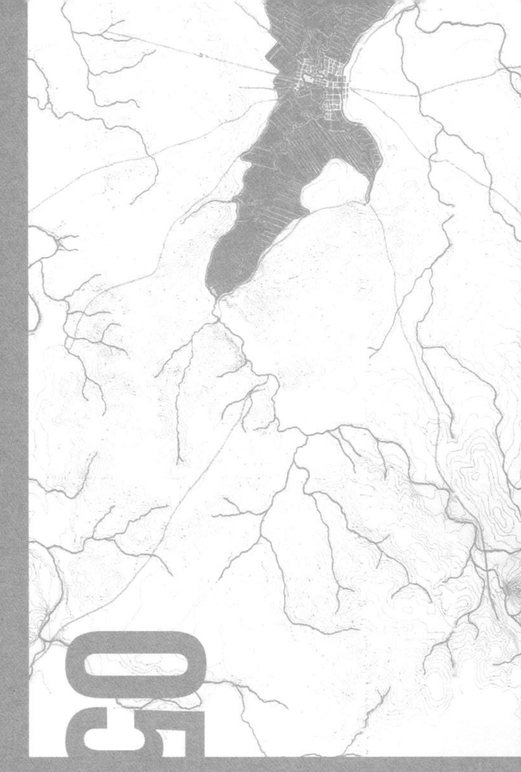

05

WEST

San Antonians in the nineteenth century knew the land west of San Pedro Creek as "Laredito," where life was no less exciting than on the Mexican border. Freighters assembled wagon trains for long hauls to Mexico and West Texas. Cowboys left to trail herds north to distant railheads. By day and night locals gathered to eat and shop at colorful outdoor markets near the flourishing red-light district. The less fortunate made their homes in creek bottoms prone to flash flooding, while more affluent residents built on a small rise known as Prospect Hill.

The railroad's arrival on the West Side in 1881 revolutionized the local shipping and cattle industries and spurred development. Streetcar lines reached to suburbs surrounding newly dammed lakes, gleaming universities rose from mesquite-studded pastures. Belgian farmers prospered on the rich soil at the town's edge. When the 1910 Mexican revolution brought in a wave of refugees, many settled on the West Side, enriching the already diverse cultural mix.

By the 1940s, much of the near West Side had devolved into the city's improvised areas. Depression-era relief projects and post-war urban renewal programs brought some of the nation's earliest public housing projects and large-scale neighborhood demolition in the name of revitalization. Two constants were Our Lady of Guadalupe Church and the Guadalupe Theater, which in the 1970s became catalysts for a new central plaza and community-based social and cultural programs.

Since then, decaying public housing projects have been replaced by more traditional neighborhoods, historic zoning has reinvigorated pre- and post-war suburbs and the Deco District promises commercial revitalization along old Fredericksburg Road. The economic base has been dramatically reshaped with the reinvention of the former Kelly Air Force Base into a gateway for international trade and aircraft maintenance. Lackland Air Force Base remains a military training center. Sea World, a scientific research campus and sprawling subdivisions envelop recently vacant farmland to create a new urban landscape.

ADDRESS
501 West Durango Boulevard

ARCHITECTS
Ford, Powell & Carson, master plan

1 THE UNIVERSITY OF TEXAS AT SAN ANTONIO DOWNTOWN CAMPUS, SINCE 1997

The University of Texas at San Antonio opened an eleven-acre campus beside an elevated expressway on the western edge of the central city in 1997. Under a master plan by Ford, Powell & Carson, since expanded, academic buildings were planned around a central open space. Between the expressway and the central courtyard, a parking structure designed by the same firm shielded the courtyard from the expressway while preserving a view of the skyline. The first structure, the Frio Street Building (1997, Humberto Saldaña), has been joined by the Buena Vista Street Building (1999,

1

2

Humberto Saldaña and Kell Muñoz Wigodsky) and the Durango Building (2001, Ford Powell & Carson). Continuing growth has been addressed by enlargement of existing buildings and expansion of the campus to the west.

ADDRESS
623 South Pecos Street

ARCHITECT
James Murphy

RENOVATED
1902, 1923, 2000

2 NR JOSÉ ANTONIO NAVARRO ELEMENTARY SCHOOL, 1886 **(PUBLIC SCHOOL NO. 8)**

This Italianate style building, originally a two-story structure with four rooms, was designed by the prolific school architect James Murphy. It was enlarged in 1902 under Henry T. Phelps and John A. Shand, who matched the existing stone construction. Later additions, including a 1923 building facing on San Fernando Street, are of brick. A 2000 renovation by Haywood, Jordan, McCowan included two additional stairways and an elevator. The complex, now a special high school campus for the San Antonio Independent School District, is named for José Antonio Navarro, a native-born signer of the Texas Declaration of Independence and later state senator.

3 NR HEIMANN BUILDING, 1909
(I&GN HOTEL, AVANCE HEADQUARTERS)

This Mission Revival style hotel was built to serve the adjacent International and Great Northern Railroad station. Finished in stucco and red brick, iron columns support second- and third-floor porches roofed in red tile. Like its companion hotel near the Southern Pacific Depot, this building fell into disrepair, burned and stood vacant for thirty years. It was renovated under Jorge Peña's Architectura International as the national headquarters of the non-profit organization Avance.

ADDRESS
118 North Medina Street

ARCHITECT
Atlee B. Ayres

RENOVATED
2001

4 NR INTERNATIONAL & GREAT NORTHERN RAILROAD DEPOT, 1908 **(MISSOURI PACIFIC DEPOT, CITY EMPLOYEES FEDERAL CREDIT UNION)**

This Mission Revival style depot replaced an earlier station built on the site after the International & Great Northern Railroad reached San Antonio in 1881. The tan brick and steel building has a Greek cross plan with a central domed space and four radiating barrel vaults. The eighty-eight-foot high dome is roofed in copper and topped with a bronze Indian, the railroad's signature motif. After closing in 1970, the building was vacant for fifteen years. Its interior was badly damaged by a fire in 1982 and by leaks after vandals stripped copper from the dome. A total renovation was completed in 1988 under James Resnick of HBE, St. Louis, for City Employees Federal Credit Union. The magnificent interior stairway was restored and the open space of

ADDRESS
123 North Medina Street

ARCHITECT
Harvey L. Page

RENOVATED
1988

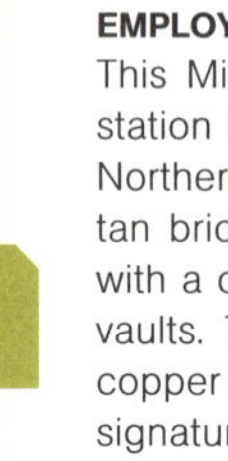

the rotunda was preserved as a lobby, while an addition for office space was added on the site of the long-demolished platform canopies. Stained glass windows were recreated and ticket windows were adapted as windows for tellers.

ADDRESS
113 Ruiz Street

RENOVATED
1946

5 NR XIMENES CHAPEL, CIRCA 1860
(CHAPEL OF THE MIRACLES)
This small, still privately owned chapel is all that remains of the family homestead of Juan Ximenes, who fought with the Texas Army during the war for independence. The simple stone structure has a square tower, gabled roof and single Gothic window in each side wall. The interior is plastered and whitewashed. Worshipers are drawn to pray before an eight-foot high wooden crucifix known as El Señor de los Milagros for its healing powers. Tradition maintains that it was moved here from San Fernando Church by the Ximenes family after the devastating fire at San Fernando in 1828. The chapel remains a popular pilgrimage spot, though an urban renewal project that demolished the surrounding neighborhood in the 1970s makes the chapel difficult to find among expressway access roads, warehouses and apartment complexes.

5

6

ADDRESS
1601 Buena Vista Street

ARCHITECT
Henry J. Harker,
Little Rock, Ark.

REHABILITATED
1984

6 NR PROSPECT HILL MISSIONARY BAPTIST CHURCH, 1911 Built to serve the surrounding Prospect Hill neighborhood, this church and attached educational wing combines Beaux Arts and Classical elements. The worship space was designed on the Akron Plan, incorporating a main and secondary auditorium separated by a moveable partition with concentric rows of curved pews. After the congregation disbanded in 1965, the church served as a community center until it was damaged by fire in 1973. The dome collapsed after a second fire, in 1980, and the building was abandoned. The 1984 conversion under John Bratton and Ernest Breig to elderly housing required installation of five lift slabs to stabilize the masonry walls. An external dome structure was installed to recreate the building's original massing.

7

7▲ MEXICAN AMERICAN UNITY COUNCIL, 1912
(CROCKETT ELEMENTARY SCHOOL)

This Prospect Hill neighborhood school, open through the 1970s, was monumentally scaled and detailed with abstract New French classical ornament. The building was expanded in 1930 under a design by Carl V. Seutter. In 1977 it was acquired by the Mexican American Unity Council for its headquarters and renovated under Larry O'Neill and Andrew Perez. The exterior was restored with the exception of newly added glazing. The grounds were landscaped as a small park.

ADDRESS
2300 West Commerce Street

ARCHITECT
Leo M. J. Dielmann

RENOVATED
1930, 1977

8 GUADALUPE THEATER, 1942
(GUADALUPE CULTURAL ARTS CENTER)

This historic theater anchored the entertainment district that thrived along Guadalupe Street in the 1930s and 1940s. Once a popular venue for stage acts and movies, the Guadalupe, like many neighborhood theaters, declined during the 1960s. After brief service as a flea market, the theater was restored by a public-private partnership as a center for the preservation and presentation of Hispanic arts. Exterior tile work and signage was restored and the interior reconstructed as multi-purpose gathering space incorporating the neighborhood's glass block and glazed-tile vocabulary. Renovations in 1984 were by Reyna-Caragonne and in 2003 by Jorge Peña.

ADDRESS
1301 Guadalupe Street

RENOVATED
1984, 2003

ADDRESS
1300 block of Guadalupe Street

ARCHITECTS
Reyna-Caragonne

9▲★ PLAZA GUADALUPE, 1984

Plaza Guadalupe was created as the focal point of the Avenida Guadalupe Association's revitalization program for this west side commercial and residential neighborhood. The plaza, built on an axis with Leo M. J. Dielmann's Our Lady of Guadalupe Church (1921), combines elements of Baroque planning and architectural imagery with those of southwestern regionalism. Light modulating screen walls and pergolas and vivid patterns and colors enliven open-air spaces. Artist Jesse Treviño's 10-by-40-foot, three-dimensional ceramic tile candleholder depicting the Virgin of Guadalupe was unveiled in 2003 between the plaza and adjacent Guadalupe Theater. Immediately to the west, Las Oficinas de Avenida Guadalupe (2006) houses health service providers. Across the street are El Progresso Community Center, a special events venue and El Parian, an affordable office building.

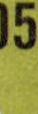

ADDRESS
411 Southwest 24th Street

ARCHITECT
James Wahrenberger

10 OUR LADY OF THE LAKE UNIVERSITY, SINCE 1896

In 1895 the Sisters of Divine Providence, a French order, established a school for girls on a site overlooking Elmendorf Lake. Soon expanded to a two-year, then to a four-year college, the school became coeducational in 1969. The original campus includes Wahrenberger's main building (1896) plus his St. Ann's Hall (1907) and Moye Hall (1922). Wahrenberger was a prolific designer for San Antonio's Catholic community, as was Leo M. J. Dielmann, who designed the Chapel (1923–28), Providence Hall (1925), Science Hall (1936) and St. Florence Library (1947). Befitting the order, the designs are suitably Gallic, with soaring towers and dormered rooflines. The chapel's spire rises 193 feet, and its Gothic style interior features a fine collection of stained glass by Munich artist Emil Frei. Alamo Architects' Flores Residence Hall (1999) incorporates beige face brick, stone details, steep pitched roofs and dormers to complement the historic buildings. Sueltenfuss Library, by Garza, Bomberger and Associates, was completed in 2000.

11

12

13

11▲ RICARDO G. SALINAS HEALTH CLINIC, 2003
Courtyards buffer this building on two sides of its large central reception area, which is adjoined by smaller waiting areas and clusters of private consultation rooms. Economically constructed shed forms emit natural light throughout. Vibrant colors, spaces of various shapes and bare fluorescent lighting arrays help create a nontraditional clinic setting.

ADDRESS
630 South
General McMullen Drive

ARCHITECTS
Sprinkle Robey

12▲ RAYMUNDO RANGEL HOUSING, 2000
Five residential buildings with common and private porches surround a communal garden providing security and community for elderly residents of this infill housing project. Passive solar elements such as deep overhangs, louvered roof vent cupolas, building orientation and rain harvesting systems help make the complex sustainable. Shapes are borrowed from neighboring bungalows. The low stone wall along the street is reminiscent of similar walls surrounding early Belgian farmhouses nearby. Colors reflect the strong Hispanic flavor of the neighborhood.

ADDRESS
1021 South
San Eduardo Street

ARCHITECTS
Sprinkle Robey

13▲ GARDENDALE ELEMENTARY SCHOOL, 1949
Reyna and Caragonne's notable 1987 classroom and kitchen addition to this school combines angled vaults, glazed tile and glass block walls, stuccoed concrete block and painted steel in a modern interpretation of the southwestern style.

ADDRESS
1731 Dahlgreen Avenue

RENOVATED
1987, 1998

ADDRESS
5757 Highway 90 East

ARCHITECTS
Ford, Powell & Carson

14▲ NELSON W. WOLFF MUNICIPAL STADIUM, 1994
San Antonio's 6,400-seat municipal baseball stadium is home to the San Antonio Missions, a Class AA team. Two stucco-clad towers at the main entrance recall the design of San Antonio's earlier ballpark, which had been modeled after its neighboring Mission Concepciòn. Wolff Stadium includes grandstand seating topped by boxes, all covered by an open-trussed metal roof structure reflecting this area's industrial construction. Grassy areas and berms flanking the first and third base lines provide informal seating and picnic areas.

14

15

16

ADDRESS
2042 West Thompson Place

ARCHITECTS
Lake/Flato

15▲ TRIPLE-S STEEL SUPPLY COMPANY, 2004
Lake/Flato created an iconic warehouse for this Houston-based steel service center by devising a kit-of-parts using structural shapes and sections found in the company's catalogue. Sunscreens were created with steel angles and galvanized Z rafters. The winged roof of the office/showroom provides daylight and recalls the facility's location beside a runway of Kelly USA, the industrial park that comprises the former Kelly Air Force Base.

ADDRESS
7183 Highway 90 West

ARCHITECTS
Sprinkle Robey

16▲★ KEL-LAC TRANSIT CENTER, 2004
This 3,000-square-foot facility provides queuing areas for sixteen VIA Metropolitan Transit buses, a sixty-seat air-conditioned waiting area, ticket office and handicapped-accessible toilet facilities. The waiting area's public art has expanses of storefront glass interspersed with colored glass panels bearing etched text. The outdoor pedestrian island providing access to bus routes includes built-in seating areas and shade trees.

17▲★ HENRY GUERRA BRANCH LIBRARY, 2004

A front plaza with a series of curved cast-in-place concrete walls for sitting and reading welcomes readers into this 14,500-square-foot branch library. The building is in two wings, one for general use and the other for staff and storage. It is oriented to maximize natural light, capture breezes and help define an existing green space to the north.

ADDRESS
7978 Military Drive West

ARCHITECTS
Sprinkle Robey

18 ST. MARY'S UNIVERSITY, SINCE 1894
(ST. LOUIS COLLEGE)
19▲★ SARITA KENEDY EAST LAW LIBRARY *NO PHOTO*

The characteristic High Victorian architectural style of James Wahrenberger was chosen for St. Louis Hall (1894), the signature building of St. Louis College. Established by the Society of Mary, a Catholic teaching order, [18] the new campus was on a promontory overlooking the then-distant suburb of West End. It first served boarding students from the order's downtown school, St. Mary's Institute. Classes were later consolidated and the school was renamed St. Mary's College and then St. Mary's University. The design of St. Louis Hall is subdivided into symmetrical groups of threes, horizontally broken by central vertical accents and brick ornament. The emphatic design discouraged later architects from integrating new construction with it, and it was not until Jones Kell's [19] Sarita Kenedy East Law Library (1984) that a caliber of design similar to Wahrenberger's returned

ADDRESS
1 Camino Santo Maria

ARCHITECT
James Wahrenberger

to the 135-acre campus. The Law Library's exterior is an unorthodox mix of arched detailing and materials. Its generously proportioned interiors are tranquil and subtly detailed. Functional design incorporates modern technology in the Alumni and Convocation Center (2000, Hastings & Chivetta, St. Louis) and in the AT&T Center for Information Technology (2003, Jerry Theis). The Gateway to Historic St. Mary's University (2004, JEK Landscape Architect) includes a dramatic portal, plazas and lush landscaping. The 100-foot Barrett Memorial Bell Tower (2006, Jerry Theis) adds a visual focal point to the campus.

ADDRESS
906 West Kentucky Street

ARCHITECT
Charles Lester Monnot, Oklahoma City

20 NR NATIONAL SHRINE OF THE LITTLE FLOWER, 1931 (OUR LADY OF MOUNT CARMEL AND ST. THERESE CHURCH) The Discalced Carmelites, a Catholic religious order, was invited to establish a mission on San Antonio's West Side in 1923. Its success led to an international campaign to build a shrine honoring St. Therese, a French-born saint known as "the little flower." The cross-vaulted church and attached monastery are built of concrete, steel and clay tile clad in gray Bedford, Indiana limestone. The exterior is sparingly decorated with Spanish Renaissance details. The main tower rises 116 feet. The secondary 72-foot tower is topped by a bronze statue of St. Therese. The interior is richly decorated with work of local and international artists and craftsmen. Wooden figures were carved in the Spanish studio of Francisco Pablo. Art glass windows represent the work of the Emil Frei Stained Glass Company of St. Louis, notably by Rodney Winfield. Marble carvings and mosaic tile work were designed by master San Antonio monument artist Louis Rodriguez. Locally produced are the wrought iron gates and grilles by Voss Metal Works and the decorative tile floors by Aztec Art Tile Company.

21 NR THOMAS JEFFERSON HIGH SCHOOL, 1932

This monumental Spanish Revival campus with its two large patios was built on a thirty-three-acre site in part by the Works Projects Administration. In 1937 United Press selected Jefferson as the most outstanding high school in America. Its domed towers, red tile hipped roofs and wrought iron balconies were elaborately embellished with cast stone ornamentation by Hannibal and Eugene Pianta and with decorative concrete tiles by Redondo Tile. The Baroque main entry is of special note. Interior spaces, notably the auditorium and library, are richly decorated with molded plaster detailing, oak wainscoting, concrete tile floors and colorful stenciling. The three-story east wing and shop were completed by Phelps & Simmons in 1963. Work in 1978 included installation of aluminum windows and construction of a girls' gymnasium and student union building.

ADDRESS
723 Donaldson Avenue

ARCHITECTS
Adams & Adams and Phelps & Dewees

22▲ FORMER BALCONES HEIGHTS CITY HALL, 1971
NO PHOTO **(SLAY ENGINEERING COMPANY)**

A diminutive municipal administration and police headquarters building set on a street of detached suburban houses, this former city hall is in the O'Neil Ford style of Modernist Regionalism. The unpretentious, domestic scale of the building is enhanced by counterposed shed roofs and a combination of variegated brown brick and cypress siding.

ADDRESS
111 Altgelt Street

ARCHITECTS
Johnson-Dempsey & Associates

ADDRESS
4804 Fredericksburg Road

ARCHITECTS
Alamo Architects

23▲ HUMANE SOCIETY ANIMAL SHELTER, 2002

Activities center around a group of buildings surrounding a landscaped park space, where visitors can spend time in the open air with potential animal family members. Animal care areas are broken into campuses of individual buildings with smaller, sunlit spaces surrounded with play yards, where animals get daily exercise or visit with potential adoptive families. Animals are housed in room-size enclosures, visible through glass walls. Large overhanging roofs and vine-covered trellises provide shelter from the elements.

23

25

ADDRESS
7900 Callaghan Road at IH10

ARCHITECT
Robert Callaway

24▲ REGISTRY BUILDING, 1972 *NO PHOTO* (U.S. GLOBAL INVESTMENTS)

Sited along the access road to a major expressway, this building is a tectonic essay in precast architectural concrete and glass. The ell-shaped plan places the main arm, a three-story office block atop partially submerged parking, alongside the access road with a smaller, two-story arm screening surface parking at the rear. Where these two arms intersect, a curving skylit lobby and circular entry stairs provide the only counterpoint to the strictly rectilinear lines of the building massing. The main elevation balances the horizontality of the basement parking and third-story attic treatment with the vertical thrusts of concrete pilasters and alternating panels of glass and concrete.

ADDRESS
800 IH 10 West

ARCHITECTS
Hellmuth, Obata & Kassabaum, Dallas

25 ONE FORUM OFFICE BUILDING, 1983 (TENNECO BUILDING)

This sixteen-story tower is wrapped by a three-story rose-colored office block, its color intensified by rose-colored reflective glass. Its stepped-back massing profile rises from the crest of Horizon Hill to look across a valley of condominiums.

27

28

26▲ MEDICAL CENTER TOWER, 1980 *NO PHOTO*

This twelve-story office tower is faced with highly contrasted bands of white precast concrete and slot-ended ribbons of reflective glazing. Deep diagonal incisions shaping the building culminate in a glazed, wedge-roofed entrance lobby. Medical Center II (1986, Marmon Barclay Souter Foster Hays) is a companion piece.

ADDRESS
7950 Floyd Curl Drive

ARCHITECT
Marmon Mok

27▲ METHODIST HEALTHCARE MINISTRIES CORPORATE HEADQUARTERS, 2005

An exterior of white poured-in-place and precast concrete with a slick finish and a custom-designed glass and aluminum window wall system is featured on this ell-shaped building with a landscaped courtyard.

ADDRESS
8109 Fredericksburg Road

ARCHITECTS
Kell Muñoz

28 CANAVAN CENTER, 1970–77

This medical-professional office complex features buildings domestically scaled and, in San Antonio's tradition of modernist regionalism, minimal in detail, blunt in profile and uniformly surfaced in light brown brick. Extensive plantings enhance the intimacy of the stepped massing and screen walls, enclosed garden courts, cedar pergolas and external stairways, all visible from inside through large glazed openings.

ADDRESS
8647 Wurzbach Road

ARCHITECTS
Ken Bentley & Associates

ADDRESS
9800 Fredericksburg Road

ARCHITECTS
Benham-Blair & Associates

29 UNITED SERVICES AUTOMOBILE ASSOCIATIONS, 1975
This vast insurance headquarters building, a third of a mile in length, is located on a 300-acre site. It contains three million square feet of space and a 2,600-car underground garage and accommodates 6,000 employees. The building's plan is skewed to conform to the contour of the site. Interior trays of office space open to an air-conditioned three-story central court that runs the length of the building. Architectural features include a composite system of precast concrete panels cladding a light steel frame, recessed ribbon windows, expressed stair towers and exposed air-handling units. A ranch house and stable on the property

were adapted for company use. Neuhaus + Taylor of Houston were the interior architects and James Keeter the landscape architect.

ADDRESS
12501 Network Boulevard

ARCHITECTS
Rehler Vaughn Beaty & Koone

30▲ UNIVERSITY BUSINESS PARK, 1985 *NO PHOTO*
This 90,000-square-foot office and service center gains distinctive identity from its deep-gridded fascia accentuated with contrasting colors and staggered massing. A two-and-a-half-foot square grid was used as the dominant visual element.

ADDRESS
5727 Farinon Drive

ARCHITECTS
Sprinkle Robey

31▲ HARRIS CORPORATION EMPLOYEE BREAKROOM, 1992 This futuristic showplace at the headquarters of Harris Corporation's Microwave Communication Division features a high-tech interior with an exposed ceiling and a custom light cone in the center. Curved and skewed storefronts were inserted into existing openings of the 1979 manufacturing building to bring a sense of the landscaping inside and to give the breakroom a strong identity as seen from the parking lot. The entry acts as an organizing device from which other ceiling and wall pieces collide and radiate.

32

32b

33

32★ THE UNIVERSITY OF TEXAS AT SAN ANTONIO, 1976 For the initial campus of the University of Texas at San Antonio at a then-remote Hill Country site, three monolithic concrete buildings penetrated by interior courts and skylit hallways were arranged around an elevated pedestrian plaza. The central plaza featured a large, light-diffusing sombrilla at the center and wooden trellises hung from cables around the walkways. Facilities were designed for 5,000 students in five academic colleges, using a master plan that provided for facilities that would accommodate 30,000 students.

ADDRESS
One UTSA Circle

ARCHITECTS
Ford, Powell & Carson and Bartlett Cocke & Associates

32b▲ UNIVERSITY OF TEXAS AT SAN ANTONIO BIOTECHNOLOGY, SCIENCE AND ENGINEERING BUILDING, 1996 In an effort to inspire and attract Hispanic science majors, the architects of this five-story laboratory research building departed from the campus's usual tan, concrete colors to reflect the colors, folklore and symbols of South Texas. The block of research laboratories was faced with limestone in a subtle grid pattern to reflect the precision and rationality of modern research. A connecting public building was inspired by the image of a votive candle, a symbol of healing along the Texas-Mexico border.

ADDRESS
One UTSA Circle

ARCHITECTS
Kell Muñoz Wigodsky

33▲ SECURITY SERVICE FEDERAL CREDIT UNION CORPORATE HEADQUARTERS, 2000 The campus environment of this 126,000-square-foot corporate headquarters on a rocky hill site is enhanced by maximum

ADDRESS
16211 La Cantera Parkway

ARCHITECTS
Marmon Mok

use of outdoor spaces. Its "green" design incorporates broad shading, reflection roofs, use of local materials, abundant natural light, natural water filtration, high efficiency cooling and lighting, recycled materials and building orientation to reduce solar gains and maximize views.

ADDRESS
9150 Wellwood Street

ARCHITECTS
Lake/Flato

34▲★ GREAT NORTHWEST LIBRARY, 1994
The main entrance of this branch library is oriented away from a major street intersection toward the more tranquil neighborhood. Simple indigenous building forms were used. The quieter book stack areas are in low, limestone-clad "pods," while zones of public activity are in high vaulted spaces with clerestory windows.

ADDRESS
14960 Omicron Drive

ARCHITECTS
Kell Muñoz Wigodsky

35▲★ ALICE P. McDERMOTT BUILDING, CANCER THERAPY AND RESEARCH CENTER INSTITUTE OF DRUG DEVELOPMENT, 1992
This corporate headquarters and laboratory research building features two-story blocks of laboratories along exterior walls, support spaces in the center and auxiliary and public functions at either end of the building. Construction materials combine native fieldstone, wood-mold brick, conventional wood windows and glazed window walls. Atop stone buttresses, preengineered columns supporting the roof structure are painted purple and exposed on the exterior of the building.

ADDRESS
14815 Omicron Drive

ARCHITECTS
Kell Muñoz Wigodsky

36▲ INSTITUTE OF BIOTECHNOLOGY, UNIVERSITY OF TEXAS HEALTH SCIENCE CENTER AT SAN ANTONIO, 1990 This first major building in the Texas Research Park promotes interaction among those studying the pathogenesis of disease by grouping administration and staff offices in suites at one end of the building, lab space in the center and common spaces at the other end. The laboratory block is framed with pieces relating to the landscape and Texas traditions.

37

38

37▲ GUADALUPE HOMES, 2000
Alazan-Apache Courts was built in 1939 as San Antonio's first public housing project. Some of its original one- and two-story concrete buildings were renovated in the 1990s, but new development took the form of the adjacent Guadalupe Homes. Its forty-three brightly colored, Craftsman-style single-family homes and two small apartment buildings create a village-like setting. The structures have large windows, pergolas, columns and front and rear porches. The tightly spaced lots, porches and sidewalks are separated by medians designed to encourage neighborhood activity.

ADDRESS
1011 South Brazos Street

ARCHITECTS
Alamo Architects

38 MAURY MAVERICK JR. BRANCH LIBRARY AND FIRE STATION NO. 49, 2006 This branch library is integrated with a grove of large trees while the nearby fire station is situated for safest exits for emergency vehicles. Both facilities are compatibly designed to make them appear as a civic center complex, a sense enhanced by the new park across the street. The buildings have exterior masonry walls in glazed patterns and feature sloping roofs that identify major components and allow light in. Each has a large pylon element that acts as a gateway to the complex. The library façade features a design by Henry Rayburn that includes a playful sign and an intricate perforated metal screen with an overlay of shading and pattern. The library's ceiling includes acoustical panels arrayed in complex waves that rise and fall throughout the ductwork.

ADDRESS
8700 Mystic Park

ARCHITECTS
Alamo Architects

ADDRESS
1103 Cincinnati

WOODLAWN LAKE Built around 1880 by George W. Russ, Alazan Creek was originally damned to create West End Lake, an eighty-acre amenity for residential growth. Street cars carried visitors to "the finest artificial lake in the south." An outdoor pavilion accommodated evening dances, and small rowboats were popular with families and couples. Today Woodlawn Lake is a popular park with jogging trails, sailboating and community activities.

ADDRESS
303 Dartmouth

ROSEDALE PARK The annual Low Rider Show and Tejano Conjunto Festivals are only a few of the cultural events held at Rosedale Park. Tejano is the folk music of Texas and Conjunto is traditional Mexican music accented with polka accordions. Together they are the blend of cultures that is San Antonio de Tejas.

ADDRESS
Wolff Stadium,
Highway 90 & Callaghan Road

MISSIONS BASEBALL Texas League Missions are the AA affiliate of the San Diego Padres. Nelson Wolff Municipal Stadium was completed in 1994 and now includes a 16-by-22-foot video scoreboard for instant replay. Get your tickets @ samissions.com.

CAPILLAS Home altars (yard shrines) maintain symbolic ties between the earthly and heavenly religious saints and have roots in the Spanish-Mexican heritage of the city. The folk art shrines are made of different materials, ranging from iron to cement sculptures–often with murals painted or clad in tile. These shrines are dedicated in honor of specific saints or virgins in the backyard or facing the street to celebrate the Catholic faith of a family.

DAY OF THE DEAD In El Día de los Muertos, an important social ritual, the first two days of November are set aside to honor the dead and the continuity of life. Families celebrate by visiting the cemeteries, setting out food and drink for departed relatives and friends, and decorating gravesites.

CEMETERIES, FLOWER STANDS, MONUMENTS

SAN FERNANDO #1, SAN FERNANDO #2
San Fernando Cemetery #1 (the name was originally applied to the cemetery located within the walls of the Alamo) was first opened in 1851. Veterans of the Texas Revolution, early San Antonio settlers and fighters in the Indian Wars are buried here. The earliest markers date from 1840. Frank Cadena (16/D/46), the last man

ADDRESS #1
Tampico and
South Colorado

ADDRESS #2
746 Castroville Road

to hang in Texas, and Col. José Navarro, a signer of the Texas Declaration of Independence, are both at rest here. San Fernando Cemetery #2, on Castroville Road, with over 100,000 burials, holds the memories of a very significant cross section of the San Antonio population. Surrounded by monument makers, whose family businesses have been here for over eighty years, and countless flower vendors, this area of town comes alive with vibrant colors at Easter, Christmas, Mother's Day and especially El Día de los Muertos.

BOTANICAS Curanderos are traditional folk doctors that prescribe medicinal herbs to cure many ills. These herbs and mixtures are offered along with candles (santos) in tall glass jars labeled "Bingo," "Peaceful Home," or "Find Work," and small charms known as milagros (miracles) in countless West Side botanicas. Pamphlets detailing lives of saints and recipes for healing are found in the many volumes on shelves for sale.

FRUTERÍAS A local store selling fresh fruit produces in a variety of presentations, dressed with salt, lemon and chili pepper. The mixed fruit cup is a favorite combination of watermelon, pineapple, cantaloupe, grapes and strawberries. At the frutería one can find other products like ice creams, aguas frescas, raspas, corn-in-a-cup, turkey legs, hot dogs and sandwiches.

PANADERÍA, TORTILLERÍAS Marranitos (little pigs), gusanos (worms), cuernos (horns)—names of some of the baked goods—are recognizable by their shapes at any of the panderías scattered throughout the West Side. Baked fresh every day, these Mexican pastries are the way to start the day. Whether traditional corn, or flour, if you are looking for tortillas, an abundance of places make them.

TAMALES Ask any native San Antonian where to get the best tamales and you may hear a hundred different answers, among them favorite restaurants, taquerías or family kitchens. The taste of a tamal is as varied as the places to find them. Traditionally, they are delicious little packages of seasoned masa or corn dough encasing various fillings of meats and spices, wrapped respectfully in specially prepared corn husks. Though tamales are a year-round favorite, they are definitely a holiday tradition. Get them early—they disappear as fast as loving hands can create them.

MURALS, GRAFFITI In the early 1980s, the Community Cultural Arts Organization began the first of more than 200 murals in the Cassiano Homes public housing development; many depict Mexican American historic and religious figures. The murals are a vivid form of cultural and political expression often dealing with specific issues in the community. You can also find many other murals, and creative graffiti, throughout the West Side.

ADDRESS
Guadelupe Street

SHOTGUN HOUSES Driving West over the Guadelupe Street bridge, you will notice a number of one-story houses built on very narrow lots and oriented both toward the street and the alley. These are a great example of the remaining San Antonio shotgun houses. Unfortunately, a number of them have been lost, but still provide an affordable housing option.

FOOD/ENTERTAINMENT

ALDO'S RISTORANTE ITALIANO Rated by many as the finest in Italian food in San Antonio, Aldo's keeps customers coming back to its romantic Italian setting. Red snapper in a white wine sauce with artichokes, pesto and crabmeat — Snapper de Aldo — is a local favorite. Fine Italian and California wines and a full bar are available to accompany your meal. Look for the bright yellow former residence north of the Medical Center.

ADDRESS
8539 Fredericksburg Road
San Antonio, Texas 78229
(210) 696-2536

BISTRO TIME A small intimate restaurant, Bistro Time is recognized throughout San Antonio for its excellent crab cakes and succulent bacon-wrapped filet mignon. A central fountain and candle-lit tables enhance elegant dining featuring French, northern European, Asian and American dishes. Lunch buffet is Tuesday–Friday.

ADDRESS
5137 Fredericksburg Road
San Antonio, Texas 78229
(210) 344-6626

DEWESE'S TIP TOP CAFÉ This business has been owned and operated by a family since the 1930s. Just as the neon sign suggests, this place is reminiscent of the Texas 60s diners. DeWese's brings in a highly diverse clientele, all looking for fast and friendly service that brings them filling and homey fare. In the tradition of the diners, they offer some of the best freshly made pies.

ADDRESS
2814 Fredericksburg Road
San Antonio, Texas 78201
(210) 732-0191

EL 7 MARES If you would like to have the opportunity to taste Mexican seafood prepared in an endless variety of offerings, this is the place to visit. You will be pleasantly surprised by the range of selection and the size of the portions. Starting with ceviche and moving on to shrimp brochette, your seafood cravings will be satisfied. But look further for other interesting offerings.

ADDRESS
3831 West Commerce Street
San Antonio, Texas 78207
(210) 436-6056

ADDRESS
16641 La Cantera Parkway
San Antonio, Texas 78256
(210) 558-6500

FRANCESCA'S AT SUNSET Located at the Westin La Cantera Resort, this restaurant offers contemporary southwestern cuisine in a setting with a great view that makes this place a good choice for a romantic evening. Celebrity chef Mark Miller has left his mark on a number of dishes on the menu, adding a bit of spice to the tasty offerings.

ADDRESS
913 South Brazos
San Antonio, Texas, 78207

GIOVANNI'S PIZZA Located just around a corner from the Plaza Guadelupe, this surprising bit of Italy is a fixture in this neighborhood. Giovanni dishes out Italian food that has even former New Yorkers come back for more. Try his most popular pizza, the Giovanni Supreme.

ADDRESS
121 North Zarzamora
San Antonio, Texas 78207
(210) 433-0111

KARAM'S Opened in 1946, Karam's serves the heart of the West Side. Homemade tamales, cabrito (baby goat) and super-chalupas are favorites of the locals. Savor the Border Patrol Plate under the guard of the impressive Toltec figures in the pleasant outdoor garden.

ADDRESS
115 South Zarzamora
San Antonio, Texas 78207
(210) 308-7300

MALT HOUSE A delicious variety of mouth-watering favorites—burgers, fries, cheese enchiladas, and fried chicken—has been the staple of the Malt House for more than fifty years. This small neighborhood former drive-in serves a malt that is better described as a chocolate sundae—spoons required. Closed Mondays.

ADDRESS
111 South Leona
San Antonio, Texas 78207
(210) 225-6060

PICO DE GALLO Another of the Cortez family culinary offerings, in addition to Mi Tierra and La Margarita, this place is famous for its colorful and bright neon sign outside and the recently added murals. Inside the atmosphere is just as festive. It's always crowded at lunch time, when you can have one of their daily specials, in addition to having a choice of many other representative Tex-Mex dishes. Puro San Antonio.

SARIKA'S THAI Located near the medical complex, Sarika's Thai may be missed in the maze of strip centers and ambulances, but it's worth the find. Whether zesty or mild, the popular curry shrimp and sweet and sour chicken dishes are served in a casual setting with tablecloths and flowers. Lunch is usually crowded; weekends are family friendly.

ADDRESS
4319 Medical Drive
San Antonio, Texas 78229
(210) 692-3200

THE SHOPS AT LA CANTERA This recently opened "destination" open-air shopping center brought a new approach and level of quality to shopping in San Antonio. The Shops at La Cantera blend the pedestrian-friendly plan of a regional mall with the ease of use of a lifestyle center in a distinctive, landscape-focused environment. This mall blends the visual heritage of San Antonio and the Texas Hill Country with the fashion edge necessary to support a setting for high-end retailers. In the wonderfully rambling layout, shoppers are tempted by an amazing range and quality of merchandise. When hungry, stop in one of the many eateries.

ADDRESS
15900 La Cantera Parkway
San Antonio, Texas 78256
(210) 582-6255

Yes, craft and artistry still exist in today's world of architecture and construction.

—BARBARA DEAN HENDRICKS

Room for Craft in the 21st Century

by BARBARA DEAN HENDRICKS

Barbara Dean Hendricks is the Building Arts of South Texas writer

In this increasingly hectic, high-pressure world, it is no surprise that corners are cut, visions are compromised, budgets are trimmed. Is there still a way to create timeless structures? Do we have still have time for quality? Do we have money for the unique? Do we have the will?

Yes, craft and artistry still exist in today's world of architecture and construction.

A few still choose this longer, harder but infinitely more rewarding path.

San Antonio and South Texas have unique needs for craftspeople. Not only are there historic and even mythic public buildings to preserve for future generations, the area boasts a wealth of unique public and private buildings spanning almost four centuries.

Unlike many faster-growing cities in which countless architectural gems were destroyed in the name of progress, San Antonio's measured growth has preserved thousands of historic homes and workspaces; created numerous historic districts; and birthed a citizenry committed to preserving its unique culture and heritage.

The artisans working today, often part of a multi-generational family craft tradition, represent woodcarving, plasterwork, metal work, tile, masonry and much more.

Their tools may date from the 1800s – as do **John Hall's** sash sticker and four head molder used to make classic wooden windows. Or they may come from an even older tradition, such as **Kurt Pankratz's** timeless blacksmith's anvil and forge. Or be on the scientific cutting edge, as is **Cisi Jary's** microscope, with which she discerns the chemical composition of ancient paint on a doorway or ceiling she is conserving.

Some trained as artists, like **Johannes Scholze**, educated in woodcarving and furniture design at a German art institute. When interviewed at the grand age of 102, he remembered many of the masterpieces he created in his 80-year career, from hard-carved balustrades at the University of the Incarnate Word to the complete carved wooden interior at Saint Dennis Chapel on the O'Connor Ranch outside Goliad.

Why choose an artist, a craftsperson, to "enhance" your building? Because true craft is much more than enhanced design. It is more than *care and concern, attention to detail* and *adherence to quality.* That very craftwork may create its meaning for future generations. As Cisi Jary said, "In some buildings you can feel the energy of the artist still there.... See their fingerprints."

If you truly incorporate the artistry of craftwork into your design, those ineffable creations, often formed by hand, can make the difference between standard and unique, between a useful structure and a beautiful building, between a good job and a work of art.

We are doubly blessed in South Texas. These talented craftspeople help us both honor our past and create a present worth preserving. Artisans like **Thomas Michael Battersby**, a "stuccoist," **Curtis Hunt**, a mason, and **Carlos Cortes**, a master at "faux bois" concrete sculptures, frequently find themselves preserving the creations of their fathers, uncles or even grandfathers.

These craftspeople keep our built treasures beautiful and functioning in a twenty-first century world. They are renewing the soul of this beautiful city as they create new works that will hopefully be preserved, in turn, by their children and grandchildren. Thus the past and the present continue to nurture and enrich us all.

Barbara Dean Hendricks, Monte Adams, Tommy Adams and Emily Thuss are documenting (through in-depth interviews and photography) many of the area's talented craftspeople for a soon-to-be-published book The Building Arts of South Texas: *Stories of Endangered Building Arts and The Craftspeople Who Keep Them Alive.*

ARCHITECTURE

NORTH CENTRAL

06

WITH THE KIND SUPPORT OF

THE DANIEL J. SULLIVAN FAMILY FOUNDATION

NORTH CENTRAL

The Gilded Age came late to San Antonio, and when it thrived in its own particular form here (1890–1930) San Antonio was the largest city in the largest state. Exceptional architects and craftsmen were drawn to the fast-growing city like a magnet. Much of their remarkably varied work is spread throughout the north central area of San Antonio. Particularly distinctive residential architecture is concentrated in the one-hundred-block area now known as the Monte Vista National Historic District, the only neighborhood of its era in Texas to have survived virtually intact.

Homes from bungalows to haciendas in Queen Anne, Prairie, Tudor and Spanish Colonial Revival styles are also scattered through the neighborhoods of Tobin Hill, Beacon Hill and Government Hill and in Alamo Heights, Olmos Park and Terrell Hills, incorporated as separate suburbs in the 1920s and 30s. Looping street plans and pocket parks in portions of Monte Vista and Alamo Heights reflect City Beautiful design features from the turn of the twentieth century.

Two groupings of institutional architecture in this region are especially distinctive–the broad cross-section of changing military styles at Fort Sam Houston and the red-brick-and-arches Modern Regionalist campus of Trinity University, designed largely by San Antonio's O'Neil Ford.

After World War II, suburban residential and commercial development crept farther northward on either side of such arteries as Broadway and San Pedro Avenue, leapfrogging Loop 410 in an evolution that made north central San Antonio a buffer between the central city and sprawling development to the north.

ADDRESS
509 Howard Street

ARCHITECTS
Richard van der Stratten and Herff & Jones

1 AURORA APARTMENTS, 1930

With Crockett Park as its front yard, the Aurora takes full advantage of its site, lording over the entire Tobin Hill neighborhood. The flamboyant character of the exterior, with its quasi-Gothic terra-cotta balcony rails and cornice enrichments, may have seemed excessive at the start of the Depression, but it results in a dramatic presence designed to attract affluent tenants. The Aurora now provides affordable housing for the elderly.

1

2

ADDRESS
601 Howard Street

ARCHITECTS
Coughlin & Ayres

RENOVATED
1985

2 NR ALEXANDER HALFF HOUSE, 1904

Built in the once-stylish Tobin Hill neighborhood, the Alexander Halff House, with its metal shingled roof and twin projections flanking the main entrance, seems almost Japanese in character, but on a scale entirely American. The arch framing the front doors recalls the work of H. H. Richardson, especially in the use of such fine materials as the polished gray granite piers. The most original details are the first-floor columns, with their quasi–Art Nouveau foliate carving. Badly damaged by fire during 1984 renovations, it was restored to its original splendor by Fisher Heck the following year and converted to office use.

ADDRESS
800 West Myrtle Avenue

ARCHITECTS
Marmon Mok

3▲★ SAN ANTONIO TRANSIT SYSTEM OFFICES, 1973

NO PHOTO **(VIA METROPOLITAN TRANSIT OFFICES)**

A picturesque array of metal-surfaced shed roofs and irregularly spaced window openings in walls of tan brick identify this two-story administration building, constructed on a flat site facing San Pedro Park. Its Modern Regionalist style incorporates a pinwheel-plan configuration and diagonal alignments to induce a sense of visual movement. Large rectangular windows and sloping roofs imbue the building with a surprisingly domestic character. The transit company's older offices (1946–48, Ayres & Ayres) face Flores Street behind this newer structure.

4a

4a▲ NR SAN PEDRO SPRINGS PARK, SINCE 1729

San Antonio's oldest designated park is on land reserved for public use by the Spanish government in the eighteenth century. Spanish soldiers and missionaries established a mission and fort near the springs as San Antonio was founded in 1718. They soon moved to a more protected site in what is today downtown San Antonio, but the abundant springs still provided water for the San Pedro acequia (1731–34), which irrigated fields along its route south past the King William Street area for another century and a half. The city officially established a reserve around the springs in 1852 and leased the area for outdoor pavilions for food, drink and entertainment. Attractions later included a small zoo, racetrack, baseball field, lake and swimming pool. As spring flow dwindled in the late nineteenth century, the park deteriorated and the city began periodic improvement efforts, which continue. A major renovation of the forty-six-acre park in 1998–2002 by Beaty & Partners and RVK included redesign of the pool to a more natural configuration, bathhouse renovations and landscape improvements. The stone blockhouse and circa 1897 bandstand were restored by Fisher Heck.

ADDRESS
1500 San Pedro Avenue

ADDRESS
1315 San Pedro Avenue

ARCHITECTS
Ayres & Ayres and John M. Marriott

RENOVATED
2007

4b SAN PEDRO BRANCH LIBRARY, 1930

San Antonio had only three branch libraries, all inadequate, when a citizens' committee recommended a first-ever bond election for library improvements. Bonds were approved and this new facility on the eastern edge of San Pedro Park opened in 1930, designed in the Spanish Colonial Revival style building with a clay tile roof. The interior featured vaulted ceilings and archways leading to flanking wings, where collections were housed in intimate settings. Two back rooms, now enclosed, were originally screened porches looking onto the park. A renovation in 2007 under Kinnison Associates included mechanical system updates and accessibility upgrades.

ADDRESS
800 West Ashby Place

ARCHITECTS
Bartlett Cocke and Marvin Eickenroht

RENOVATED
1963, 2001

4c SAN PEDRO PLAYHOUSE, 1930

This Greek Revival style theater set back from the northwest corner of San Pedro Park was inspired by the design of the city's 1859 market house, demolished for the widening of Market Street. To placate the San Antonio Conservation Society, which was organized in 1924 to save the market house, the city salvaged the market's Doric columns for use in the planned play-house. Architects Bartlett Cocke and Marvin Eickenroht deemed the columns too damaged for reuse, but through photography and careful measurements and tracings replicated them in new stone. Sculptor Gutzon Borglum served as consultant for the project. Built as part of the nationwide Little Theater movement, the facility, which now seats 400, is reportedly the nation's oldest municipally built playhouse still in use. It was enlarged in 1963. A complete renovation was undertaken in 2001 by Killis Almond and Associates.

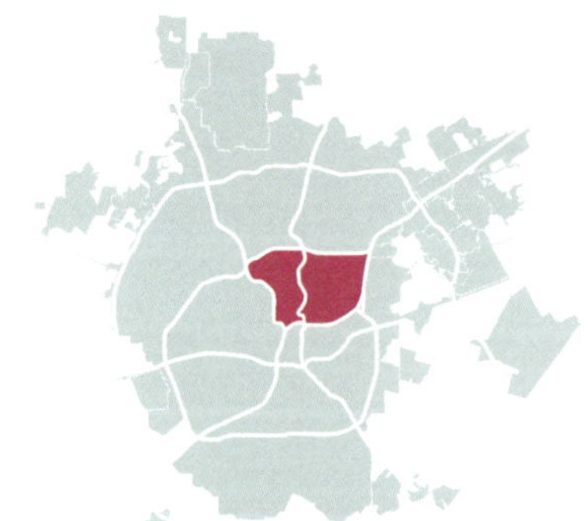

5

6

7

5 NR WOMAN'S CLUB OF SAN ANTONIO, 1904
(WOODWARD HOUSE)

Built as the home of carriage dealer David J. Woodward, this Classical Revival home was acquired as a clubhouse in 1926 by the Woman's Club of San Antonio, organized in 1898 and the city's oldest women's civic and social organization. The dark interior hardwood was imported from Russia. Paneling and the grand staircase sweeping to large rooms on the second floor make the house ideal for entertainments.

ADDRESS
1717 San Pedro Avenue

ARCHITECTS
Coughlin & Ayres

RENOVATED
1927, 1996

6 & 7▲ TEMPLE BETH-EL, 1927

The design of Temple Beth-El deftly combines square and spherical forms, unified by the consistent use of terra-cotta ornament and clay tiles. In this most Spanish of Texas cities, even a synagogue is designed with decidedly Iberian-Renaissance-style ornament, most notably the marvelous cornice of scallop shells. The contrast between the earth tones of tiled dome and the whitewashed stucco of the exterior is no small part of this building's appeal. Consulting architect with Seutter & Simons was Albert S. Gottlieb of New York. In 1947 six remodeling projects, including the Hannah Hirschberg Chapel, were completed according to the designs of N. Straus Nayfach. Additional renovations and the Barshop Auditorium were completed in 1983. Renovations under Marmon Mok in 2003 included construction of the [7] Dreeben Family Pavilion, a twenty-seven-foot square domed structure with a link

ADDRESS
211 Belknap Place

ARCHITECTS
Seutter & Simons, New York

RENOVATED
1947, 1983, 2003

to the main temple. It includes a limestone wall facing toward Jerusalem that evokes the image of the Western Wall. The north and south glass walls are infused with images of the Tree of Life and the seven branches of the Menorah.

ADDRESS
310 West Ashby Place

ARCHITECT
Carl von Seutter

8 KOEHLER HOUSE, 1901
(KOEHLER CULTURAL CENTER)

Sculptured friezes, massive stone verandahs, Palladian windows and a polygonal turret are among the details of the rusticated stone exterior of this three-story Richardson Romanesque mansion built by brewer Otto Koehler. A newspaper description at the time of its opening termed the house "a perfect palace and a picture in dressed white limestone." Architect Carl von Seutter had worked for James Riely Gordon, but on this design he turned away from the polychromed Romanesque of his mentor toward a more free-spirited and individual style. The house occupies an entire city block, its grounds originally landscaped by Boerne nurseryman G. A. Schattenberg. The six-foot iron and concrete fence surrounding the property was designed by Charles Boelhauwe. The home is now the Koehler Cultural Center of adjoining San Antonio College.

8

9

ADDRESS
505 Belknap Place

ARCHITECTS
McAdoo & Wooley

9 NR JAY ADAMS HOUSE, 1893

This Queen Anne confection was the builder's show-house for Jay Adams's Laurel Heights subdivision, one of more than a dozen components that now make up the Monte Vista National Historic District. Its stone was quarried from nearby San Pedro Park. Designed by Solon McAdoo and Albert Wooley, the eight fireplaces, handcut oak paneling, circular parlor, ballroom, octagonal fern house and the carriage house have survived with little change. The metal griffins flanking the porch steps are among the finest late nineteenth century architectural details in San Antonio.

10 NR CHRIST EPISCOPAL CHURCH, 1914

Atlee Ayres had to walk less than two blocks from his new home on Belknap Place to oversee construction of Christ Episcopal Church, itself two blocks closer than another Ayres-designed church on the same street (Laurel Heights Methodist Church, 1909). Christ Church was faced with buff-colored brick from Kansas, with most original stonework of hard Cedar Park white limestone. The English Gothic style is reinforced by the squat proportions of its central entrance tower, topped by three finials on each side. The skylit dome and radiating decorative beams over the sanctuary foreshadow Ayres's treatment of the ceiling in the rotunda of Municipal Auditorium. A brick parish hall designed by John M. Marriott was added at the rear in 1929 and extended in 1948 by a larger wing designed by Atlee B. and Robert M. Ayres. A renovation in 1958 was overseen by J. Fred Buenz, who also oversaw conversion of an Atlee Ayres–designed carriage house (1908) nearby for general use. The 1975 renovation under Vernon Helmke included replacement of the stained-glass window above the entrance with a bronze sculpture of a welcoming Christ by Austin's Charles Umlauf. A two-story education building on the French Place side of the church campus was designed by O'Neill Conrad Oppelt and built in 1992.

ADDRESS
510 Belknap Place

ARCHITECT
Atlee B. Ayres

RENOVATED
1958, 1975

ADDRESS
131 East Kings Highway

ARCHITECT
Henry T. Phelps

11 NR IKE KAMPMANN HOUSE, 1922

The centerpiece of this home is the Richardson Romanesque arched stone entrance salvaged from an earlier Kampmann House on Avenue E, removed to make way for the Scottish Rite Cathedral. The carving is said to have been done by an unknown Italian stonecutter who strolled by as the first house was being built in 1880. Architect Henry Phelps successfully integrated the arch as a dramatic contrast to the newer unadorned limestone wall surfaces. The handling of the projecting bay on the east elevation of the house is particularly effective.

11

12

13

ADDRESS
126 East Kings Highway

ARCHITECTS
The Kelwood Company

12 NR McNEEL HOUSE, 1925

Set far back from the street by a verdant lawn, the McNeel residence provides us with one local firm's interpretation of the Spanish Colonial Revival style. The rambling nature of numerous houses by Ayres & Ayres is not present here; this house is more block-like, the only break coming with the large porte-cochere. The characteristic Spanish Colonial love of texture is provided by the barrel-tile roof and the Plateresque ornament set above the main entrance. While not in the same league as the firm's masterpieces, the Casino Club and the Aztec Theater, this is nevertheless an impressive work.

ADDRESS
101 East Kings Highway

ARCHITECT
Ralph Cameron

13 NR HORNADAY HOUSE, 1929

In the context of San Antonio architecture, Ralph Cameron is not well known for his residential work, yet he made the most of this particular opportunity. This is a fairly typical piece of Colonial Revival work except for the incredible front entrance. The almost-Baroque daring with which the architect recesses the door behind a monumental broken-pediment Palladian entry screen enhances the entire design. Against the power of the entrance, the paneled shutters with their jigsaw cutouts appear almost whimsical.

14 NR STOWERS HOUSE, 1925

Yet another variant of the ever-popular Spanish Colonial Revival style, the Stowers House relies on changes in fenestration to emphasize the style's asymmetrical nature. The inset entrance, with its extremely attenuated Solomonic columns, is the sole penetration into the mass of the house, while the polygonal bay forming its east end attempts to break out of the generally rectangular form.

ADDRESS
131 West Lynwood Avenue

ARCHITECTS
Adams & Adams

15 NR HERBERT KOKERNOT HOUSE, 1928

While not as grandiose as the same firm's Morgan House on Alameda Circle, the Kokernot House is more accessible by virtue of its site placement. Once again Spanish Colonial Revival asserts itself as the dominant style of the 1920s in the more affluent suburban neighborhoods. Its entrance is notable for its Solomonic corkscrew columns with massive finials and scrolling.

ADDRESS
115 East Lynwood Avenue

ARCHITECT
Russell Brown, Houston

16 NR HOGG HOUSE, 1924

This is the first great work in the Spanish Colonial Revival style with which Atlee B. Ayres became most strongly associated during the coming decade. Built for Thomas Hogg, son of Texas Governor James Hogg, its massing is focused on the monumental cylindrical stair tower, which serves as the hinge on which the plan pivots. The austere character of the elevations is highlighted by some splendid details, most notably the massive front door with its tiny window barred in

ADDRESS
202 Bushnell Avenue

ARCHITECTS
Ayres & Ayres

wrought iron. The house was expanded by the same firm in the 1950s when a series of rooms was added to the east end, but the character of the original design was maintained.

ADDRESS
323 Bushnell Avenue

ARCHITECTS
Ayres & Ayres

17 NR MANNEN HOUSE, 1926

When designing houses in the Spanish Colonial Revival style, the Ayres firm made consistent use of angled plans, with two masses meeting in an obtuse angle. The Mannen residence is one of the smaller of this breed but is characteristically well detailed. The arcaded verandah on the ground floor and the wood balcony wrapping around the second are the most regionally

17

18

appropriate elements. The original character of façade openings to the right of the doorway has been changed significantly by the installation of fixed sheets of plate glass.

ADDRESS
240 Bushnell Avenue

ARCHITECTS
The Kelwood Company

RENOVATED
1982, 2001

18 NR THE BUSHNELL APARTMENTS, 1926

The seven-story Bushnell Apartments were built to appear as "a lofty Spanish palace." The elaborate entry is anchored on either side by what seem to be two slightly projecting towers topped by tile-roofed rooms with frontal balconies above the level of the roof garden. Cast stone Spanish Colonial Revival details contrast nicely with the plain stucco exterior. An innovative feature at the time was installation of two high-speed automatic elevators that did not require attendants, equipment that is still in use. Builder was the Kelwood Company, which consisted of architect Robert B. Kelly and real estate partner Harvey C. Wood. The Bushnell was renovated in 1982 under Rehler, Vaughn, Beaty & Koone. Joe Stubblefield's 2001 rooftop terrace provides dramatic views of the city.

19★ UNIVERSITY PRESBYTERIAN CHURCH, 1954

Milton Ryan, with characteristic ingenuity, designed this small church to make the most of a low budget and readily available materials. The shape of the roof, the mullion cross of the glazed central bay and the organ loft, displayed beneath the peak of the steeply pitched roof, identify the building as a church. Its pink-red brick surfaces relate it visually to the adjacent buildings of Trinity University. Ryan also designed the attached Education Building (1955).

ADDRESS
524 Shook Avenue

ARCHITECT
Milton A. Ryan

20▲ RUBLE CENTER OF TRINITY BAPTIST CHURCH, 1923 **(McKINLEY ELEMENTARY SCHOOL)**

The adaptive reuse of this former neighborhood school as an annex to Trinity Baptist Church (1960, Bartlett Cocke) is a minor work of virtuosity. Under Chumney, Jones & Kell (1983), low-cost industrial building components were assembled in a lively, articulate manner, especially in the design of a large multipurpose room inserted in an ell-shaped crook at the back of the building. This addition, in actuality a pre-engineered metal shed, is faced with a shimmering screen of glass block set in a brightly colored armature of exposed steel sections. On the street elevation, only the panels of glass blocking the old loggia openings hint at the dramatic transformations behind.

ADDRESS
419 East Magnolia Avenue

ARCHITECTS
Phelps & DeWees

RENOVATED
1983

ADDRESS
2504 North St. Mary's Street

ARCHITECT
Emmett T. Jackson

21 ST. SOPHIA GREEK ORTHODOX CHURCH, 1926

San Antonio's Greek immigrants first worshipped with a visiting priest at St. Mark's Episcopal Church, but as the community grew after World War I members raised enough money to build their own church in 1926. Emmett Jackson's Byzantine Revival design was detailed with inlaid tile, fine brickwork and cast-stone pieces. A tile mosaic in the central arch over the entry depicts the double-headed eagle of the Byzantine Empire. An interior apse screen was imported from Greece. Icons on the barrel-vaulted interior were painted by longtime pastor Ergon J. Zografos. Stained glass

windows were installed in the 1960s. Additions include the rectory (1955) and the education and the community hall (1961).

TRINITY UNIVERSITY, SINCE 1952

Since its founding in 1869, Trinity University had campuses in two locations in Texas before moving to temporary quarters in western San Antonio, pending completion of a final campus. That 117-acre campus opened in 1952, still uncompleted, north of downtown San Antonio. Its location in a former rock quarry and garbage dump with craggy contours dictated a nonconventional campus design. Master planners placed athletic facilities on the level ground to the south and dormitories at the base of a rocky bluff, accessible by stairways to main buildings on the rugged slopes above. Low rooflines of the upper campus buildings were designed to appear as if they formed an Italian town on a hill, dominated by a cathedral [22] (Parker Chapel) and its campanile [22b] (Murchison Tower). Cost considerations led to pioneer use of economic Lift-Slab construction methods recently developed at the same time by Trinity trustee Tom Slick and New York architect Phillip Youtz. Use of red brick in campus buildings created a pleasing, unified ensemble of structures that do not compete with each other. Donors were not allowed, Ford once pointed out, to demand monumental naming entrances "with a capital E." Despite cost restraints, several individual structures achieve architectural distinction.

ADDRESS
One Trinity Place

ARCHITECTS
Master plan by O'Neil Ford and Bartlett Cocke; William Wurster, Boston, consulting architect

ADDRESS
Trinity University

ARCHITECTS
O'Neil Ford and Bartlett Cocke

22 MARGARITE B. PARKER CHAPEL, 1966

The 166-foot T. [22b ▲] Frank Murchison Tower (1964), a concrete-filled red brick structure that rose at an estimated rate of two and a half feet per day, serves as the campanile for nearby Parker Chapel. The chapel draws from O'Neil Ford's celebrated design with A. B. Swank of The Little Chapel in the Woods (1939) at Texas Woman's University in Denton. Its nine interior parabolic arches, faced in brick, support an overhanging copper roof. Ford's multi-talented brother Lynn executed many details, among them the carved wooden doors and screen, light fixtures, a lead mantel and the chancel cross. Windows were designed by Ruth Dunn.

23

24

ADDRESS
Trinity University

ARCHITECTS
Ford, Powell & Carson and Bartlett Cocke & Associates

23▲ ELIZABETH COATES LIBRARY, 1979

This unusually programmed, four-story building is set in a hollow below surrounding campus buildings. To compensate for this anomaly, it is entered on its third-floor level. The two upper levels of the reinforced concrete-framed, cruciform-planned building are finished in brick. Accentuating the library's serrated profile are glazed corner bays that harbor reading nooks.

ADDRESS
Trinity University

ARCHITECTS
O'Neil Ford and Bartlett Cocke

RENOVATED
2005

24★ RUTH TAYLOR THEATER, 1966

Along with the Chapman Graduate Center (1965), the Ruth Taylor Theater marks Ford's turn toward a Modern Regionalist vernacular, demonstrated in this theater's use of standing-seam metal-covered shed-roofed masses, segmental arches, slit windows and brick detail. Working with Trinity's theatrical director Paul Baker, Ford and his associate Arthur J. Rogers designed the building to house three distinct theater spaces, each flexible and readily adaptable for various types of performances. Renovation under Kell Muñoz with Michael R. Howard of New Orleans in 2005 again used Lift-Slab construction techniques. The interior was reconfigured and a new floor added. Aluminum composite panels were added to improve the visual transition to the higher elevation of the newly rebuilt Northrup Hall nearby.

25

26

25▲★ LAURIE AUDITORIUM, 1971

Laurie Auditorium consists of a partially exposed drum-like substructure of reinforced concrete and the Sid W. Richardson Communications Center, a brick-faced, shed-roofed classroom building oriented toward the courtyard of the Ruth Taylor Theater. The massive semicircular structure with its 3,000-seat auditorium was set on a steeply sloping downhill site to minimize the impact of its bulk on the campus, while giving it a public aspect from East Hildebrand Avenue to the north. The garage, its interstitial bays filled with vertical cedar slats, also provides an outdoor terrace for the auditorium above.

ADDRESS
Trinity University

ARCHITECT
Ford, Powell & Carson and Bartlett Cocke & Associates

26▲★ COATES UNIVERSITY CENTER, 1952

Built as the Trinity Student Union, this was one of the original campus structures. Set at the edge the stone bluff overlooking the lower campus, its glass walls and broad porches are strongly horizontal to harmonize with the natural landscape. Following remodeling in the early 1970s, the building was renovated and expanded in 1987 by Chumney/Urrutia, which included former Bartlett Cocke partner Patrick Chumney. The 60,000-square-foot addition makes a bold and colorful design statement utilizing steel, glass, brick and terrazzo finishes in the style of traditional campus construction.

ADDRESS
Trinity University

ARCHITECTS
O'Neill Ford and Bartlett Cocke

RENOVATED
1987

ADDRESS
Trinity University

ARCHITECT
Robert A. M. Stern Architects, New York

PHOTOGRAPHER
Peter Aaron/Esto

27 NEW NORTHRUP HALL, 2004

Trinity's original Northrup Hall, a two-level, administrative/classroom structure that was one of the original Lift-Slab buildings on the new campus, was replaced by a four-story building that sacrificed somewhat the chapel's dominance of the profile of campus buildings in order to gain additional administrative space on the increasingly crowded campus and spectacular fourth-story views of downtown. At the nexus of the new Northrup Hall's two wings, a multi-story transparent lobby serves as a passageway and creates a welcoming lobby space for those in transit. The space opened the campus to the site visually and physically and

27

28

become a principal entrance to the campus. Inside the lobby's glass enclosure, a steel-framed grand staircase appears to float upward vertically for all four floors. During the changes, Miller Fountain (1966, O'Neil Ford & Associates and Alex Caragonne) was relocated to the west end of the building and set in a small amphitheater to create an outdoor gathering space.

ADDRESS
106 Oakmont Court

ARCHITECT
The Kelwood Company

RENOVATED
1982

28 NR SELIGMANN HOUSE, 1925
(WILLIAM KNOX HOLT CONTINUING EDUCATION CENTER)

The Seligmann House represents Robert B. Kelly's approach to Spanish Colonial Revival on a grand scale. The monumental massing of the Seligmann House recalls the stage-set design that Kelly drew upon with great success in a different context—the Aztec Theatre downtown. The home was renovated under DeLara Almond to become a continuing education center for Trinity University.

29

30

29 ALAMO STADIUM, 1940

Magnificently sited overlooking the downtown skyline and Brackenridge Park on thirty acres of the city's original Spanish land grant, this 23,000-seat limestone and concrete stadium was built for the San Antonio Independent School District by the WPA. Known from its low profile of irregularly shaped stone construction as "The Rock Pile," it is the state's largest high school football stadium. A double row of palm trees leads to the entrance decorated by a 60-foot long series of four ceramic tile murals designed by Ethel Wilson Harris. The murals, fabricated by WPA workers in Harris's local Mexican Arts and Crafts Studio, depict a century of local sporting activities, ranging from rooster races to the district football teams of 1940. Bronze plaques honor former district players who have gone on to become All-Americans.

ADDRESS
760 Stadium Drive

ARCHITECTS
Phelps, Dewees & Simmons

30 FRANK MURCHISON HOUSE, 1939

O'Neil Ford's first building commission in San Antonio was for this horizontally extended one- and two-story house of stone and cedar. The house is pulled out, one room deep, across its sloping site. Ford and Swank turned its back to the street while opening the garden elevation to the downhill slope and the prevailing breeze. The blind, gabled end walls with exposed stone chimney stacks, the shallowly pitched copper roof and the cantilevered, south-facing balcony recall the mid-nineteenth century building traditions of San Antonio

ADDRESS
9 Ironwood Road,
Olmos Park

ARCHITECTS
O'Neil Ford and
Arch B. Swank Jr.

and central Texas. The horizontality and openness of the house, however, identify it as Modern in the spirit of the American Regionalist movement of the 1930s.

ADDRESS
303 Devine Road,
Olmos Park

ARCHITECT
William McKnight Bowman

31 ROBERTSON HOUSE, 1930

With the Webb and Newton houses around the corner on East Olmos Drive, the Robertson House forms what is likely the finest trio of late 1920s residences in San Antonio. Bowman's design, featured in the April 1930 issue of *The Architectural Forum*, takes its inspiration from the great villas of the Veneto, though on a much smaller scale. In the true tradition of the Italian villa, the second floor contains the greatest room, a vast drawing room that bisects the second floor and is apparent on the exterior in the form of the arcaded loggia overlooking the sweeping front lawn. The only element needed to complete the mood would be replacement of Devine Road with a body of water.

ADDRESS
810 East Olmos Drive,
Olmos Park

ARCHITECTS
Ayres & Ayres

32 JONES HOUSE, 1927

The formal symmetry of the Jones house makes for an interesting comparison to the adjacent Newton house, both completed the same year. The Jones House is actually an enlarged version of a house designed by Ayres & Ayres five years earlier, but on a much larger site than its prototype. The concentration of ornament around the entrance portico is judiciously balanced by the rather austere character of the rest of the exterior walls.

ADDRESS
800 East Olmos Drive
Olmos Park

ARCHITECTS
Ayres & Ayres

33 NEWTON HOUSE, 1927

With its beautifully landscaped site, the Newton House is one of the best efforts of Ayres firm. While this is a large house, an informality is apparent in the seemingly random placement of fenestration on the outside walls. The entrance tower hints at the design of the Atkinson House, now the McNay Art Museum, which was to follow on the heels of the Newton commission. The sculptural molding that frames the front door is unusual in the firm's work and adds an element of three-dimensionality to the otherwise flat surfaces of the walls.

34 WILLIAMSON HOUSE, 1968

Exterior wall faces and turns reveal the simple interior plan of this residence, nestled into a mature landscape of tall oaks and lush ground cover. Individual rooms radiate like a series of shed-roofed pavilions around a two-story core. Vertical accents rival the trees through tall chimneys of Mexican brick, board-and-batten siding of stained cedar, slender window units, and banks of French doors. The horizontal earth is confirmed by the gently-sloping roofs covered with flat Saltillo tiles. The combined effect reveals a contemporary interpretation of the Arts and Crafts Movement from the early 1900s.

ADDRESS
303 Park Hill Drive,
Olmos Park

ARCHITECT
Flowers & Maxwell

35 TURNER HOUSE, 1928

The Turner House is one of the gems of Olmos Park and of San Antonio at large. While well known for his design of the modern San Antonio River Walk, Hugman was clearly capable of more than stage set architecture. This is one of the best Spanish Colonial Revival houses in the city, combining the monumental simplicity of the eighteenth-century originals and the inventiveness of the revival. The highlight of the house is the small room topped by a dome on scroll brackets, which appears to have been copied from the great mission church of San Xavier del Bac near Tucson.

ADDRESS
214 Park Hill Drive,
Olmos Park

ARCHITECT
Robert H. H. Hugman

ADDRESS
300 Alameda Circle, Olmos Park

ARCHITECT
Russell Brown, Houston

36 MORGAN HOUSE, 1929

This low-key Mediterranean villa contains more than 20,000 square feet of living area, but its enormous size is skillfully concealed from passersby. The house is set back from the traffic circle it faces, and the growth of trees has further screened it from the eyes of the curious.

ADDRESS
505 East Mandalay Drive, Olmos Park

ARCHITECT
Birdsall P. Briscoe, Houston

37 CLEMENS HOUSE, 1947

Birdsall Briscoe, one of Houston's most assured eclectic architects, excelled at southern regionalized versions of neo-Adam and Regency genres. This outstanding Georgian-style house, designed in 1941 but not

36

37

38

39

begun until 1946, exemplifies his grand manner, with its noble, south-facing portico looking out across a terraced garden toward East Wildwood Drive and its scarcely less honorific north-facing motor-court elevation. Briscoe even pressed the garage into this double-fronted composition so that it serves as an architectural terminus for cross axes that traverse the east garden.

ADDRESS
300 Paseo Encinal, Olmos Park

ARCHITECT
George Louis Walling, Austin

38 NEGLEY HOUSE, 1929

This house benefits from one of the loveliest sites in Olmos Park. Its heavily wooded setting seems to be a natural part of the landscape. Stone for its walls came from the old Nat Washer store downtown, which makes the house appear to be much older than its construction date.

ADDRESS
835 Contour Drive, Olmos Park

ARCHITECT
John F. Staub, Houston

39 SEELIGSON HOUSE, 1939

Houston's foremost eclectic architect, John F. Staub, designed this monumental stone country house as a regionalized, suburbanized French chateau. Its symmetrical main block is flanked by low, shed-roofed appendages that extend outward to tie the house to its site. Oriented to take advantage of the prevailing breeze and downhill views, the house reveals both entrance and garden elevations to passersby.

40

41

42

40▲ 100 WEST OLMOS DRIVE, CIRCA 1940
(KENWOOD MERCANTILE COMPANY)
A 4,000-square-foot commercial building at West Olmos Drive and McCullough Avenue in Olmos Park was transformed into an 18,000-square-foot office building with a new two-story office building, separated from the renovated one-and-a-half-story building by an exterior courtyard. Proximity to the street reinforces the urban street sense.

ADDRESS
100 West Olmos Drive, Olmos Park

REDESIGNED
1990, O'Neill Conrad Oppelt

41 THE ARGYLE, 1859
Built as a two-story headquarters for a 1,400-acre ranch then two miles from San Antonio, the Argyle was named by a developer for having a setting similar to his Argyleshire homeland in Scotland. A third floor and the southwest wing were added and the building opened as a hotel in 1891. In 1907 the front three-story verandahs were replaced with the Argyle's signature columns and deeper verandahs, giving the building the aura of an antebellum mansion. The Argyle was purchased in 1955 and renovated as a private club benefiting what is now San Antonio's Southwest Foundation for Biomedical Research.

ADDRESS
734 Patterson Avenue, Alamo Heights

RENOVATED
1890, 1955

42★ LIGHT HOUSE, 1962
At first glance this unobtrusive yet dramatic house appears to consist only of a transparent pavilion floating in a subterranean garden. Closer examination reveals a low, backup wing, ell-shaped in plan, to which

ADDRESS
300 Argyle Avenue, Alamo Heights

ARCHITECT
Brooks Martin

the pavilion is discreetly attached. Tan-colored brick, cedar siding and posts and the crisp rectilinear of the overhanging roof decks are in the San Antonio tradition of Modernist regionalism.

ADDRESS
401 Torcido Drive, Alamo Heights

ARCHITECT
George Washington Smith, Santa Barbara, CA

43 MAVERICK-ZACHRY HOUSE, 1929
This is the only Texas work by the noted California architect responsible for creating Spanish Colonial Revival architecture's Santa Barbara style, based on such elements as thick stuccoed walls with deep openings for windows and doors and heavy overhangs with carved wooden corbels. Smith tended to rely on less complicated massing than did many who practiced in the style. Well screened from the road by trees, this house is arranged around a large central courtyard. Access from the outside is provided by a simple doorframe set in the otherwise planar exterior wall. Dramatic interior ceilings recall those of the Alhambra. This is considered one of the most impressive courtyard-oriented homes built in the nation at that time.

43

45

44

ADDRESS
400 Torcido Drive, Alamo Heights

ARCHITECT
Isaac Maxwell

44 SCHOENBAUM HOUSE, 1985
Schoenbaum means "beautiful tree" in German, and the clients here chose to build a house befitting their name. The structure is carefully nestled among native vegetation, with the entry stair and retaining walls creating additional space for plantings. The house folds over its site with double-wythe walls of handmade Mexican brick, highlighted by standing-seam metal roofing and terrace paving of Arkansas ledgestone. The architect designed and made all light fixtures, doors, panels and other details, giving the house what he called "contemporary regional" detailing.

ADDRESS
218 Acacia Street, Alamo Heights

REDESIGNED
1990, Lake/Flato

45▲ ACACIA HOUSE, CIRCA 1955
A cramped 1,600-square-foot one-story 1950s bungalow was transformed in 1990 into a 2,900-square-foot, two-story house open both in plan and to the outdoors. A large screened porch extends the living space into the backyard, while the master bedroom floats in the tree canopy overlooking Olmos Basin.

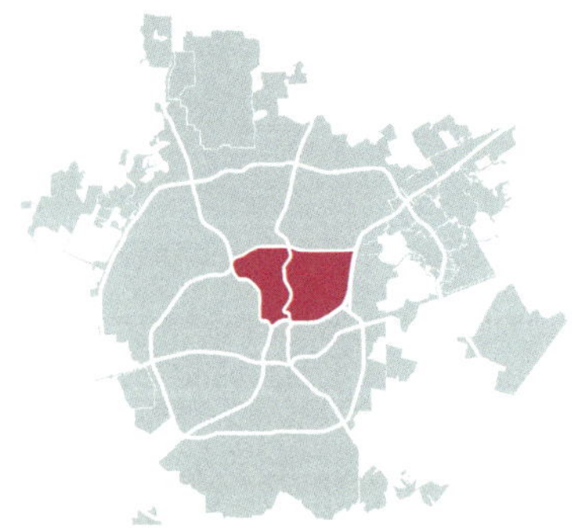

46▲ CITY OF ALAMO HEIGHTS SWIMMING POOL, CIRCA 1955 The municipal swimming pool owned by the City of Alamo Heights had fallen into disrepair, and its new lessee sought improvements. Making few physical changes to the pool and associated structures, Jones Kell transformed the facility's appearance with large planes of cool colors, masking any crudeness in the building while giving a soft brightness to the heat of a San Antonio summer day. Bolder colors mimic those of annual Fiesta events and of area flowers.

ADDRESS
250 Viesca Avenue, Alamo Heights

RENOVATED
1990

47▲ ALAMO HEIGHTS POOL SHADE STRUCTURE, 1994
The wavelike form of this shade structure over the dining patio of the City of Alamo Heights Swimming Pool recalls water, a Fiesta dress, sombrero and tent.

ADDRESS
250 Viesca Avenue, Alamo Heights

ARCHITECTS
Kell Muñoz Wigodsky

48 LANG HOUSE, 1953
After California Modernist architect Harwell Harris came to Austin in 1951 to direct the University of Texas School of Architecture, he designed a number of houses across the state. This is one of several inspired by Frank Lloyd Wright's Usonian houses of the 1930s and 40s. Vertically accentuated pink brick panels bracket horizontal expanses of lapped wood siding that serve as fascias above banked windows. Reticent on its public side, the house opens to a south-facing rear garden and downhill slope.

ADDRESS
700 Alta Avenue, Alamo Heights

ARCHITECTS
Harwell Hamilton Harris, Austin

ADDRESS
11 St. Luke's Lane, Alamo Heights

ARCHITECT
Henry Steinbomer

49 ST. LUKE'S EPISCOPAL CHURCH AND SCHOOL, 1955

Henry Steinbomer sited this formidable complex of church and school buildings on the eastern ridge overlooking Olmos Basin and designed it in a mannered contemporary version of neo-Gothic. The lofty interior of the church is carried on laminated wood members and lit through stunning panels of stained glass executed by Cecil Casebier with semi-abstract designs based on the Apostles' Creed. Steinbomer's extremely attenuated bell tower and spire are highly visible from the nearby expressway. An administration, library and computer lab building by Lake/Flato was added in 1998 and a middle school addition was built in 2002.

49

50

51

ADDRESS
809 College Boulevard, Alamo Heights

ARCHITECTS
Lake/Flato

50 GEIBEL HOUSE, 1995

This house was planned as a compound of buildings meandering among beautiful large oak trees in harmony with this neighborhood's simple bungalow roof forms. To give the most open land possible to gardens and living area, the house was placed at the front of the lot. The structures surround an inner private courtyard, a more family-oriented west courtyard and a series of outdoor rooms. Building materials were chosen for their natural beauty and low maintenance—limestone, sandstone, integral color stucco, standing seam metal and oiled wood.

ADDRESS
251 Castano Avenue, Alamo Heights

ARCHITECT
Richard Mogas

51 CHRISTIAN HOUSE, 2006

This contemporary home fits seamlessly into the fabric of an established neighborhood. The first floor is an example of today's preference for an open, casual lifestyle. Walls are limited and are virtually transparent from front to back. Curtains on recessed tracks can divide spaces and offer privacy from the street. Limestone planters in the front yard tie into the Cartesian grid of the house and help serve as a transition to the street.

52

53

54

52▲ CLEAR CHANNEL COMMUNICATIONS HEADQUARTERS, 2000

Native Texas limestone anchors this three-level building to its site, a former cement quarry. Dress of the stone in low relief, rough-hewn blocks allow it to blend with glass, steel, slate and maple to convey an aesthetic befitting a high-tech company. Technical innovations include sculptured steel awnings, trellises and sunshades to adjust interior temperatures to the extremes of the Texas climate.

ADDRESS
200 East Basse Road

ARCHITECTS
Overland Partners

53▲ LIFSHUTZ HOUSE, 1987

The 5,400-square-foot Lifshutz House contains many architectural Southwest regional elements found in Ford, Powell & Carson's earlier houses, such as vaulted ceilings, deeply recessed window openings and smooth, natural colored stucco walls. Ceilings are wood and plaster and floors are both of both new and reused wooden floors. The interior courtyard can be shaded by drawn cloth shading devices.

ADDRESS
363 East Terra Alta Avenue

ARCHITECTS
Ford, Powell & Carson

54 MERCANTILE BANK BUILDING, 1981
(LAREDO NATIONAL BANK BUILDING)

This six-story, 220,000-square-foot bank and office building acknowledges its location at the intersection of an interstate highway loop and a major arterial street by the curvature of its main elevation, which cuts into the building above a three-story, glazed banking hall. The architectural designer, Richard Keating, combined

ADDRESS
40 North East Loop 410

ARCHITECTS
Skidmore, Owings & Merrill, Houston

light-toned granite-clad spandrels, reflective window glass and metallic gray mullions in this sleek, understated composition.

ADDRESS
84 North East Loop 410

ARCHITECTS
Neuhaus + Taylor, Houston

55 CENTURY BUILDING, 1973

Century Building's long, low shape was determined by then-current height-and-setback restrictions due to its proximity to San Antonio International Airport. One of the first speculative office buildings to be constructed along Loop 410, it was also the first building in the city to be surfaced entirely in gold reflective glass. Neuhaus + Taylor designer Elmo Valdes inserted an air-conditioned garden court beneath the tiled plane of the front elevation.

55

58

56

57

ADDRESS
1250 North East Loop 410

ARCHITECTS
Rehler Vaugh Beaty & Koone

56 NORTH FROST BANK BUILDING, 1981

Knife-edged profiling, a sloped-glass lobby roof and a neutral, gridded sheath of silver reflective glass imbue this eleven-story office building with its image. A deep, horizontal shadow line between the tenth and eleventh floors implies a distinction between cap and shaft.

ADDRESS
2635 Brookhurst Drive

ARCHITECT
John H. Kell Jr.

57 KELL HOUSE, 1972

For a heavily wooded corner site verging on a shallow ravine, John H. Kell Jr. designed his stepped-level, double-faced house with a flat roof. A steel-framed, glazed pavilion containing the major living rooms projects from the rear of a cubic, brick-faced block, its glazing compacted into gridded metal bays. This makes for a sensuous, provocative juxtaposition of contrasting vocabularies, which Kell developed into a brash new architectural language in subsequent work.

ADDRESS
3920 Harry Wurzbach Highway

ARCHITECTS
Lake/Flato

58▲ ZINFANDELI'S RESTAURANT, 1988
(CRUMPETS RESTAURANT)

This restaurant building sited in a dense stand of live oaks uses a palette of metal siding, plywood wall and exposed wood studs to create an artful, vaulted environment. Glass walls visually connect the interior dining spaces with the shady deck areas outside.

59

60

61

59★ ST. PIUS X CATHOLIC CHURCH FAMILY CENTER, 1995 This link between the St. Pius X sanctuary and church school is strengthened by a shaded front courtyard that can be used as an outdoor room for church festivals and that also serves as the focal point for all three buildings. A wood slat ceiling and exposed ceiling structure make the 600-seat auditorium feel more like an outdoor space and thus works with the outdoor courtyard as one large space.

ADDRESS
3919 Harry Wurzbach Highway

ARCHITECTS
Kell Muñoz Wigodsky and Jerry Theis

60 FRIENDS MEETING HOUSE, 2005
To achieve a quiet, sheltered, contemplative setting for meditative worship, the Friends Meetinghouse is detached from its urban context and oriented to the back of a courtyard surrounded by mesquite and acadia trees. The design was inspired by the functional and simple spaces of early meetinghouses and built to a human scale with simple materials.

ADDRESS
7052 North Vandiver Road

ARCHITECTS
Lake/Flato

61▲ SUNSET RIDGE SHOPPING CENTER, 1950
The 1950s design of this shopping center had remained so popular that its renovation in 1989, by the same firm that originally designed it, simply enhanced the appearance and focused on the front covered pedestrian walkway. New gazebos were added to the walkway at intervals to break the center into recognizable areas and provide seating areas. Uplighting at night illuminates the gazebos' canvas roofs. Shifted structural grids, updated tile patterns and new concrete joint pat-

ADDRESS
6400 North
New Braunfels Avenue

ARCHITECTS
Jones Kell

RENOVATED
1989

terns make subtle textured additions to the original design. Additional landscaping at varying heights provides softness and separation from adjacent parking.

ADDRESS
6000 North
New Braunfels Avenue

ARCHITECTS
Ayres & Ayres

62 & 63 MARION KOOGLER MCNAY ART MUSEUM, SINCE1929 (ATKINSON HOUSE) One of the finest Spanish Colonial Revival homes designed by Ayres & Ayres is that completed in 1929 [62a] for Mrs. Marion Atkinson, now known as Marion Koogler McNay, a trained artist who contributed some designs for the tilework, iron gates and grills and patterns for ceiling beams. The various segments of the rambling house enfolded a central patio [62b] on three sides. A central

62a

62b

63

reception hall provided access to wings on either side and, between twin tile-covered stairways sweeping to the upper floor, opens onto the courtyard. The surrounding acreage was landscaped with Southwest plantings, gardens and ponds. Mrs. McNay willed her collection of modern art and her estate to become a museum, which opened in 1954. Between 1969 and 1985, Ford, Powell & Carson supervised a series of five additions that extended the original house and also enclosed the patio, requiring relocation of the independent San Antonio Art Institute that had occupied the former aviary. That led to construction of the Art Institute's nearby Jones Building [63] (1975, Flowers & Maxwell), marked by its curving entry of stout brick columns with elaborate bases and capitals, corbelled brick piers and radiating brick paving, all dominated by the notched wooden portales that shade the north and south entrance courts. After the Art Institute closed in 1992, ownership of its property passed to the McNay Art Museum. In 2003 the McNay demolished a postmodern Art Institute building designed in the 1980s by Charles Moore in preparation for construction of a major wing, designed by French architect Jean-Paul Viguier and scheduled to open in 2008. That will extend to the east the basilica-plan Leeper Auditorium Building (1994, Overland Partners), its pavement tiles made by the same Mexican company that did those for the original home.

64

65

64 BENTLEY HOUSE, 1982

This tan brick house built by Ken Bentley for his family is a series of box-like masses configured around protected outdoor spaces. Stone belt courses accentuate the horizontality of the façade screen, which is pierced by two bays of cast-stone louvers to maintain privacy without blocking the prevailing breeze.

ADDRESS
511 Morningside Drive, Terrell Hills

ARCHITECT
Ken Bentley

65 OAK COURT, 1936
(LUTCHER BROWN HOUSE)

The greatest house in San Antonio by this important firm, Oak Court represents the climax of a decade of outstanding residential design that began with the Thomas Hogg House in 1924. Its form and scale result from a close partnership between Robert M. Ayres and H. Lutcher Brown, whose fortune derived from forests and paper mills in Louisiana and who greatly admired that state's plantation houses. While not a replica of any specific colonial or antebellum structure, Oak Court borrows details from such distinguished sources as the Mathias Hammond House in Annapolis, whose doorframe inspired the enlarged version dominating the front elevation of the Brown house. Through the walled estate's magnificent iron gates one can still enjoy the vista down the straight azalea-lined drive to the home.

ADDRESS
636 Ivy Lane, Terrell Hills

ARCHITECTS
Ayres & Ayres

ADDRESS
13 Elmcourt, Terrell Hills

ARCHITECTS
Lake/Flato

66 PACE HOUSE, 1998 (ELM COURT RESIDENCE)

Like traditional courtyard houses, this turns its back to the street and focuses inward. A glass-enclosed gallery encircles a square sculpture court, with the main living spaces behind a thick, limestone-clad wall. Light is brought in through clerestories, shaded monitors and cupolas.

66

68

ADDRESS
105 Newberry Terrace, Terrell Hills

ARCHITECT
Milton A. Ryan

67★ SCHERR HOUSE, 1953 *NO PHOTO*

Together with its next-door neighbor at 111, this house exemplifies Ryan's deft, constructivist approach to modern architecture. Economy and exposition of structure, maximum lightness and transparency, unassertive massing and responsiveness to sloping sites characterize both houses, still splendidly maintained.

ADDRESS
939 Garraty Road, Terrell Hills

ARCHITECT
O'Neil Ford

68 JOHN MURCHISON HOUSE, 1942

Designed for the brother of Ford's first San Antonio house client, Frank Murchison, this two-story house of variegated pink brick and cedar with twenty rooms and 12,000-square-feet is even larger and more expansive than the first. Set atop the crest of a low, originally wooded hill, it is one room deep, being elongated horizontally in thin wings. Since the prevailing breeze and favored views were toward the public street rather than away from it, the main entrance is from the rear of the house to preserve the downhill slope, since sold and developed, as a sweeping garden. Steel was in scarce supply when the house was built, so oil-sucker rods from oil rigs were used for the 45-foot steel piers beneath the foundation.

69

70

71

69★ DUNWOODY HOUSE, 1951

This is one of six houses Milton Ryan designed and built speculatively in the 600 and 700 blocks of Elizabeth Road between 1948 and 1951. He described this ethereal home as his "pipe dream." Horizontal steel angles welded to a network of steel pipe columns and struts anchor the floating roof and floor planes. Walls sandwiched between alternate from panels of redwood plywood to fixed and operable glazing units. Taking advantage of the sloping site, Ryan placed a carport beneath the house. The front door is approached from ground level by a gangplank ramp and a boomerang-shaped terrazzo terrace.

ADDRESS
735 Elizabeth Road, Terrell Hills

ARCHITECT
Milton A. Ryan

70 CHITTIM HOUSE, 1922

The Chittim House, one of the early homes in Terrell Hills, benefits from its large and beautifully landscaped corner site. An unusual one-story design from the Ayres firm, it makes extensive use of shelter-giving verandahs, framed by a series of columns with Mudejar-style capitals.

ADDRESS
501 Elizabeth Road, Terrell Hills

ARCHITECTS
Ayres & Ayres

71 MARSHALL STEVES HOUSE, 1964

This 14,000-square-foot Spanish Colonial hacienda, a departure from O'Neil Ford's progressive style, conceals interior richness behind austere exterior walls. The house consists of pavilion units projected from a lateral, one-hundred-foot-long gallery interspersed with patio gardens. Architectural detailing imported

ADDRESS
501 Elizabeth Road, Terrell Hills

ARCHITECTS
O'Neil Ford and Associates

from San Miguel de Allende in Mexico was incorporated into the design. Masons were brought in from Mexico to construct the home's most distinctive feature, a series of brick vaults called bovedas that topped the central hallway. Stewart E. King & Associates did the landscaping.

ADDRESS
400 Wiltshire Avenue, Terrell Hills

ARCHITECTS
Ford, Powell & Carson

72 WINTER HOUSE, 1981

The Winter House is a more informal and congenial work than Ford, Powell & Carson's better-known work around the corner, the Marshall Steves House. The large size of the site permits a rambling plan of one-story units framing an entrance courtyard. The vistas

72

73

74

from the house are oriented away from the street with the exception of the rooftop terrace, clearly identified by the trellis.

ADDRESS
222 Austin Highway, Alamo Heights

REDESIGNED
2006, John Grable

73▲ 222 AUSTIN HIGHWAY, CIRCA 1935

John Grable Architects resurrected this 1930s motor lodge as a spare, minimalist office building by stripping the structure to its core. Elemental and reclaimed materials such as longleaf pine and unfinished carbon steel are enhanced by sculptural daylighting and define the simple palette for three office units.

ADDRESS
5424 Broadway, Alamo Heights

ARCHITECTS
Adams & Adams

RENOVATED
1986

74 MAGNOLIA OIL COMPANY, 1930

Dallas-based Magnolia Oil tended to hire local architects as the expanding company built the most elaborate Spanish Colonial Revival service stations in Texas. Its red Pegasus flying horse remained a corporate emblem for successor companies through Mobil Oil. After Mobil closed this station, its renovation as a retail outlet included enclosing the former service area and its exposed wood brackets and beams within glass walls. Guardianship of the familiar Pegasus neon sign was turned over to the San Antonio Conservation Society to assure the sign's preservation atop the building.

75

76

75★ LA QUINTA APARTMENTS, 1964
This twenty-four-unit complex of row houses on two contiguous corner lots is built above depressed parking and focused inwardly on austere, enclosed communal spaces. Wall planes on sand-surfaced brick punctuated by segmentally arched door and window openings ally these houses with the Modern regionalist vernacular. James Keeter was responsible for landscape design.

ADDRESS
185 Terrell Road, Alamo Heights

ARCHITECT
Chris Carson

76 SISTERS OF CHARITY OF THE INCARNATE WORD MOTHERHOUSE CHAPEL, 1907 The dominant exterior feature of this bright reddish brick chapel is its bell tower with four trumpeting angels on each corner, recalling those on the tower of H. H. Richardson's 1870s Brattle Square Church in Boston. Pews in the vaulted nave face each other rather than the altar, in the form of those in medieval European monasteries where monks would sing liturgical choruses to each other. The chapel was restored in 2006 using Pittsburgh-based liturgical art and design specialist Rohn & Associates Design. The chapel was originally an eastward extension of the five-story motherhouse (1900, Alfred Giles) that was demolished in 1988 and replaced by a similar structure.

ADDRESS
4301 Broadway, Alamo Heights

ARCHITECT
Fred B. Gaenslen

RENOVATED
2006

ADDRESS
4301 Broadway,
Alamo Heights

ARCHITECT
Attributed to Jules Poinsard

RENOVATED
1985, 2004

77 NR BRACKENRIDGE VILLA, 1852
(SWEET HOMESTEAD, FERNRIDGE)

This home was built near the headwaters of the San Antonio River by James R. Sweet, a city alderman whose purchase of the headwaters land effectively gave him control of the city's water supply and triggered a long-term controversy. The raised one-story cottage with Greek Revival symmetry and detailing was purchased along with the headwaters land by George W. Brackenridge, who in 1886 added a high Victorian three-story wing that included a dining room with walls covered by tooled elephant hide. Brackenridge, who became San Antonio's leading philanthropist,

77

78

78

sold his estate in 1897 to the Sisters of Charity of the Incarnate Word, who used the home as their motherhouse until constructing their own immediately to the east. Brackenridge Villa now houses offices and meeting rooms for the adjoining campus of the University of the Incarnate Word.

ADDRESS
4307 Broadway,
Alamo Heights

ARCHITECT
Jones Kell

78★ SISTERS OF CHARITY OF THE INCARNATE WORD LONG-TERM CARE FACILITY AND MOTHERHOUSE, 1989

On a fifteen-acre site bordering the University of the Incarnate Word campus on the north, Jones Kell Architects designed a complex including a 150-bed independent living structure, a 60-bed extended care facility and other amenities. The buildings are positioned on the curving land, highlighting large trees in natural outdoor courtyards. A small stream was developed as a contemplation path from the more formal garden at the upper portion of the site to the wildflower field in the lower portion. Also included in the project was a new motherhouse for the Sisters of Charity of the Incarnate Word, inspired by the design of the previous motherhouse (1900, Alfred Giles). The exterior marble stairway to the second floor and its columned portico were rescued from the original motherhouse and reinstalled on the new structure.

79 UNITED SERVICES AUTOMOBILE ASSOCIATION, 1956 (AT&T) This spectacular 1950s period piece first housed the second headquarters built for the United Services Automobile Association. Composition, fenestration and materials change with orientation, and there are intense color contrasts between the white Georgian marble and the turquoise porcelain enamel spandrel panels. The original building was substantially enlarged in 1962. When the incipient financial services giant moved to new quarters in far northwestern San Antonio, this building became a regional office of Southwestern Bell, now AT&T.

ADDRESS
4119 Broadway

ARCHITECTS
Phelps, Dewees & Simmons and Ayres & Ayres

BRACKENRIDGE PARK, SINCE 1901

Most of the land surrounding the upper reaches of the San Antonio River remained property of the City of San Antonio under Spanish land grants until the 1850s, when the city began selling portions off. The headwaters and some land on either side of the river below were sold and eventually acquired by George W. Brackenridge, whose private waterworks pumped water up through present-day Mahncke Park to a hilltop reservoir to store for use of the city below. In the 1890s Brackenridge's artesian wells downstream obviated his need for the headwaters of his riverfront land. In 1899 he donated 199 acres to the City of San Antonio for a public park, that was named in his honor, and opened in 1901. By the 1920s, additional donations, by Emma Koehler and Bexar County, enlarged the park to 344 acres. Attractions included an 18-hole golf course (1916), the Zoological Garden and a lily pond later named the Japanese Tea Garden (both 1917), the Witte Memorial Museum (1926), the Sunken Garden Theater (1930) and Pioneer Hall (1937). The park was reconfigured in the 1960s when a long-debated expressway sliced along its western acreage. Recent bond-funded renovations by Humberto Saldaña and Associates (2003) and Rialto Studios (2006) have refurbished pavilions and landscape features, converted roadways to hike-and-bike trails and introduced public art.

80

ADDRESS
3805 Broadway

ARCHITECTS
Ayres & Ayres and Phelps & Dewees

80 PIONEER HALL, 1937

This boldly scaled yet simple building with Renaissance classical detailing was constructed to house collections commemorating early Texas trail drivers as part of the state's centennial celebration. Its design recalls the United States post office and federal building on Alamo Plaza, also completed in 1937. Planned expansion of the adjacent Witte Museum is to incorporate the building. A bronze cast of the maquette of Gutzon Borglum's Trail Drivers Memorial, designed in San Antonio in the 1920s, is displayed outside the entrance.

81 IRON BRIDGE, 1890

This elaborate iron bridge originally carried what is now South St. Mary's Street over the San Antonio River downtown. The largest of several erected in San Antonio in those years by the Berlin Iron Bridge Company, it is believed to be the last surviving lenticular arch bridge in Texas. After a series of devastating floods, the bridge was replaced by a sturdier structure and moved in 1925 to this river crossing at Lambert Beach, once a public swimming pool. It was refurbished by the National Youth Administration in 1937–38. Other remaining iron bridges by the same manufacturer still carry traffic over the river at Presa, Crockett and Convent streets.

ADDRESS
Brackenridge Park

ARCHITECTS
Berlin Iron Bridge Company, East Berlin, Connecticut

82 BATH HOUSES, 1924

In 1915, City Commissioner of Parks Ray Lambert undertook improvements in the north part of Brackenridge Park. His swimming beach in the river adjacent to an old water works pumphouse was an instant success. Lambert enlarged the beach in 1925 and built this concrete and stone bathhouse, designed by Emmett Jackson. Scalloped window openings gave the simple structure an air of sophistication. Partially roofed with clay tile, it was mainly an open-air structure. It was converted to a playscape in 1992.

ADDRESS
Brackenridge Park

ARCHITECT
Emmett T. Jackson

ADDRESS
Brackenridge Park

CRAFTSMAN
Dionicio Rodriguez

83 NR PEDESTRIAN BRIDGE, 1926

This elaborately detailed faux bois work simulating an arbor of woven wooden limbs is considered one of the masterpieces of Mexican-born artisan Dionicio Rodriguez. The pedestrian bridge spans the old Water Works channel and the Upper Labor Acequia in the northern part of the park. Rodriguez, already a skilled faux bois craftsman when he arrived in San Antonio in 1925, traveled throughout the United States creating works for both public and private clients. Other pieces, including shelters, benches and the entry arch to the Japanese Tea Garden, are found throughout the park.

83

84

85

ADDRESS
Brackenridge Park

ARCHITECT
Emmett Jackson

84 JOSKE PAVILLION, 1927

This stone park shelter overlooking the river was completed as a memorial to local merchant and civic leader Alexander Joske. The structure's thick battered walls, stout-beamed ceiling and buttressed, polygonal chimney stack combine to express a spirit of whimsical exaggeration. At the north end of the pavilion is an operatic stair with a landing that spans an arched recess opening outward between chunky masonry colonettes.

ADDRESS
Brackenridge Park

85 NR JAPANESE TEA GARDEN, 1917
(SUNKEN GARDEN)

Park Commissioner Ray Lambert's creative vision for Brackenridge Park is perhaps best expressed in his dramatic transformation of an abandoned rock quarry and cement works into a lushly landscaped sunken water garden. Using prison labor, Lambert incorporated remaining industrial stacks and kilns with new features, including a thatched roof pavilion, cascading water fall, ponds, walkways and bridges to create a fanciful public garden. First known as the lily pond, the site was soon called the Japanese Sunken Garden after the Jingu family moved here to operate a teahouse. After Pearl Harbor the family was forced to move, and the site was renamed the Chinese Sunken Garden, as still inscribed on the 1942 Oriental-influenced gate by Dionicio Rodriguez. The site, rededicated in 1984 as the Japanese Tea Garden, is being renovated under the auspices of the Friends of the Park.

86

87

86▲ & 87▲ WITTE MEMORIAL MUSEUM, SINCE 1926

The city had already broken ground for a museum in San Pedro Park when it received Alfred Witte's bequest to construct a similar facility in Brackenridge Park. Ayres & Ayres adapted its plans to the new site. The original three-arched main entrance was replaced in a modernistic remodeling and addition (1961, Henry Steinbomer and Bartlett Cocke) and a new entry flanked by monumental figures sculpted by Charles Umlauf. The riverfront back yard includes a replica log cabin built by NYA workers in 1939. Three historic buildings—the Ruiz, Twohig and Navarro houses—were relocated to the grounds in the early 1940s under the direction of Historic Buildings Foundation architects Henry Steinbomer, Marvin Eickenroht and J. Fred Buenz. Overlooking the back yard is Prassel Auditorium (1988, O'Neil, Conrad and Oppelt) [87], a regional work of beige and red brick with a broad, tile-roofed verandah. The H-E-B Science Treehouse (1997, Lake/Flato) [86] overlooking Brackenridge Park and the San Antonio River combines native limestone walls, arches and tile roofs with cupolas, spires, crenellations and balconies. An elevated walkway leads to a multi-level treehouse supported by two full-size faux bois oak trees by artisan Carlos Cortes, a skilled practitioner of the craft popularized locally by his predecessor, Dionicio Rodriguez.

ADDRESS
3801 Broadway

ARCHITECTS
Ayres & Ayres

ADDRESS
555 Funston Place

LANDSCAPE ARCHITECTS
James E. Keeter and George G. Cook

88 & 89 NR SAN ANTONIO BOTANICAL GARDEN, SINCE 1980 The San Antonio Botanical Garden rises in a former limestone rock quarry above the eastern end of Mahncke Park. Separate native areas display the diverse Texas ecology and pioneer architecture. Other features include gardens for children and the blind and an authentically designed Japanese garden. The amphitheater is set in a stone-lined reservoir, a remnant of George Brackenridge's nineteenth-century San Antonio Waterworks. The dramatic glass towers of Emilio Ambasz's Lucile Halsell Conservatory (1988) [88] rise from a sculptural earthwork carved into the hillside and provide a half acre of greenhouse space

88

89

90

for a variety of tropical and desert plants. Entrance to the Botanical Garden is through the two-story rusticated stone Richardson Romanesque Sullivan Carriage House (1896, Alfred Giles) [89], dismantled at its original downtown site, reassembled here and opened in 1995 with a restaurant and gift shop on the ground floor and meeting rooms and offices upstairs.

ADDRESS
3303 Broadway

ARCHITECTS
O'Neil Ford & Associates

90★ INTERCONTINENTAL MOTORS, 1963
This exceptional auto showroom and maintenance building was built on the site of Quinta Urrutia (1918, Porfirio Treviño), the exotic Spanish- and Moorish-influenced residence of the noted Mexican exile Dr. Aureliano Urrutia. O'Neil Ford and his associate Howard Wong's design for the three-acre site preserved mature trees as the setting for a glazed, cruciform sales pavilion set on an elevated, coved, back-lit base. The maintenance block was set behind the showroom. Careful detailing of the exposed concrete structural components and brick and glass enclosure are unusual among buildings of this type. Original finishes included ornamental lighting fixtures by ceramicist Martha Mood and beaten copper planting troughs by Lynn Ford.

91

92

91★ MULBERRY TERRACE APARTMENTS, 1960

The design of these two fourteen-unit garden apartments on a sloping site necessitated floating the rear blocks over parking stalls at the downhill end of the property. The units enjoy generous shares of outdoor space enclosed with horizontal wood-slat privacy screens. Panelized wall surfaces feature extensive glazing. Exposed outdoor stairs cantilevered from brick planes and a network of pedestrian bridges animate the common spaces. Original landscaping was by Stewart E. King and James Keeter.

ADDRESS
1305 and 1315
East Mulberry Avenue

ARCHITECT
Allison B. Peery

92 PEARL BREWERY, SINCE 1894

The San Antonio Brewing Association purchased an old brew house on this site beside the San Antonio River in 1887. Six years later the company hired August Maritzen, one of the foremost brewery architects of the day, to design the new facility that became known as Pearl Brewery. Maritzen's brick brew house (1894), with its arched windows and mansard-roofed tower, was San Antonio's tallest building at the time. Local architects contributing to the complex include Otto Kramer, who designed the elliptical-shaped brick stables building (1894); Albert F. Beckmann; who supervised construction of Maritzen's 1897 stock house and other buildings; and Adams & Adams (1939), Leo M. J. Dielmann (1930s and 1940s) and Bartlett Cocke (1950s). The brewery survived Prohibition by manufacturing non-alcoholic products and resumed beer production in

ADDRESS
312 Pearl Parkway

ARCHITECTS
August Maritzen, Chicago;
Albert F. Beckmann

1933. After the twenty-two-acre plant closed in 2001, it was purchased for multi-use redevelopment according to a master plan by Lake/Flato in consultation with Ford, Powell & Carson. Pearl Parkway, the boulevard to the brewery from Broadway, has been landscaped and its public works rebuilt through a public-private partnership. Long-term site development and landscaping, which incorporates old brewery hardware and equipment, is by Rialto Studios. These are to interface with planned river channel improvements and provide river passenger barge access.

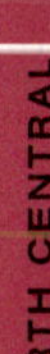

93

94

93 WAREHOUSE, CIRCA 1960
(CENTER FOR FOODS OF THE AMERICAS)

ADDRESS
312 Pearl Parkway

RENOVATED
2006

This nondescript warehouse was adapted in 2006 by Lake/Flato to house a culinary arts college. The design opened new windows in the outer brick walls and introduced an interior steel structure, echoing the brewery's industrial vocabulary. The building is accessed from a concrete loading dock–style porch that provides views of student chefs at work. A shade structure and plain metal awnings offer sun protection.

94 PEARL STABLE, 1894

ADDRESS
312 Pearl Parkway

ARCHITECT
Otto Kramer

RENOVATED
circa 1955, 2006

The brewery's neoclassical, elliptically shaped stable with its exceptional brickwork once housed as many as sixty horses used for hauling wagons filled with bottles and kegs of beer to outlets throughout the city. When Pearl completed conversion of its operations to motorized vehicles in 1918, the stable building became a beer warehouse. Converted in the 1950s to an entertainment venue, the stable was fully renovated in 2006 as a state-of-the-art event facility by Ford, Powell & Carson, also charged with renovating the historic brew house, stock house and boiler house.

95 PEARL BREWERY GARAGE, 1939
(AVEDA INSTITUTE SAN ANTONIO)
The brewery's utilitarian garage structure has been dramatically transformed into the San Antonio Institute of AVEDA, a cosmetology and esthiology teaching facility and salon. Durand-Hollis Rupe and Lake/Flato accurately restored the building's exterior and adapted the interior, preserving original industrial-style features including the wooden roof structure, steel bow trusses, skylights, steel sash windows and concrete floor. Lighting, piping and ducting were woven into the structure. The garage includes classroom spaces, an open styling salon, intimate rooms for spa treatments, a sales gallery and support spaces, as well as an adjoining restaurant featuring organic, locally purchased products. The design team is also renovating the nearby Full Goods Warehouse (1974) as office, retail, restaurant and residential space. Between the garage and expressway, the can recycling building is being converted to residential and retail use by Durand-Hollis Rupe.

ADDRESS
312 Pearl Parkway

ARCHITECTS
Adams & Adams

RENOVATED
2005

96▲★ SOUTH TEXAS BLOOD AND TISSUE CENTER HEADQUARTERS, 1994 This highly insulated limestone and steel-trellised headquarters building, the largest of its kind in South Texas, includes a donor center, laboratories and support spaces. It incorporates optimal solar orientation and natural daylighting. The gray water retrieval and processing system, designed to irrigate

ADDRESS
6211 IH 10 West

ARCHITECTS
Overland Partners

the surrounding landscape with rain and cooling system water, was the largest in North America when it was completed in 1994. Interpretive exhibits and signage make the center more user-friendly.

ADDRESS
7150 IH 10 West, Balcones Heights

ARCHITECT
Kell Muñoz Wigodsky

97▲ FIRST UNITARIAN UNIVERSALIST CHURCH, 1998

This church campus, first comprised of a courtyard and four surrounding buildings, was extended and completed with the addition of this 400-seat sanctuary in 1998. A large skylight above the dais emits refracted daylight through glass prisms, creating "natural" stained glass. The sanctuary floor is colored concrete finished to expose the limestone aggregate. Interior finishes—

including wood paneling, exposed wood structure and use of leaf patterns in the ceiling and floor—are all natural references to the trees in the courtyard, which is viewed through a glass wall.

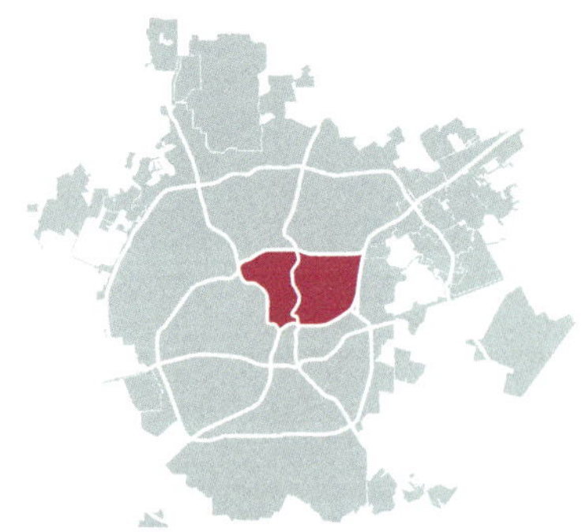

FORT SAM HOUSTON, SINCE 1879

Fort Sam Houston, begun in 1876, was established to supply forts on an Indian frontier sufficiently distant that the new installation's only protected walled area surrounded the Quadrangle quartermaster depot. Major expansions beyond the Quadrangle included the distinctive grouped buildings of Staff Post (1881–85) for officer housing, Infantry Post (1885–1906), Cavalry and Light Artillery Post (1905–12) and New Post (1928–39), east of North New Braunfels Avenue on the site of the World War I–era Camp Travis. In the early twentieth century, Fort Sam Houston was the nation's largest Army post. It was the scene of the first military aircraft flights in Texas and supplied Gen. John J. Pershing's pursuit of Pancho Villa along the Mexican border. Several divisions formed and trained here during both world wars. Since then the 3,000-acre post has become the Army's center for medical training. It is also the home of U.S. Army North with its homeland defense missions, of U.S. Army South, which oversees Army and National Guard operations in Central and South America, and of numerous other commands and functions, including Brooke Army Medical Center with its noted burn treatment center. Fort Sam Houston's more than 900 registered historic buildings are by far the most at any American military installation.

ADDRESS
East Grayson Street near North New Braunfels Avenue

98a NR THE QUADRANGLE, 1879

The first structure at Fort Sam Houston was the limestone-walled Quadrangle, built to house supplies and workshops moved from the Army's longtime depot at the Alamo. Forming the southern wall facing Grayson Street is a two-story row of offices entered through a central sally port that also leads into the Quadrangle. The tower in the center originally screened a water tank, replaced in 1882 with a four-sided clock. Its design was inspired by a European tower admired by the then U.S. Army Quartermaster General, Montgomery Meigs.

98b

98c

ADDRESS
Infantry Post

ARCHITECT
Alfred Giles

98b LONG BARRACKS, 1887

Built to house eight companies of troops, the two-story Long Barracks extend for 1,081 feet along Infantry Post's former parade ground. Its central feature is a three-story crenellated stone central bay with an arched sally port leading to the consolidated garrison mess hall (1891). Verandahs across the front of the building were enclosed in the 1930s but set to be replaced in their original form during a restoration project being planned in 2007.

ADDRESS
Infantry Post

ARCHITECT
Alfred Giles

RENOVATED
1996

98c BAND BARRACKS, 1893

The only building of its type remaining in the Department of Defense inventory, the Band Barracks faces the midsection of the former Infantry Post parade ground, much of it now occupied by latter-day housing units. This siting allowed the band to play for parades from the third-story belvedere, thus being sheltered from the summer sun. Damaged by fire, decay and vandalism, the Band Barracks was nearly demolished, along with other historic military structures, but, like the others, was rescued and restored. The public-private restoration partnership, under Fort Worth's Komatsu Rangel, also replaced the long-missing belvedere.

98d

98f

98e

98g-1

98d GIFT CHAPEL, 1909 Gaining its name from its financing by gifts from civilian and military personnel, this Neoclassic chapel was designed by a well-known San Antonio ecclesiastical architect. It was dedicated by President William Howard Taft. The chapel is noted for its classic columned entrance and copper-roofed dome. Its interior is lined with flags of the nation's states and territories and of units stationed at the post. The organ installed in 1969 includes chimes donated by Mrs. Dwight D. Eisenhower, who came to Fort Sam with her husband as a newlywed and returned with him when he was reassigned here again just prior to the outbreak of World War II.

ADDRESS
Fort Sam

ARCHITECT
Leo M. J. Dielmann

RENOVATED
1993, 2006

98e BROOKE GENERAL HOSPITAL, 1938 Built at the head of Arthur MacArthur Field near the site of Camp Travis's frame hospital, the eight-story Brooke General Hospital is a monumental piece of Spanish Baroque architecture, with brick and cast stone walls, tile and terrazzo floors and red tile roofs. Its monumental entrance portico extends from the façade, its projecting central section culminating in a square tophouse set back and capped by low-pitched tile roof sections rising from each side. The facility had an initial capacity of 418 beds. The building was flanked at an angle by smaller, three-story quarters in a similar style for nurses to the west and enlisted men to the east. The 1938 facility was renovated and restored under Insite Architects for office use.

ADDRESS
New Post

ARCHITECT
Edwin V. Dunstan, U.S. Army

RENOVATED
2004

ADDRESS
New Post

ARCHITECT
A. F. Dershimer, U.S. Army

98f FORT SAM HOUSTON THEATRE, 1935

The tower of what appears to be a Spanish mission poking incongruously from the streetscape along the southern edge of Fort Sam Houston's main parade ground regularly generates surprise. The landmark is actually the modestly designed post theater, a structure built with numerous step-backs from the multi-arched loggia to the shell of the 1,200-seat auditorium. Included in the design are the faux belltower and, an ornate columned medallion announcing the style as Spanish Colonial Revival.

98g-2

98g-4

98g-3

98g-5

98g HOUSING UNITS, 1886–1939

Nowhere is the diversity of Fort Sam Houston's architecture more apparent than in its landmark housing units. The earliest are those along Staff Post, designed by Alfred Giles. Facing the parade ground west of the Quadrangle, fifteen sets of Italianate two-story officers' quarters were completed in hammer-dressed rustic rubble with stones in three sizes. Elegance ascended from the [98g-1] Captains' Quarters to [98g-2] Field Officers' Quarters to the [98g-3] Commander's House, now known as the Pershing House. Next came a similar assemblage, of brick, facing the parade grounds of Infantry Post, the most notable example being that post commander's home, now known as the [98g-4] Stillwell House (1886). Along the parade grounds of Cavalry and Artillery posts are red and buff brick two-story gabled barracks on the south and, on the north, a line of two-story family quarters for officers, including, at the eastern end, what is known as [98g-5] Eisenhower House (1912). Spanish Colonial Revival was at the height of its popularity when Ayres & Ayres designed New Post's barracks, ninety-four noncommissioned officers bungalows south of Arthur MacArthur Field and, to the north, two-story homes for company grade officers. The most distinctive New Post residence is Commander's House (1939). In 2007 Fisher Heck was supervising design in a five-year project to renovate and restore 386 historic post housing units.

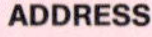

FORT SAM HOUSTON NATIONAL CEMETERY During the Mexican War, the U.S. Army established a quartermaster depot in San Antonio and was named the headquarters of the U.S. Army, Eighth Military District in 1849. The Army Post was officially established in 1875 and Fort Sam Houston was constructed the following year, but the cemetery was not designated until 1926. Burials from the post first took place at the city cemetery, which was donated to the federal government in 1867. sixty acres were added to the cemetery in 1931, and it

ADDRESS
1520 Harry Wurzbach Road
San Antonio, Texas 78209
(210) 820-3891

became known as the San Antonio National Cemetery. Renamed again in 1937, Fort Sam Houston National cemetery is the resting place of over 110,000 veterans and family members since Word War II, including 340 general officers and 27 graves of the "Buffalo Soldiers." For more information visit: www.cem.va.gov.

BRACKENRIDGE PARK In 1899, 343 acres were donated to the City of San Antonio by Colonel George W. Brackenridge to create Brackenridge Park, home to the San Antonio Zoo and many other family attractions and outdoor activities including the Brackenridge Eagle train, Japanese Tea Gardens, Brackenridge Golf Course and Witte Museum.

ADDRESS
3910 North St. Mary's Street
San Antonio, Texas 78212
(210) 736-9534

SAN ANTONIO ZOO In 1914, Colonel Brackenridge placed buffalo, elk, deer, monkeys, a pair of lions and four bears on the land he had deeded to the city. This collection of animals became the San Antonio Zoo, today home to over 3,800 animals representing 750 species. Events and activities abound for children and families. Observe elusive Attwater's Prairie Chicken or even spend the night at the zoo–the programs are endless. Open 365 days a year. Check out the zoo at www.sazoo-aq.org.

PHONE
(210) 734-7184

PHONE
(210) 735-7455

BRACKENRIDGE EAGLE A miniature replica of a 1863 steam locomotive travels a two-and-half-mile loop around the park delighting children and adults alike.

PHONE
(210) 821-3120

JAPANESE TEA GARDENS The Japanese Tea Gardens were constructed in 1917 by prison laborers over an abandoned stone quarry. A brick smokestack and lime kilns are still evident among the floral arrangements, water lily ponds and waterfall. Natural limestone cliffs carved nearby were transformed into the Sunken Gardens Theater.

ADDRESS
3801 Broadway
San Antonio, Texas 78209
(210) 357-1900

WITTE MUSEUM Discover the ecological history of Texas and view visiting galleries from Texas artists. Visit www.wittemuseum.org to learn more. The Witte Museum, located on the banks of the San Antonio River in Brackenridge Park, was created with the sudden death of businessman Alfred Witte. His bequeath of $65,000 to the City for a natural science museum to be located in Brackenridge Park surprised and delighted city leaders.

ADDRESS
555 Funston Place
San Antonio, TX 78209
(210) 207-3250

SAN ANTONIO BOTANICAL GARDEN The San Antonio Botanical Center is more than a 33-acre living classroom in which to explore the world of plants. Community events sponsored by the Botanical Society—*Shakespeare in the Park, Gardens by Moonlight, Concerts Under the Stars* and *Walk Across Texas* during Fiesta—are San Antonio favorites. Visit the Lucile Halsell Conservatory which is a sculpted set of glass forms, housing an exhibition hall, tropical house, desert house, palm house, fern room and an orangey. Visit www.sabot.org for event dates and tickets.

CONCRETE BUS STOP, CIRCA 1927 This trolley stop-turned-bus stop, the only known example of this form by Dionicio Rodriguez, remains a masterpiece of faux bois design in spite of a few missing limbs. The piece was donated by Rodriguez's patron, the president of San Antonio Portland Cement Company, to the City of Alamo Heights as a waiting area in the median of Broadway for transit patrons. Three large tree trunks with surrounding seats support a gabled palapa roof that shades riders. When the median was removed

ADDRESS
Broadway at Patterson Avenue, Alamo Heights

CRAFTSMAN
Dionicio Rodriguez

in 1931, the stop was relocated and two original end sections with branch handrails were removed. The northernmost tree trunk seat also appears to be missing, but these long-ago changes do not diminish the importance of this unique work.

PARCHMAN STREMMEL GALLERY Located in Olmos Park, Parchman Stremmel shows regionally and nationally recognized contemporary American and Latin American artists. The gallery presents paintings, sculpture and works on paper in a variety of styles.

ADDRESS
110 West Olmos Drive
San Antonio, Texas 78212
(210) 824-8990

J R MOONEY GALLERY Nationally known for its quality framing and representation of San Antonio and South Texas Artists; one of the company's most famous early clients was Porfirio Salinas. Salinas, whose artwork was owned by Presidents Kennedy and Johnson, was a client of the gallery and was represented by the gallery until his death in 1973.

ADDRESS
8302 Broadway
San Antonio, Texas 78209
(210)-828-8214

PEARL PARKWAY The restoration and adaptive reuse of the historic Pearl Brewery, under the vision and execution of local architects and landscape architects, is creating an urban community through thoughtful education, restoration, food and xeriscape landscape.

ADDRESS
312 Pearl Parkway
San Antonio, Texas 78215
(210) 212-9539

FOOD/ENTERTAINMENT

ADDRESS
8400 North New Braunfels Avenue
San Antonio, Texas 78209
(210) 824-0116

BARN DOOR Yes, The Barn Door is really a barn door. Despite the homey checkered plastic tablecloths, this is a San Antonio institution. There is a butcher shop inside, and the atmosphere is casual. The story of old Texas is told with pictures of cowboys and horses on the walls. You can find mouthwatering steaks, chicken and seafood and the place is suited for a business lunch, first date or family night out.

ADDRESS
8142 Broadway Street
San Antonio, Texas 78209
(210) 930-9393

BETO'S LATIN GRILL A hand with a heart in the palm sums up Beto's made-by-hand philosophy. The mood is festive with bright yellow stucco walls and 1950s style vinyl chairs; the clientele is mostly yuppie, young couples and families. There is outdoor covered seating and a play area with a sandbox for the kids. Order a mojito, and this is the place to chill, even in the heat.

ADDRESS
218 East Olmos Drive
San Antonio, Texas 78212
(210) 828-3141

BISTRO VATEL Tucked in a tiny Olmos Park shopping center, chef Damien Vatel's Bistro Vatel captures the feel of a Parisian eatery, complete with specials listed on a chalkboard and tables draped in white cloths and a piece of butcher paper; an authentic Parisian bistro that specializes in real French cuisine.

ADDRESS
1720 Blanco Road
San Antonio, Texas 78212
(210) 732-6480

BLANCO CAFÉ Get ready for Mexican food like abuela used to make, and lots of it. A tiny place on the inside, but it's inexpensive, laid-back and delicious. Wake up early for a breakfast taco made with homemade tortillas, or stop by at lunch for an enchilada or tortilla soup.

ADDRESS
5050 Broadway
San Antonio, Texas 78209
(210) 826-0069

BROADWAY 5050 The name is the address. The bar and restaurant have been recently renovated, and the place has changed from watering hole to hip neighborhood bar. You might want to freshen your knowledge of Quentin Tarantino movies; the menu has everything from the Royale with Cheese, the Butch and the Big Kahuna, and even the Vincent Vega.

CAPPY'S Seafood and steaks are featured at this casual, upscale dining room, nestled in the historic district of San Antonio known as Alamo Heights. It's a family-owned and -operated restaurant and has been in the same location for more than thirty years. Call ahead for reservations.

ADDRESS
5011 Broadway Street
San Antonio, Texas 78209
(210) 828-9669

CASBEER'S Nothing but good food and good music. Five days a week, this neighborhood cafe features local musicians as well as touring artists. Take a closer look at the menu, and you'll find the Kinky Burger, homage to Kinky Friedman's run for the governor in 2006. While the campaign may be over, the burger remains by popular demand. With each burger sold, one dollar goes to the Utopia Animal Rescue Ranch, which was co-founded by Kinky Friedman.

ADDRESS
1719 Blanco Road
San Antonio, Texas 78212
(210) 732-3511

CHRIS MADRID'S This is not your ordinary burger joint. It's the mecca for burger lovers and is even on AOL's list to top 15 burgers to eat before you die. While it may be easy to find in the historic Midtown section of downtown, good luck trying to find a place to park. But once inside, the line moves fast and the food is fresh. Burgers are the main dining course, and you'll find six varieties and two sizes, the regular and the macho. It's a quaint, family-friendly restaurant with everyone from business execs to city leaders to college students.

ADDRESS
1900 Blanco Road
San Antonio, Texas 27821
(210) 735-3552

CIAO LAVANDERIA At Ciao Lavanderia authentic and traditional Italian dishes like cioppini, paninis and gourmet pizzas straight from the wood-burning oven are a delight.

ADDRESS
226 East Olmos Drive
San Antonio, Texas 78212
(210) 822-3990

ADDRESS
3920 Harry Wurzbach Road
San Antonio, TX 78209
(210) 821-5454

CRUMPETS RESTAURANT & BAKERY Voted one of Esquire's 100 best restaurants, Crumpets offers the most unusual–a special collaborative expedition between Far-Flung Adventures and Crumpet's chef Francois Maeder. Participants are treated to a three-day rafting trip through the spectacular Santa Elena Canyon of the Río Grande in Big Bend National Park while enjoying marinated shrimp, rack of lamb, quail and beef Wellington with eggs benedict appearing for breakfast. Evening meals are accompanied by a

selection of fine wines and other beverages; musicians join the guests and perform at campsites. Sign up at www.crumpetsa.com.

ADDRESS
6498 North New Braunfels Avenue
San Antonio, Texas 78209
(210) 828-1111

EZ'S BRICK OVEN & GRILL "Let's go someplace easy" was the concept Cappy Lawton developed for this health-conscious custom-blended "fast-food" restaurant. Opened originally in an empty grocery store; the neon counter and the four-cheese pizza are what's cookin' at EZ's.

ADDRESS
7701 Broadway Street
San Antonio, Texas 78209
(210) 828-9050

FREDERICK'S The previous owner grew up in his parents' Vietnamese restaurant in Paris, and the influence is evident in the menu. The combination of flavors from the East and the West make the cuisine exciting and unusual. Frederick's has also been voted as the most romantic restaurant in San Antonio. You may not see it from Broadway, but the restaurant is just blocks from the Quarry Golf Course. It is closed on Sundays and reservations are recommended.

ADDRESS
400 East Josephine Street
San Antonio, Texas 78212
(210) 224-6169

JOSEPHINE ST CAFÉ Try the t-bone and wilted salad – it's all good. The main dining room houses a huge indoor tree trunk, and in keeping with its next-door neighbor, the Liberty Bar, the booths tilt at improbable angles.

LA FONDA ON MAIN Established in 1932. What appears to be a local neighborhood restaurant has been a favorite in San Antonio to many famous visitors and celebrities alike. Franklin Roosevelt, John Wayne and Yul Brenner have all dined at this quaint tiled-roofed residence acquired by Cappy Lawton in 1990. Enjoy Mexican cuisine on the patio with a frozen margarita or cold beer. Truly a San Antonio gathering spot.

ADDRESS
2415 North Main Avenue
San Antonio, Texas 78212
(210) 733-0621

L'ETOILE Simple sophistication. A two-star French restaurant, and the menu here is constantly changing. You'll find an elegant atmosphere inside, as well as private rooms and fine wines. L'Etoile caters to a cosmopolitan crowd, providing lighter fare and a more diverse take on traditional French cuisine.

ADDRESS
6106 Broadway
San Antonio, Texas 78209
(210) 826-4551

LIBERTY BAR The leaning structure was mentioned in the *New York Times* in a "36 Hour Visit." Best bread pudding in town and always fresh brown-paper tablecloths invite sketching. In the 1920s a flood forced the tilt that exists today. Each time a patron calls the building inspector the report is always "in fine shape." Check out the unusual menu at www.liberty-bar.com.

ADDRESS
328 East Josephine Street
San Antonio, Texas 78212
(210) 227-1187

LOS BARRIOS Bring your appetite and some patience, as finding a table on Friday night may be nearly impossible. But the margaritas keep on flowing and the mariachi bands keep on playing. The plates of food are big enough to feed an entire family, but save room for sopapillas, fried Mexican deserts dipped in honey.

ADDRESS
4223 Blanco Road
San Antonio, Texas 78212
(210) 732 6017

OLMOS PHARMACY The place for a chocolate shake or malt since 1938. Slide into a booth or take a swivel seat at the counter and dig into a juicy cheeseburger. Or if lemonade cools you off, get it fresh squeezed. This is the malt shop your grandparents would have gone to.

ADDRESS
3902 McCullough Avenue
San Antonio, Texas 78212
(210) 822-3361

ADDRESS
5800 Broadway
San Antonio, Texas 78209
(210) 822-6151

PALOMA BLANCA Paloma Blanca (white dove) bills itself as an oasis for the mind and spirit, right in the heart of San Antonio, and that's exactly what you get. It's more upscale and refined, the atmosphere more Mexico City than low-key San Antonio. The architecture is hacienda-inspired, with whispering palms and flowering landscape, and the patio is perfect for a lazy Sunday afternoon. Tequila tastings are held the last Thursday of each month.

ADDRESS
4100 McCullough Avenue
San Antonio, Texas 78212
(210) 821-5338

PANCHITO'S RESTAURANT Arrive early on Fridays and enjoy awesome drink specials and a talented musician performing while you dine. Try the bacon-wrapped shrimp plate, pricey but delectable, or the Olmos Tacos—different and tasty. Service is friendly and prompt.

ADDRESS
4230 McCullough Avenue
San Antonio, Texas 78212
(210) 829-5050

SHIRAZ If you're ready for Persian cuisine order the fesenjan, a chicken breast baked in a sweet walnut pomegranate sauce. Beef lovers will thoroughly enjoy the ghormeh sabzi, which consists of sauteed beef with parsley, cilantro and green onions. Vegetarian selections are in the offing along with a wonderful selection of wines. Do not miss dessert! The Persian ice cream is made with vanilla, saffron and rosewater, it is a delicious treat that your palette will not forget.

ADDRESS
1133 Austin Highway
San Antonio, Texas 78209
(210) 824-8686

SILO A truly unique visual and dining experience; seafoods and beef and the freshest possible produce are complemented by live entertainment Thursday–Saturday. Bookings for groups and events are welcome.

TACO CABANA It started in 1978 as a taco stand, and almost thirty years later, Taco Cabana is a fast food giant in San Antonio. The colorful pink and turquoise cabanas dot almost every corner around town. Their tortillas are made by hand, with a variety of salsas to choose from. You can sip on margaritas inside or outside on the patio, or if you don't have time to relax, go through the drive thru to take a taco home. Most locations are open 24 hours, perfect for late-night hunger attacks. Check out the original on the corner of Hildebrand and San Pedro.

ADDRESS
3310 San Pedro Avenue
San Antonio, Texas 78212
(210) 733-9332

TACO TACO Located at the corner of Hildebrand and McCullough, Taco Taco is a small intimate café that serves breakfast until 2 pm. The chilaquiles are a local favorite. The eggs are fluffy, cheese is appropriately orange, peppers carry bite and tortilla strips are crisp. Expect a wait at the door on weekends.

ADDRESS
145 East Hildebrand Avenue
San Antonio, TX 78212
(210) 822-9533

ADDRESS
2403 North St Mary's Street
San Antonio, Texas 78212
(210) 735-5471

TEKA MOLINA Try the puffy tacos, but don't bring your credit cards, as they're not accepted. This taco house is open early in the morning but closes at 7p.m. Monday through Friday.

ADDRESS
5005 Broadway
San Antonio, Texas 78209
(210) 826-6411

TWIG BOOKSHOP AND CAPPYCINNOS Grab a cup of coffee and meander through one of the largest architecture book sections in town. This independent bookstore also has some of the best selections of local authors and children's books.

He was a bigger-than-life character
who made good copy and
knew how to capture it.

—MARY CAROLYN GEORGE

O'Neil Ford, FAIA

by MARY CAROLYN GEORGE

Mary Carolyn George is a noted historian and writer, who has written a book about O'Neil Ford

In the course of the twentieth century, Texas could claim an impressive roster of fine architects, but none were as celebrated nationally—even internationally—as O'Neil Ford. And none were as revered or reviled. He was a bigger-than-life character who made good copy and knew how to capture it. O'Neil Ford , son of Bert and Lula Belle Ford, was born at Pink Hill, near Sherman, Texas, on December 3, 1905. His creative bent was nurtured by his parents, who sought educational opportunities for their children. He attended a progressive elementary school in Sherman where drawing was incorporated into every phase of the curriculum. After Bert Ford died in a railroad accident, Mrs. Ford moved her family to the college town of Denton. Neil assumed the responsibilities of breadwinner at twelve. He developed a flair for persuasive showmanship to obtain jobs for himself and his younger brother, Lynn, who gained fame as a wood-carver, and his sister, Authella, skilled in working with copper. He perfected his technique throughout his life to bring in jobs for his architectural firm or to lobby for favorite environmental or political causes. During his high school years, Ford haunted the library at the nearby college where the librarians encouraged his passion for reading. He entered North Texas State (now the University of North Texas) in 1924, but economic pressures forced him to abandon his efforts to get a formal education after two years. Ford subsequently enrolled in an architecture course from the International Correspondence School of Scranton, Pennsylvania. His lack of university training became part of his mystique. In 1924, he and his uncle traveled through the Alsatian and German communities of Castroville and Fredericksburg. Ford was deeply impressed by the simplicity and beauty of the vernacular architecture he saw there and the experience decisively influenced his later work.

From 1926 to 1932, Ford worked in the office of Dallas architect David R. Williams, a leading spokesman for Texas vernacular architecture, where he served his apprenticeship. Flamboyant, extravagant and often outrageous, Williams became Ford's role model. He responded to Ford's abilities as a designer, and together they produced a number of fine regional houses of native brick, wood and stone in north central Texas. Ford was also influenced by the tradition of the English Arts and Crafts Movement and the works of Greene and Greene in California, especially attempts to synthesize architecture and the visual arts. In an attempt to carry on this tradition, he enlisted the skills of his siblings as well as artists Jerry Bywaters and Thomas Stell who collaborated on many projects, stenciling walls and making mosaics. During the Great Depression, the young architect worked on Work Projects Administration and National Youth Administration projects, and with the Rural Resettlement Administration.

Ford formed his first partnership in 1937 with Arch Swank in Dallas. Their major job was the Little Chapel in the Woods on the campus of Texas Woman's University, Denton, constructed by NYA trainees with interior craft elements by college art students. The task of translating ideas into something that could be built fell to Jerry Rogers who did the working drawings for the chapel. The reconstruction of La Villita by the WPA precipitated Ford's move to San Antonio, where he took Jerry Rogers as his partner (1939–53). Their research into building systems including the Youtz-Slick lift slab and stressed concrete was put to the test in 1949 when they received the commission to design a new campus for Trinity University in San Antonio, along with Bartlett Cocke and Harvey P. Smith, who soon stepped aside. From 1953 to 1965, O'Neil Ford and Associates with Richard Colley of Corpus Christi did a number of buildings for burgeoning Texas Instruments, both in Texas and abroad. Among the best-known work for TI was the Semiconductor Building in Dallas (1958), which made use of a new structural system of thin concrete shells known as hyperbolic paraboloids, developed by Mexican architect Félix Candela. In 1967, Ford formed a partnership with Boone Powell and Chris Carson. Bright young people fresh out of architecture schools were eager to work in this innovative office, and Ford's best work was accomplished in collaboration with talented youth. Campuses for Skidmore College in New York and the first phase of the University of Texas at San Antonio are notable examples of the firm's work during Ford's final years.

O'Neil Ford devoted much energy to serving causes dear to his heart, including the National Council on the Arts, the American Council for the Arts in Education, and the Foreign Buildings Operation of the State Department. He also garnered many honors—elevated to the AIA College of Fellows (1960) and honorary doctoral degrees from four universities. The first endowed chair in the School of Architecture at the University of Texas at Austin was named for Ford. In 1940, Ford married Wanda Graham, who served as president of the San Antonio Conservation Society (1955–57) and played a prominent role in the community. O'Neil Ford died on July 20, 1982, in San Antonio.

ARCHITECTURE

1. San Antonio International Airport - Terminal One
2. Los Patios Garden Center
3. Episcopal Church of the Reconcilation
4. Saint Mary's Hall
5. Northeast Baptist Medical Office Building
6. Plaza at Thousand Oaks
7. United States Postal Service General Mail Facility
8. Bartlett Cocke Construction Company Offices
9. Morton House
10. Holy Trinity Catholic Church
11. Cornerstone Church
12. Promontory Pointe Pool Pavilion
13. Kich House
14. St. Francis of Assisi Catholic Church
15. Frost Bank DeZavala Branch
16. St. Andrew Presbyterian Church
17. Churchill Baptist Church
18. Churchill National Bank
19. Slimp House
20. SASA Building
21. EEHO Mexican Restaurant
22. Harvey Sculpture Studio
23. Galleria Nord

ARCHITECTURE

NORTH

07

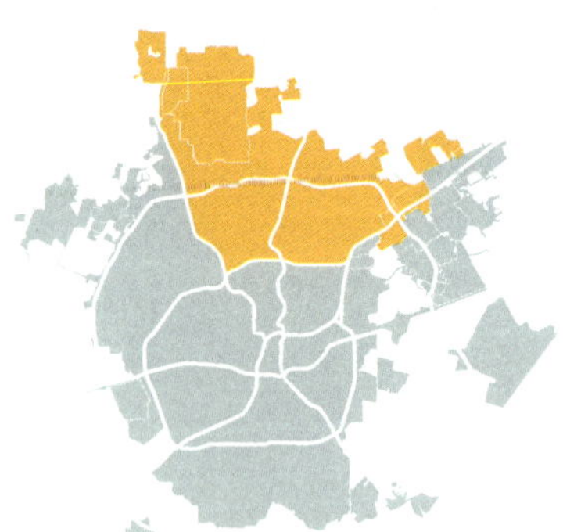

NORTH

The amorphous suburban area north of the central segment of San Antonio's Loop 410 began to grow in the 1960s, as the Hill Country's rolling foothills attracted increasing amounts of residential and commercial development. The region remains anchored in its center by San Antonio International Airport and McAllister Park.

Some developments coalesced as separately incorporated suburbs—Castle Hills, Shavano Park, Hollywood Park and Hill Country Village—grew in the 1950s in the six miles between Loops 410 and 1604. A smaller separate suburb, Balcones Heights (west sector), remains just inside Loop 410. Contemporary land annexation by San Antonio, however, left most of the region within the corporate limits of San Antonio.

By the late 1990s, increasingly dense development was spreading on either side of US 281 north beyond Loop 1604 to the limits of Bexar County. A few small stone farmhomes and outbuildings, some restored, remain as reminders of the farms and small ranches that once dotted the area.

ADDRESS
139 Airport Boulevard

ARCHITECTS
Heery & Heery, Atlanta; Marmon Mok Partnership; W. E. Simpson Company

1 ▲★ SAN ANTONIO INTERNATIONAL AIRPORT TERMINAL ONE, 1984 The precision of industrial construction and environmental technology combined with a spirited acknowledgment of San Antonio's architectural character to produce this first stage of a four-phase program that is replacing San Antonio International Airport's old main terminal building (1952, Ayres & Ayres). Terry Sargent, chief designer for Heery & Heery, contributed to the terminal's checkered pink concrete masonry units and silvery aluminum banding, exposed tubular steel trusses and lightweight acrylic, plastic and perforated steel vaults, all of which produce the brilliant contrasts of texture and color associated

1

2

with San Antonio. The vaults lend the main concourse level a strong sense of spatial definition and admit filtered daylight through transverse ribbed slots. The adjacent 1,300-car parking garage is surfaced with Adoquin stone. The central mechanical plant masquerades as a sculptural piece and fountain. Marmon, Mok & Green did the landscape architecture.

ADDRESS
2015 N.E. Loop 410

ARCHITECT
Frank Welch

2 ★ LOS PATIOS GARDEN CENTER, 1971 Notwithstanding its proximity to Loop 410, this specialty shopping center is set on a quiet, wooded, thirty-three-acre estate along Salado Creek. Ambience, not the domination of architecture, is what was aimed for, making Los Patios charming without being contrived. Understated small-scale, shed-roofed and stucco-faced buildings are connected by pergolas and galleries and by landscaped courts discretely inserted amid the trees. The gallery, the first and the most carefully detailed building, is a combination house-and-store that incorporates a cast-stone Spanish-style portal salvaged from San Antonio's demolished Missouri-Kansas-Texas Railway Passenger Station (1915, Frederick J. Sterner). Soon added were the Gazebo (1973) and Hacienda (1977) by Frank Welch Associates and Carrington Weems & Associates.

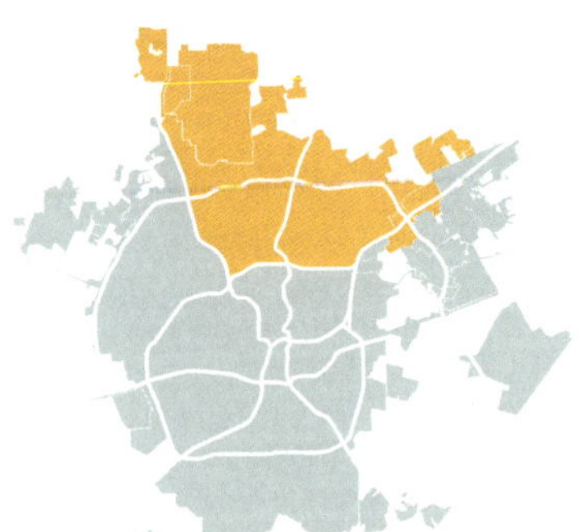

3★ EPISCOPAL CHURCH OF THE RECONCILIATION, 1974 The liturgical centrality of the Eucharist prompted the square planning and pyramidal massing of this suburban church, which occupies its flat, wooded site with dignity and authority. The outer walls, laid up in wide courses of salvaged limestone, are indented on three sides to provide deep-set, enclosed garden bays, screened from the outside by wooden slats. The high, copper-clad lantern rising above the central worship space recalls in its shape the vernacular buildings of the central Texas countryside. A later addition (1987) by Frank Welch Associates received a TSA design award.

ADDRESS
8900 Starcrest Drive

ARCHITECTS
Ford, Powell & Carson

ADDITION
Frank Welch

4 SAINT MARY'S HALL, 1968
The original campus of this small private school for girls set on a large, wooded tract represents O'Neil Ford at his best. Cloistered passageways, some of arched masonry construction and others of cedar post-and-beam construction, ring a series of garden courts to join the compactly cluttered, domestically scaled campus buildings. Regional design elements include low-pitched, standing seam metal roofs, punctuated by clerestory bands or up thrust sheds; simple but carefully articulated wood joinery; and walls of dun-colored Mexican brick. The architecture merges with the cultivated landscape to achieve the paradoxical goal of romantic regionalism: that dream of tranquil timelessness that seeks to evade history in order to become nature.

ADDRESS
9401 Starcrest Drive

ARCHITECTS
Ford, Powell & Carson and Bartlett Cocke & Associates

ADDRESS
8715 Village Drive

ARCHITECTS
Marmon Mok

5▲ NORTHEAST BAPTIST MEDICAL OFFICE BUILDING, 2000 This six-floor medical office building is directly connected to a five-level parking garage. The tower connecting the two houses a full-height atrium and elevator core. The building also houses an ambulatory surgical center.

ADDRESS
2845 Thousand Oaks Drive

ARCHITECTS
Riehm Owensby Guzman

6▲ PLAZA AT THOUSAND OAKS, 1984 *NO PHOTO*
Punctuated by roofed pyramidal tower bays, this office and retail center frames a motor court and pedestrian concourse. Plantings and fountains are allied with variations in massing, materials and colors to create a sense of identity.

5

7

ADDRESS
10410 Perrin Beitel Road

ARCHITECTS
Marmon Mok and Phelps Simmons Garza

7★ UNITED STATES POSTAL SERVICE GENERAL MAIL FACILITY, 1977
This low-set, long-spread, 300,000-square-foot building combines a post office, regional mail-handling operations and a vehicle maintenance garage. A metal-panel wall system cladding the steel-frame structure contributes to the building's quiet, imperturbable look. The building's horizontality counters the gently rolling landscape in which it is set. Glazing recessed in deep slots along the west elevation provides dark wells of shadow that underscore the building's horizontal expanse. A projecting vertical bay denotes the post office's front door.

ADDRESS
8706 Lockway Street

RENOVATED
1982

8▲ BARTLETT COCKE CONSTRUCTION COMPANY OFFICES, 1982 *NO PHOTO*
This pecan-shaded wooden frame farmhouse, an anachronism in this industrial area, was converted to offices under Jones Kell in 1982 along with a 5,000-square-foot addition of red brick walls inspired by the farmhouse's brick chimneys. Other walls of glass blocks diffuse sunlight and views of surrounding industries.

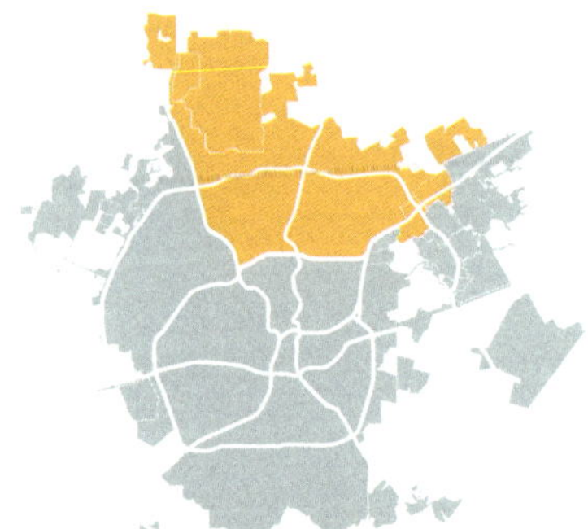

9★ MORTON HOUSE, 1982

Living space in this contemporary residence is efficiently managed with three gabled pavilions linked by wraparound galleries and accented by tall chimneystacks. Its regional architecture is reflected in the rough stone walls and sheet-metal roofs, which reflect an early adoption of imported materials.

ADDRESS
12590 Judson Road

ARCHITECT
Frank D. Welch

10▲ HOLY TRINITY CATHOLIC CHURCH, 1991

A sanctuary for 600 was doubled in size in 2001 during the second phase of construction for this church. Natural materials complement the Hill Country surroundings. Stained glass 150 years old was salvaged from a cathedral in Baltimore.

ADDRESS
20523 Huebner Road

ARCHITECTS
O'Neill Conrad Oppelt

11▲ CORNERSTONE CHURCH, 1987

In-house television and radio broadcast facilities are included in the state-of-the-art design for this church. Exterior brick pilasters develop the structural grid of the sanctuary, which can seat 4,000. The first phase included three additional office and classroom buildings and parking for 1,300 cars. Later phases included a gymnasium/dining complex, chapel, two additional education buildings and an outdoor meeting hall.

ADDRESS
18755 Stone Oak Parkway

ARCHITECTS
Jones Kell

ADDRESS
2151 Balmoral Place

ARCHITECT
Michael G. Imber

12▲ PROMONTORY POINTE POOL PAVILION, 2001

This pool pavilion where suburbia meets the Hill Country is a simple, bold structure with timber frame construction with a pool, two change rooms, an office and mechanical space, all spread apart in a footprint that increases the overall scale to monumental stature. The additional space can be used as an outdoor pavilion for the neighborhood.

12

13

15

14

ADDRESS
419 Tower Drive

ARCHITECT
Bernard Harris

13 KICH HOUSE, 1959

Original public areas of this house were preserved in 2001; the addition was designed by Sprinkle Robey. It featured oversize glass openings that blur the line between the interior and the Hill Country landscape surrounding this home. Smaller windows on the north and south afford privacy from neighbors, provide ventilation and create controlled views. Carefully detailed red oak floors, porcelain tile, polished stone and custom birch millwork pieces finish the interior.

ADDRESS
4201 De Zavala Road

ARCHITECTS
O'Neill Conrad Oppelt

14 ST. FRANCIS OF ASSISI CATHOLIC CHURCH, 2002

The octagonal shape of this church's sanctuary is intended to create a spirit of unity that fosters an inward focus and allows parishioners to encircle the alter. High windows allow light to fill the space through the steel and wood roof framing to create a warm and uplifting experience.

ADDRESS
13226 Vance Jackson Road

ARCHITECT
Marmon Mok

15▲ FROST BANK DE ZAVALA BRANCH, 2000

Located in a commercial and retail area, this branch bank utilizes steel, glass and aluminum to create a modern and contemporary feeling. Interiors feature regional materials of quarried limestone and oak.

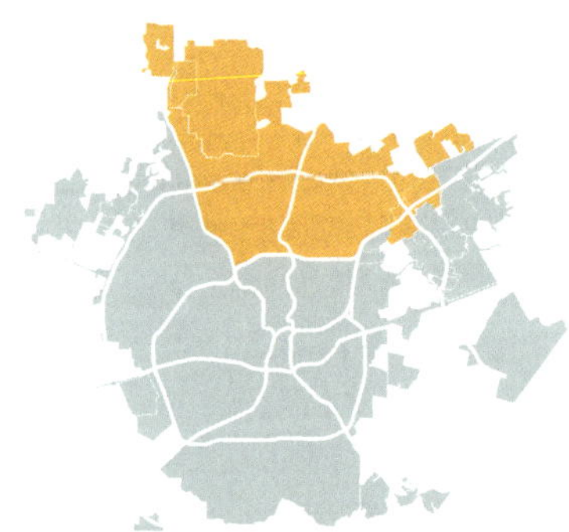

16★ ST. ANDREW'S PRESBYTERIAN CHURCH, 1963

The influence of Louis I. Kahn on American architecture in the 1960s is evident in this suburban church, which is square in plan, braced by low corner buttresses and organized internally in a diagonally rotated cross-axis. The cubic lantern at the apex of the pyramidal, wood-shingled roof admits daylight at the center of the worship space. Bands of corbelled indentations along the tan brick walls and O'Neil Ford's familiar light fixture fabrications are the only concessions to ornament in this austere but unintimidating building. A low administration and assembly wing adjoins the church on the west.

ADDRESS
8231 Callaghan Road

ARCHITECTS
O'Neil Ford and Howard Wong

17▲ CHURCHILL BAPTIST CHURCH, 2000

Set among native live oaks, this 15,000-square-foot facility's nine classrooms and gymnasium create a focal point as they open onto an exterior courtyard. Natural finish metal cladding and painted stucco wainscot tie the building to the land and reflect the landscape's colors. The kitchen enables the facility to accommodate large sit-down gatherings as well as worship services.

ADDRESS
12499 Vista View Street

ARCHITECTS
Sprinkle Robey

18▲ CHURCHILL NATIONAL BANK, 1975 *NO PHOTO*

This 2,300-square-foot interim facility, which has been razed, was constructed of four portable building modules and a portable steel vault. Despite its portable elements, the structure achieves visual distinction by a strong diagonality in form and detailing.

ADDRESS
10000 San Pedro Avenue

ARCHITECTS
Marmon Barclay Souter
Foster Hays

ADDRESS
1746 Lockhill-Selma Road

19 SLIMP HOUSE, 1931 (THE LODGE)

When this two-story rock country home was completed on the crest of a rise by the Chester Slimp family, it afforded a clear view of downtown San Antonio. It was dubbed "The Castle on the Hill," a name said to have evolved into the naming of the surrounding latter-day suburb as Castle Hills. A high-ceilinged art studio with pine rafters from East Texas built for Mrs. Slimp in 1936 is now the private dining hall for the restaurant that occupies the home.

19

20

ADDRESS
601 Northwest Loop 410

ARCHITECTS
Hellmuth, Obata & Kassabaum, Dallas

20★ SASA BUILDING, 1980 (PYRAMID BUILDING)

The serrated profile of this nine-story, 240,000-square-foot corporate headquarters for San Antonio Savings Association rises in dramatic setback terraces at the crest of a small hill facing the intersection of Loop 410 and San Pedro Avenue. Recessed horizontal ribbon windows are shielded with Texas Cordova Limestone-shielded spandrels. These originally harbored troughs for plants that cascaded over the sides, giving the building the sense of emerging from a Mayan jungle.

ADDRESS
9307 Broadway

ARCHITECT
Davis Sprinkle

RENOVATED
1988

21▲ EEHO MEXICAN RESTAURANT, 1988 *NO PHOTO*

This former diner was renovated under Davis Sprinkle with a new monumentally scaled sculptural piece that comments on roadside architecture and pokes fun at Mexican restaurant iconography. New inside walls contrast with the existing architecture through use of form and color. Through perforated openings, a folded wall enclosure allows glimpses of operations of a tortilla machine.

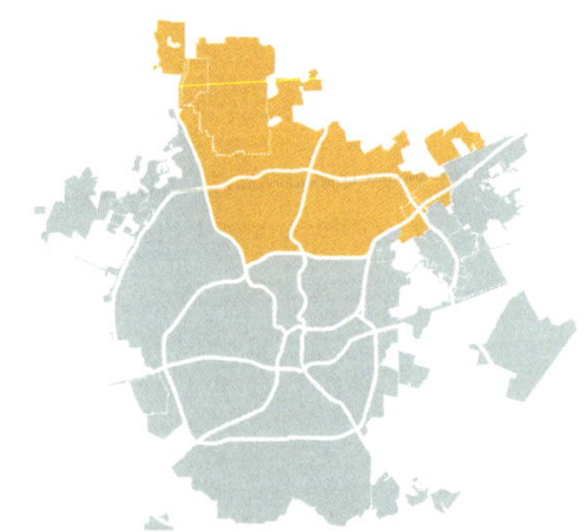

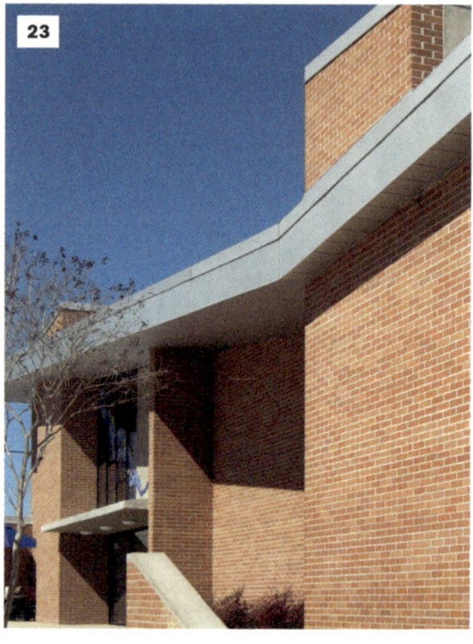

22▲ HARVEY SCULPTURE STUDIO, 1983 *NO PHOTO*

This 1,500-square-foot studio and gallery for fabrication and display of steel sculpture utilizes such expedient methods and materials as pre-engineered steel framing, an infill of red clay tile units, and metal roofing and doors to achieve spectacular effects. Painting of exposed steel results in kaleidoscopic profusion. Principal interior spaces overlook a small garden on the downhill side of the site.

ADDRESS
411 West Rhapsody Street

ARCHITECTS
Chumney Jones Kell

23 GALLERIA NORD, 2006

Load-bearing brick supports the exposed steel structure of this Modernist gallery's asymmetrical, wing-like roof, creating a soaring interior space ideal for larger paintings and sculptures. A curving stairway reaches a mezzanine with smaller display rooms. Above the entry canopy is an abstract design by Peery executed by Cavallini Stained Glass Studios. Opposite the entry, a glazed wall looks out to the fountain and pool in a walled sculpture garden.

ADDRESS
2009 Northwest Military Highway

ARCHITECT
Allison Peery

ADDRESS
2303 North Loop 1604 West
San Antonio, Texas 78258
(210) 408-2029

BIG'Z BURGER JOINT This, the newest of the Chef Andrew Weissman family's ventures, exhibits his amazing culinary creativity. It's not your typical burger joint, instead offering such experiences as a pound Angus burger topped with Applewood smoked bacon and a sunny-side-up egg. You may also want to sample the homemade habanero catsup.

ADDRESS
2015 Northeast Loop 410, at Starcrest
San Antonio, Texas 78217
(210) 655-6171

LOS PATIOS AND GAZEBO AT LOS PATIOS Five minutes from the airport, this twenty-acre eco-friendly wooded hideaway alongside Salado Creek has been a San Antonio destination for almost forty years. Visitors can combine their lunch at the Gazebo, featuring a broad menu, with a visit to the garden center, the salon, any of several boutiques or a walk along the nature trail. If you head this way on a Sunday, you will be able to partake in their delicious Sunday Lunch Buffet.

ADDRESS
1746 Lockhill Selma
San Antonio, Texas 78213
(210) 349-8466

THE LODGE RESTAURANT OF CASTLE HILLS Opened by prize-winning chef Jason Dady in 2001, this adaptive reuse of the "Hollywood-style" mansion (from which surrounding Castle Hills derives its name) creates an elegant, intimate setting for fine dining. Surrounded by majestic live oaks, you will dine on an array of the freshest ingredients, combined in a style that is a fusion of the best of the French and Italian cooking traditions.

ADDRESS
Artisans Alley
555 West Bitters Road
San Antonio, Texas 78216
(210) 496-0555

BIN 555 RESTAURANT AND WINE BAR Chef Jason Dady and his family expanded their culinary offerings at this innovative new establishment "hidden" in Artisans Alley. With an innovative menu featuring small, midsize and large plates, a wood-burning oven and a lengthy wine list predicated on "55 bottles for $55," diners can be extremely creative in their approach to dining. Come as a group and share a wide array of offerings.

MAGNOLIA PANCAKE HAUS Sometimes even San Antonians need a break from Mexican food. If it's breakfast time, they head to this North Side institution, which wins accolades for their variety of pancakes, omelets, French toast and the sort of soul-warming breakfast food that reminds one of weekends at Grandma's house.

ADDRESS
606 Embassy Oaks, Suite 100
San Antonio, Texas 78216
(210) 496-0828

EL MIRASOL ALTA COCINA An excellent place to go to be served an authentic Mexican cuisine. It has a very pleasant environment, especially on the patio, on a nice

ADDRESS
3489 Blanco Road
San Antonio, Texas 78216
(210) 479-8767

day. Try their ceviche and the enchiladas covered with the best chipotle sauce in town. Also, don't forget to order one of their margaritas with an "attitude."

LA HACIENDA DE LOS BARRIOS The Barrios family tradition continues in this location. The attractive environment offers a setting that is receptive to families and large parties. The menu includes an extensive list of Tex-Mex dishes and a variety of classic Mexican plates. The cabrito and a flaming marinated beef and pork combination should satisfy your taste buds. Their specialty margaritas should be given a consideration.

ADDRESS
18747 Redlands Road
San Antonio, Texas 78259
(210) 497-8000

EL JARRO DE ARTURO Popular for celebrations, family-owned El Jarro provides live music and dancing on weekend nights. A festive interior with extensive colorful tilework generates an appropriate mood for tasting their contemporary, expansive menu of Tex-Mex and south-of-the-border specialties. Try one of the chef's specials.

ADDRESS
13421 San Pedro Avenue
San Antonio, Texas 78216
(210) 494-5084

CAFÉ PALADAR In one of the newer establishments in San Antonio, Chef Brian West, another "graduate" of Bruce Auden's "academy" (Biga), features a menu with distinct Latin flavors. A variety of tapas is available for sampling, followed by entries, many of them infused with a Spanish "accent". The ancho chili Mexican chocolate cake is hard to resist.

ADDRESS
18322 Sonterra Place
San Antonio, Texas 78258
(210) 798-7200

Move your eyes north on city maps, farther into well-to-do suburbs, and more and more of the roads abandon grids and follow the earth's topography.

—PATRICK DRISCOLL

Suburban Sprawl

by PATRICK DRISCOLL

Patrick Driscoll is a reporter for the San Antonio Express News

When standing in front of the Alamo wondering what's original stonework and what's a restorative attempt, you're surrounded by neighborhoods that were molded by regimented Spanish plazas, a skeleton of acequias and related footpaths that flowed with the land, a spoke of trails going to other settlements and later a web of trolley lines.

Though not as famous as the River Walk, these neighborhoods and their shifting street grids are part of the history and charm of San Antonio. They help make the city as unique as it is.

But not far away is another world, one much like Anywhere, USA. These are the car suburbs that deluged and encased so many cities after World War II.

At the dawn of the 1960s, North Star Mall and Wonderland Shopping City opened on Loop 410, when it was a much narrower road running past farms, fields and forests. The malls stood proudly in lakes of asphalt like naked beacons for the booming development that would follow.

Loop 410 itself is a defining landmark for these suburbs. Part of the road was laid on top of the old Loop 13 that joined most of the city's military installations, by 1967 the new Loop 410 had finished encircling the city. The 49-mile freeway has no beginning, no end and no connection to downtown.

City maps show the town's old patchwork of tight grids loosening as they approach Loop 410, and then, like sharp lines of ink hitting a wet spot, they reach the loop and scatter.

People who live north of Loop 410 are called Looplanders, and it's not hard to find some who never or rarely go downtown. The places they live in are called subdivisions rather than neighborhoods, a reference to how land is divided and sold.

Looplanders sort of have their own downtowns – drive-thru versions. Over the years, jobs and housing massed around the Medical Center and Wonderland Shopping City, now called Crossroads of San Antonio mall, and around San Antonio International Airport and North Star Mall. High-rise buildings, many of them glittering with reflective glass, gave the two areas their own skylines, and the often congested stretch of Loop 410 between them, now the widest and busiest roadway in San Antonio, is their main street.

Loop 410 is the address for the Century Center, the city's first building to be covered entirely in gold glass; the Mercantile Bank Building, with a curving facade that echoes the freeway; and the SASA Center, nine serrated stories of limestone surfaces and windows. On Interstate 10 is the One Forum Office Building, a 16-floor tower of rose-colored concrete and glass.

Move your eyes north on city maps, farther into well-to-do suburbs, and more and more of the roads abandon grids and follow the earth's topography. Cul-de-sacs reign and empty tracts of land grow between fences, streets and buildings. The U.S. Census shows that population per square mile in this sprawling area is about half of what it is inside Loop 410.

The open spaces are another defining feature of these suburbs, which were built where flatlands to the south give way to lush rolling hills to the north. Many open spaces are simply unimaginative dead spots, often just serving to separate and buffer, but others are treasured natural areas.

Two of the city's largest preserves, McAllister Park and Walker Ranch Historic Landmark Park, totaling nearly 1,000 acres, managed to get carved out along creeks and floodplains. And some developers were sensitive enough to preserve native trees or riparian areas in their projects, such as the wooded area that's home to Saint Mary's Hall, a private school.

To see the worst, look at the huge drainage ditch just west of Nacogdoches Road, a gross transformation of Salado Creek that sits ignored behind houses. For the best, follow Salado Creek south to Loop 410, where in the freeway's shadow the Los Patios Garden Center was modestly inserted into 33 acres of woods next to a scenic pool of water.

08

ARCHITECTURE

BEYOND SAN ANTONIO

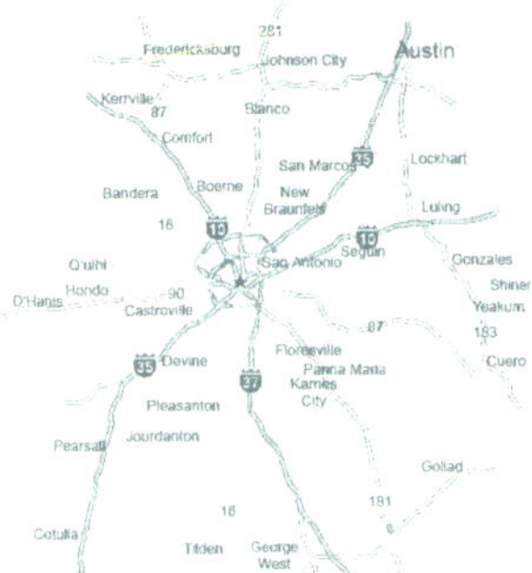

The landscape surrounding San Antonio is dotted with agricultural and ranching communities founded largely by European immigrants in the mid to late nineteenth century. Many of these, long tied to San Antonio as the center of trade and commerce, have evolved into getaways for both residents and visitors. In any direction from San Antonio, one can enjoy a wide range of architecture from vernacular to sophisticated revival styles. Notable are the courthouses that anchor county seats—each town's most substantial and imposing structures at the time of construction. Eight nearby towns have been selected for economic assistance in commercial district revitalization under the National Trust for Historic Preservation's Main Street program, administered in the state by the Texas Historical Commission. They are Cotulla, Goliad, Gonzales, Kerrville, Luling, New Braunfels, San Marcos and Seguin.

Also, just beyond the immediate environs of San Antonio are several AIA award winners. All draw on the region's vernacular architectural motifs of limestone and rough-hewn wood.

Two residential award winners are inaccessible to the public, however. Hill Country Jacal [A] (1988, Lake/Flato), near Pipe Creek, bears the Spanish term for a cabin of mud and sticks. It is a weekend retreat on a rock ledge overlooking a creek with a screened cedar pole structure oriented toward the prevailing summer breeze and thick limestone walls sheltering the living space from northwest winter winds. This project won a National AIA and TSA Award.

And the David Straus Ranch House [B] (1983, O'Neill & Perez) near Castroville has multiple buildings influenced by Spanish and early Texas styles among outdoor courtyards. This project received a TSA Award.

Other award winners include:

1

2

3

ADDRESS
194 South Main, Boerne

ARCHITECTS
Marmon Mok

1▲ FIFERV HEALTH, 1906
(NATIONAL BANK OF COMMERCE BRANCH)
This banking branch maintains the architectural character of the Texas Hill Country, incorporating a theme that reflects the original limestone bank of 1901 and the historically significant buildings of the region. Classical cast stone elements and the traditional veranda emphasize the bank's main entrance. The imagery of dormers creates an illusion that the building is less than three-stories and reflects the importance of scale in a small town.

ADDRESS
1300 South Main Street, Boerne

ARCHITECTS
Lake/Flato

2▲ FROST BANK, BOERNE BRANCH, 1988
(FIRST NATIONAL BANK)
Situated near the historic downtown district of Boerne, and carefully sited in a stand of native Live Oak trees, the architecture of this 6,000-square-foot bank draws on the traditional Hill Country vernacular.

ADDRESS
9090 Fair Oaks Parkway, Fair Oaks Ranch

ARCHITECTS
Lake/Flato

3▲★ FROST BANK, FAIR OAKS BRANCH, 1988
(FAIR OAKS NATIONAL BANK)
Created as a series of double-height octagonal metal silos joined by single-story flat-roofed office wings, this 5,000-square-foot bank building is clad in rough-textured bands of buff and gray limestone with galvanized metal roofs and deep metal-framed punched windows.

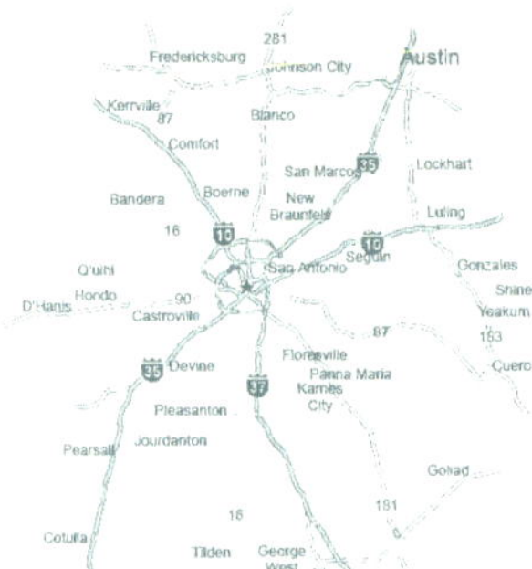

4▲★◉ GOVERNMENT CANYON VISITOR CENTER, 2005

Government Canyon State Natural Area is this Visitor Center, which floats in a field of native grasses and restored oaks at the mouth of the canyon. The exposed pipe structure suggests the canyon's rich ranching history. The building demonstrates sustainable water use practices by conserving water, collecting rainwater, minimizing run-off and contaminants and reducing the use of ground water. The Visitor Center includes an exhibit hall, gift shop, classrooms, offices, outdoor exhibit pavilion, amphitheatre and interpretive trails.

ADDRESS
12861 Galm Road, San Antonio

ARCHITECTS
Lake/Flato

5▲ LEON SPRINGS ELEMENTARY SCHOOL, 1991

Built on the site of an 1890 one-room house, the Northside Independent School District's Leon Springs Elementary School draws from Texas Hill Country architectural motifs. Masonry and wood structures have exterior walls of split-faced masonry block and windows trimmed in a contrasting smooth-faced block and accentuated by ceramic tile medallions. Metal shed roofs and canopies complete the design.

ADDRESS
23881 IH 10 West, San Antonio

ARCHITECTS
Marmon Mok

6▲★ JOE MCMULLAN INSURANCE AGENCY, 1870
(GILL SAVINGS & LOAN, BANDERA BRANCH)

An abandoned nineteenth century historic one-story stone house overlooking a state highway was renovated and adapted as a savings and loan branch office. Twentieth century additions were removed and exterior finishes were restored to their original state.

ADDRESS
285 TX Highway 16 South, Bandera

ARCHITECTS
O'Neill & Perez

SOUTH

The vast brush country of South Texas lies beyond the Medina River and the rolling hills of the Post Oak Belt. Springs, rivers and creeks sustain vegetation and wildlife in an often inhospitable environment. The region was sparsely populated until the late 1800s, when railroads drew increasing numbers of settlers who farmed and ranched. In the early 1900s, shallow oil and natural gas fields and coal and uranium mining diversified the economy. Land leases for hunting later became an important economic generator.

COTULLA

Established in 1882 as a rail stop on the ranch of Polish immigrant Joseph Cotulla, this county seat prospered largely because of the sheep and cattle industry and vegetable farming. Its oldest brick structure is the 1883 Gallman Building. The 1931 Art Deco La Salle County Courthouse was designed by San Antonio architect Henry T. Phelps. Lyndon B. Johnson taught in 1928–29 at Cotulla's Welhausen School (1926), a classically influenced building designed by Austin's Charles Page. The Brush Country Museum is housed in a restored bungalow.

TILDEN AND GEORGE WEST

Tilden and George West are county seats of sparsely-populated McMullen and Live Oak Counties. Tilden, named county seat in 1877, features a small but dignified Classical Revival courthouse designed in 1930 by W.C. Stephenson. The Neoclassical Live Oak County Courthouse (1919) by Alfred Giles is a legacy of the town's founder and namesake, George West, who used his own funds to attract the railroad and construct public buildings, bridges, roads, a waterworks and hotel on his South Texas ranch.

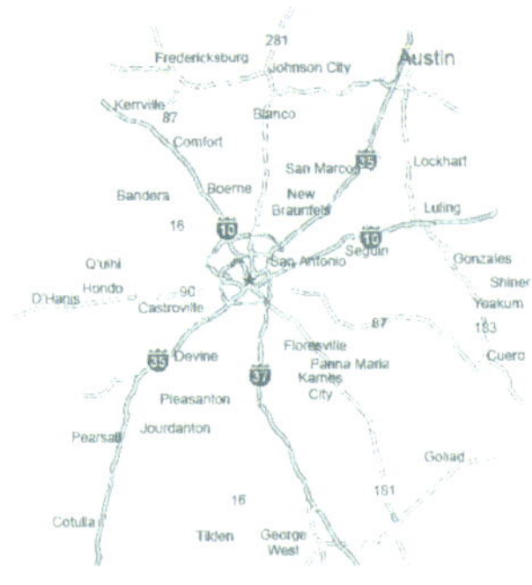

PLEASANTON AND JOURDANTON

Pleasanton, founded in 1858, was the seat of Atascosa County until 1909, when developers promoting irrigated farmland organized Jourdanton, a new railroad town, five miles away. In 1912, Henry T. Phelps's Mission Revival style Courthouse with third-story belvederes was built on a circular lot set in Jourdanton's otherwise regular grid. Phelps also supervised construction of the brick Atascosa County Jail with its crenellated towers (1915). A replica log building across from the courthouse represents the county's first courthouse, built in 1856 in the small town of Navatasco. Other notable buildings in the two towns are Pleasanton's 1874 Rock School House of locally quarried red sandstone (now painted), today part of a church complex, and Jourdanton's Mission Revival style St. Matthew's Catholic Church. The area's best-preserved agricultural complex, the Korus Farmstead, begun by Polish immigrants in the nineteenth century, can be seen on US 281 near the intersection of Farm Road 536. Also nearby is the pre-railroad town of Poteet, its economy largely based on irrigated farming, notably strawberries, celebrated each April at one of the state's oldest and largest agricultural festivals.

EAST

The economy of the Blackland Prairie and Upper Coastal Plain east of San Antonio was based on agriculture and farming, and, later, oil. A network of roads and rail lines connected rural communities to larger cities and shipping points, including San Antonio. Many of these towns have preserved their architectural fabric.

SEGUIN

In the heart of Seguin, thirty-five miles northeast of San Antonio and the seat of Guadalupe County, is the Seguin Commercial Historic District. Its 120 buildings, constructed between 1885 and 1925, are largely

low-rise brick buildings surrounding the WPA-built Art Moderne Courthouse (1935) by W.L. Wirtz and A.W. Harris. Other buildings include J. Riely Gordon's Nolte National Bank (1898), Atlee B. Ayres's Aumont Hotel (1912) and Citizen's State Bank (1905) and Leo M. J. Dielmann's C. E. Tips Building (1890) and Park Hotel (1915). The Greek Revival Zorn House named Sebastopol was built in 1855 of a primitive form of concrete used extensively in this area. The campus of Texas Lutheran University, founded in Brenham in 1891 and moved to Seguin in 1912, is located on the west side of town.

LOCKHART

Lockhart, thirty miles southeast of Austin, established in 1848 and the seat of Caldwell County, is renowned for its barbeque restaurants. Its Second Empire limestone and sandstone courthouse's (1894), designed by Henri E. M. Guindon though often attributed to Alfred Giles, was restored by Ford, Powell & Carson in 2000. The surrounding National Register commercial district is among the best preserved in the state. The Dr. Eugene Clark Library (1899) nearby is one of Texas's oldest continuously operating municipal libraries.

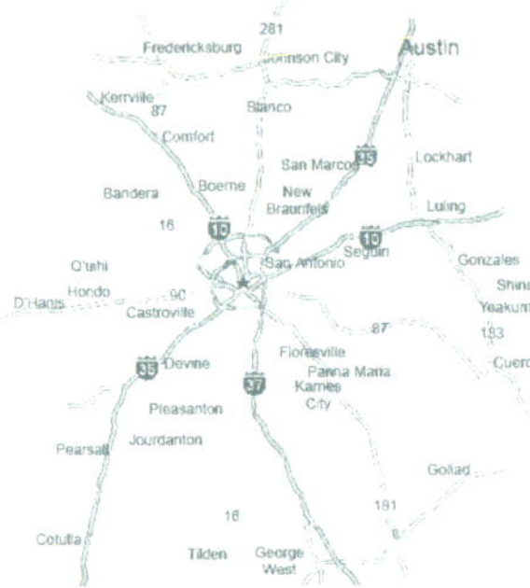

LULING

Luling, established in 1874, is on the San Marcos River fifteen miles south of Lockhart in southern Caldwell County. Originally a riverfront milling community surrounded by rich agricultural lands, it later became known for its oil fields, watermelon crop and fine barbeque. As in many Texas towns, its linear commercial district is bisected by rail lines. One- and two-story brick structures include the Walker Brothers Building (1885), now the Central Texas Oil Patch Museum. At the river crossing on the edge of town, the City of Luling is preserving and redeveloping the Zedler Mill (1875).

GONZALES

Gonzales, seat of Gonzales County, was surveyed in 1825 by Green DeWitt, who laid out a network of squares and boulevards. The fifteen-block National Register Historic District encompasses the original town plan. In the main square is James Riely Gordon's 1894 Romanesque Revival courthouse with its central tower. Also of note are Gordon's Kennard House (1895) with its glass and pottery chip mosaic gable, and the Dilworth House (1907), as well as Atlee B. Ayres's Hoskins and Hopkins houses, both designed in 1911. The site in 1835 of the first skirmish of the Texas Revolution, Gonzales later became a railroad community and shipping center.

SHINER

The agricultural lands surrounding the western Lavaca County railroad town of Shiner, incorporated in 1890, attracted Czech and German immigrants. The town's finest architectural statement is James Wahrenberger's Romanesque Revival Sts. Cyril and Methodius Catholic Church (1921), noted for its imported stained-glass windows and interior painting. Other landmarks are a log cabin (1853), the restored Opera House (1895), Louis Ehler's Cigar Factory (1895) and the 1927 city hall. Shiner is the home of the state's oldest independent brewery, Spoetzl Brewery, founded in 1909.

YOAKUM

Yoakum, settled in the 1830s, was incorporated in 1889 after the arrival of the railroad. A center for the cattle trade, it became known for its leather industry and bills itself the "leather capital of the world." The commercial district contains many fine, intact brick structures. Noteworthy is the former municipal power plant (1931), converted to the public library by Reitzer/Cruz in 1990.

CUERO

Cuero was incorporated in 1875 and the next year was chosen as the seat of De Witt County. Midway between the coastal port of Indianola and San Antonio, Cuero was settled by German immigrants, many of whom moved inland after devastating hurricanes. It thrived because of its rail connections to San Antonio and Houston and became known for its turkey industry. The 1897 Romanesque Revival courthouse by A. O. Watson is its most imposing structure. Cuero's three National Register districts contain a remarkably high number of well preserved, pre-1936 residential and commercial buildings. Among the vernacular buildings are many of Romanesque Revival and Neoclassical design. The work of Victoria architect Jules Leffland is well represented. Designs by San Antonio architects include Atlee B. Ayres's houses for the Hamilton family (1918 and 1939), Beverly Spillman's Cook House (1923) and Fred B. Gaenslen's St. Michael's Catholic Church (1931).

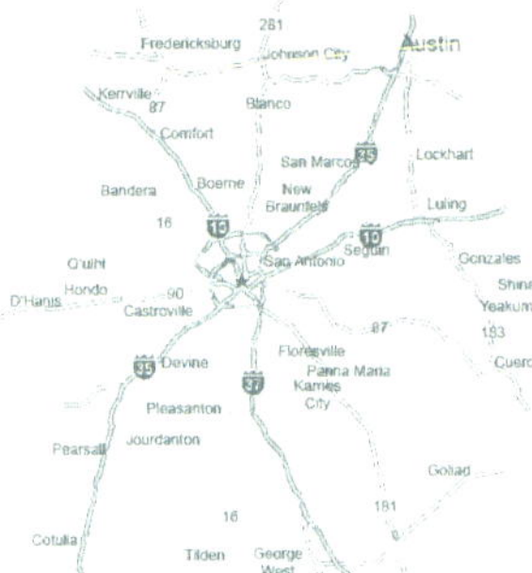

GOLIAD

Goliad, among the state's oldest Spanish colonial municipalities, dates to 1749, when Mission Espiritu Santo and Presidio La Bahia were relocated to their present location on the San Antonio River. Residents played key roles in the fight for Texas independence, and the Goliad Massacre helped galvanize support for the revolutionary cause. Goliad was incorporated and named the county seat during the Republic of Texas period. The dramatic 2003 restoration of Henri E. M. Guindon's limestone Second Empire courthouse (1894) by TWC Architects replaced the missing ornate clocktower and four cupolas, destroyed by a hurricane in 1942. The surrounding Courthouse Square Historic District is one of the most complete in the state. In addition to the mission and presidio, fine Victorian era residences are also found in this Main Street city.

HELENA AND KARNES CITY

Helena, now little more than a ghost town, served as the seat of Karnes County from 1854 until bypassed by the railroad and supplanted by Karnes City in 1894. The old stone courthouse (1873) serves as a museum and the post office, jail, Ruckman House and Sickenius Farmhouse have been restored. The clock tower and turrets of John Cormack's 1894 Karnes County courthouse in Karnes City were removed during remodeling in the 1920s, but plans are being made for the building's restoration.

PANNA MARIA

Panna Maria, which claims to be the nation's oldest permanent Polish settlement, was established in 1854 near the confluence of Cibolo Creek and the San Antonio River, fifty-five miles southeast of San Antonio. The farming community is centered on St. Mary's of the Immaculate Conception Church (1877), a Gothic Revival building with richly painted interior. The adjoining St. Joseph's School (1868) serves as a museum. Stone vernacular residences and mercantile buildings and ruins of other structures are encompassed in the Panna Maria National Register Historic District.

FLORESVILLE

Floresville, thirty miles southeast of San Antonio, was established as the county seat of Wilson County in 1873. Its agricultural economy was based on cattle, cotton and, later, peanuts, leading to Floresville's claim to being the "Peanut Capital of Texas." Alfred Giles' stately Wilson County Courthouse (1884) blends Second Empire and Italianate influences. James Riely Gordon's 1887 Wilson County Jail stands at the northeast corner of the courthouse square. Also facing the square is the Acadia Theatre (1911), restored in 1999.

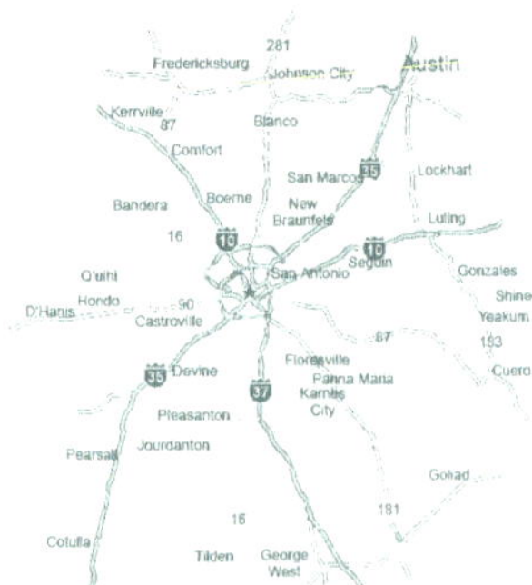

WEST

West of Sán Antonio the Balcones Escarpment divides the northern Edwards Plateau and Hill Country from the southern Rio Grande Plains. The Frio, Medina and Sabinal rivers rise and fall with flood and drought, and Medina Lake, impounded by a dam built in 1913–the fourth largest dam project in the country at the time–provides water to irrigate extensive farmlands. The region's economy remains based on the farming and ranching that drew Polish settlers in the nineteenth century.

BANDERA

Founded in 1856 as the country set of Bandera County, this town on the Medina River was noted for lumber mills, gins and raising of livestock, including sheep and goats. Post-Civil War cattle drives established Bandera's reputation as "the cowboy capital of the world," as the town is still known. The 1890 courthouse, a three-story rusticated Renaissance Revival stone building designed by B.F. Trester, stands in the center of the town square. Two blocks away is Alfred Giles's cut stone one-story jail (1881) with its castellated parapet. Beside that is the previous courthouse, a two-story rubble stone building (Henry White, 1869) now converted to a library. The recently restored St. Stanislaus Church (1876), convent (1874) and school (1922) were built to serve the town's large Polish Catholic community. The Frontier Times Museum showcases the collection of J. Marvin Hunter, whose *Frontier Times* magazine documented the history and achievements of pioneer Texans.

CASTROVILLE

This community on the Medina River was founded by Henri Castro, who brought Alsatian immigrant farmers here in 1844. In the European tradition, Castro divided his sixteen-league tract into small lots surrounded by larger farm plots. Many homes built of stone and stone and timber between 1844 and the 1880s are encompassed in the Castroville Historic District. St. Louis Catholic Church (1870) overlooks the town square,

which is surrounded by one- and two-story commercial structures. The 1879 Medina County Courthouse, sold when the county seat moved to Hondo in 1892 and remodeled in 1936, is used as city offices. The riverfront Landmark Inn complex, including the two-story inn, a house, store and a stone mill structure dating to the 1850s, is operated as a bed-and-breakfast by the Texas Parks and Wildlife Department.

HONDO, QUIHI AND OLD D'HANIS

West of Castroville on Highway 90 is Hondo, the railroad town founded in 1882 and established as the Medina County seat ten years later. Hondo was an economic center for agricultural and ranching operations, and later the site of an Army air field. The 1892 Medina County Courthouse, originally of Italianate design by Martin, Byrnes & Johnston, was altered by removal of its clock tower in 1941 and by addition of wings in 1942. Near Hondo are the historic communities of Quihi (1845) and Old D'Hanis (1848), both settled by Henri Castro's Alsatian colonists. European-style limestone cottages, some in ruins, still stand in Quihi. In Henri Castro's fourth colony, Old D'Hanis, seventeen vernacular structures dating from the mid to late nineteenth century are encompassed by the D'Hanis National Register District. Although many of the structures are in ruins, Old D'Hanis is still a good example of a European colonial village in Texas.

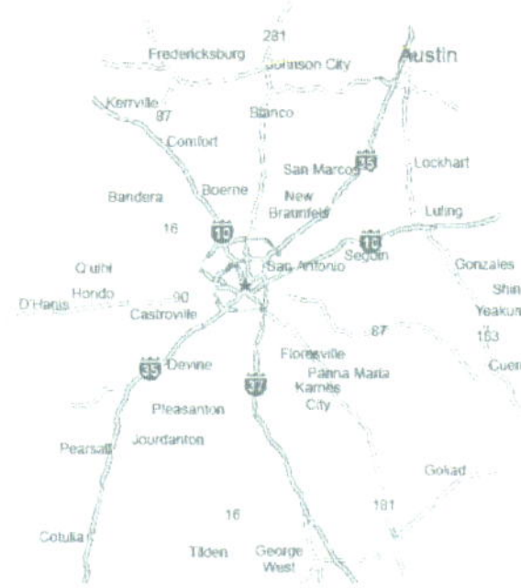

DEVINE

Thirty miles south of San Antonio off IH 35 is Devine, founded as a railroad town in 1881. Completion of Medina Dam in 1913 transformed the surrounding area into irrigated farmlands, producing vegetables and grain to be shipped by rail. Devine's old main street paralleling the rail lines retains turn-of-the-century brick commercial structures, including the Devine Opera House. Other buildings of note include the Driscoll Public Library (1988), housed in a converted brick lumber warehouse, and the limestone St. Joseph's Catholic-Church (1922). The Big Foot Wallace Museum displays pioneer furnishings and memorabilia in replica pioneer buildings.

PEARSALL

Pearsall, the seat of Frio County, is beyond Devine on IH 35 fifty-five miles southwest of San Antonio. Originally part of a sheep ranch, the town was platted in 1882 after the railroad arrived. In 1884 the county seat moved here from Frio Town, eighteen miles away. The P.J. Pauly and Brothers Frio County Jail (1884), reflecting Classical and Italianate influences, is Pearsall's oldest building and serves as a museum. Much of the town was swept by fire in 1890. The 1904 Frio County courthouse by Henry T. Phelps was remodeled in the 1930s and again in 1950. The modest wood-framed Pearsall Presbyterian Church (1885) is the town's oldest church in continuous use.

NORTH

North of San Antonio, the Texas Hill Country rises to the Edwards Plateau. Settlers who braved this rugged terrain in the nineteenth century found ample timber and rock to build homes and mercantile buildings, many of which survive. Picturesque communities smaller than those listed below are also worth a visit. Wimberly, at the convergence of Cypress Creek and the Blanco River, features a collection of specialty shops and lodgings located in nineteenth century buildings. Fischer is noted for its still functioning 1876 general store and a finely crafted wooden dance hall, now a popular location for special events. The renowned Luckenbach

store and dance hall were made famous by the likes of Willie Nelson and Jerry Jeff Walker, and the Twin Sisters dance hall still holds monthly dances.

BOERNE

Boerne, thirty miles northwest of San Antonio, was settled in 1852 and ten years later became the county seat of Kendall County. The Italianate courthouse in the center of town is a hybrid design comprised of Alfred Giles's 1910 façade added to Philip Zoeller and S.F. Stendeback's original structure (1870) and Charles Buckel's second floor (1886).

Other notable buildings include the Dienger Building (1887), now the public library; the Boerne public school (1910) transformed into the City Hall; the city-owned Kulmann-King House (1880s) and Alfred Giles's Boerne High School (1910), now city offices. Overlooking the main plaza is the restored Greek Revival style Ye Kendall Inn (1859, 1878) with its double galleries. Entering Boerne from the south is the original small stone structure for St. Peter's Catholic Church (1867).

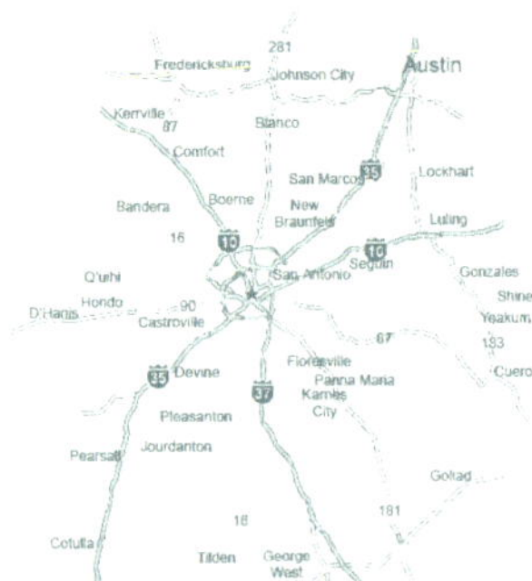

BLANCO

Sixty miles northwest of San Antonio is Blanco, which dates to the 1850s and was the original seat of Blanco County, organized in 1857. An eight-block residential and commercial National Register district surrounds Frederick Ernst Ruffini's Second Empire style courthouse (1885). The courthouse was abandoned 1890 when the county seat moved to Johnson City. After serving a variety of uses, it was renovated in 1998 as a special events' venue. The old Blanco County Jail (1877), Cage Building (1908) and Adrian Conn house (1872) are among the district's notable structures, many of them of native limestone.

COMFORT

Comfort is an especially well preserved German immigrant community. Much of the original settlement is encompassed within a National Register district featuring fachwerk and limestone structures including work of prominent San Antonio architects. The August Faltin building (1879) and Comfort Post Office (1910) are both by Alfred Giles, while the 1916 Schwethelm Building was designed by Lou Harrington.

JOHNSON CITY

Johnson City, on the nineteenth century route between Austin and Fredericksburg, is on land donated by ancestors of President Lyndon Baines Johnson. After the county seat was moved from Blanco in 1890, Henry T. Phelps's Classic Revival courthouse was completed in 1916. The Lyndon B. Johnson National Historical Park chronicles the Johnson family from its settling in the Hill Country through the presidential years. The park encompasses the Johnson settlement and the LBJ Boyhood Home, both in town, and the LBJ Ranch Headquarters complex, fourteen miles to the west. The Sauer-Beckmann Farmstead adjoining LBJ State Park

offers a glimpse of farm life from 1900 to 1918. Also near Johnson City is Stonewall, known for its peach orchards and vineyards.

FREDERICKSBURG

Fredericksburg is perhaps the quintessential Texas German Hill Country community. First settled in 1846 and then consisting largely of log structures, the town evolved into a sophisticated center of German culture and architecture. The town's wide-ranging, carefully preserved inventory of residential and commercial structures reveals log, fachwerk, limestone and brick structures spanning simple vernacular to high Victorian to early twentieth century pattern book design.

Alfred Giles's 1882 Italianate Gillespie County Courthouse, now the public library, stands next to Edward Stein's Moderne 1939 courthouse. Giles's Bank of Fredericksburg (1898) and the White Elephant Saloon (1888) are Main Street landmarks. Leo M. J. Dielmann's Gothic Revival St. Mary's Church (1906) adjoins the 1861 church. The reconstructed unique Vereins-Kirche on Pioneer Square and the Johann Michael Tatsch house (circa 1855), with its massive chimney, are also among the 350 contributing buildings in the Fredericksburg National Register Historic District.

SAN MARCOS

Colonized in 1846, San Marcos was made the county seat of Hays County two years later. The city features substantial brick architecture constructed as the town developed into a commercial center serving the surrounding agricultural and ranching region. Texas State University (formerly Southwest Texas State University) dominates the hill overlooking town. The Beaux-Arts style Hays County courthouse (1908) by C. H. Page & Brothers was restored in 1998 by Ford, Powell and Carson. The Belvin Street Historic District features residential architecture dating from 1878 to 1910, including Carpenter Gothic, Second Empire, Eastlake and Colonial Revival influenced designs.

NEW BRAUNFELS

Less than thirty minutes north of San Antonio, New Braunfels still reflects the strong influence of German settlers who founded the town in 1845. James' Riely Gordon's Romanesque Revival 1899 Comal County Courthouse (restored in 2007 by Volz Architects) overlooks the town square, with its Victorian-influenced bandstand. Some of the state's finest vernacular architecture includes the half-timbered Lindheimer home, one of the oldest structures in New Braunfels, and the fachwerk building housing the Museum of Texas Handmade Furniture. Several blocks from the square, the Sophienburg Museum showcases the area's early history.

KERRVILLE

Kerrville's pioneer settlers were Anglo-Americans and Germans who established a mercantile community here after Kerr County was created in 1856. The town became an important shipping point for surrounding ranches. Wealthy merchants and cattlemen built substantial architect-designed stores and homes, many by San Antonio designers, notably Alfred Giles. Giles's 1885 courthouse was replaced by Adams & Adams's Beaux-Arts building in 1926. Other works by Giles include the Captain Charles Schreiner mansion (1879–95), the Schreiner Store and Bank (1882 and 1893) and the Italianate Masonic Building (1890).

09

The architecture of the city is a process of evolution involving the overlapping ideas and influences of those architects who practice here. Following are brief profiles of twelve architects whose careers have been influential in shaping the architecture of San Antonio.

FRANCOIS PIERRE GIRAUD, 1818-1877

Giraud was a cosmopolitan gentleman who was enveloped by and no doubt contributed to San Antonio's international flair. He was born in Charleston, South Carolina, to French parents who sent him to Mt. St. Mary's College prep school in Maryland from 1830 to 1834. He later returned there to teach chemistry from 1842 to 1847.

He was trained as a metallurgy engineer at the *Ecole Centrale des Arts et Manufactures* in Paris, graduating in 1842. Giraud came to Texas in 1847, and by 1848 was the first city surveyor of San Antonio. While he worked on the first buildings at the Ursuline Academy, he surveyed the grounds of the five old Spanish missions, and helped the Catholic Church establish its claim to their ownership. In 1852 he persuaded the city to preserve San Pedro Springs as a city park.

During the Civil War, Giraud served as a Confederate captain of engineers, assigned as chief engineer of defenses at Galveston in 1865. He returned to work on Ursuline Academy in 1866, and begun construction of the new San Fernando Cathedral in 1868.

As soon as Reconstruction ended in Texas, Giraud was able to hold public office and served as mayor of San Antonio from 1872 to retirement in 1875.

ALFRED GILES, 1853-1920

Born the son of a wealthy Englishman, Alfred Giles apprenticed in London and attended night courses at the University of London. He came to San Antonio in 1873 and worked for a master builder John H. Kampmann, who taught him the characteristics of local building materials.

By 1875 Giles had his own office, booming with San Antonio after the arrival of railroad from Houston. He married Annie Laurie James in 1881 and had eight children; two sons later practiced architecture in his office. After his mother's death in 1885 in London, Giles retired briefly to England with his family. He soon sold his holdings there and returned to Texas in 1886.

That year Giles and his wife's family acquired several thousand acres of hill country west of San Antonio near Comfort. Giles was content to develop the livestock ranch and pursue choice architectural commissions by lengthy commute, rather than regain what had been the foremost practice in San Antonio.

When railroads opened Mexico to the 20th century, Giles opened a branch office in Monterrey. He produced numerous public buildings throughout Mexico before the 1914 revolution.

Giles died at his ranch while still actively heading the Alfred Giles Company in San Antonio.

JAMES WAHRENBERGER, 1855-1929

A native Texas born in Austin, Wahrenberger was an early beneficiary of a European education. He was first sent at age 14 to Philadelphia to study at West Pennsylvania Academy, then in 1872 he journeyed to Zurich, Switzerland, to study mathematics. At Karlsruhe, Germany, he concentrated for three years on architecture at the Polytechnic Institute.

After an extended tour of Europe, Wahrenberger returned to Austin.

Wahrenberger's proposal in 1881 for the new state capitol was judged second place. In 1882 he opened a practice in San Antonio with Albert Felix Beckman (1855-1900), who had also been educated in Germany. They acted as local architects for the St. Louis firm of E. Jugenfeld and Co. for the erection of the Lone Star Brewery.

A subsequent second-place award, for the Bexar County Courthouse in 1891, perhaps kept Wahrenberger from entering the mainstream of a statewide practice. He maintained his Austin contacts, designing a Victorian fantasy home there in 1893 for George Washington Littlefield–rival of San Antonio's own G.W. Brackenridge.

Wahrenberger received several noteworthy commissions from Catholic groups at the turn of the century. He attained an elder statesman role in the San Antonio architecture community before his death at age 74.

JAMES RIELY GORDON, 1864-1937

Born in Virginia, Gordon moved to San Antonio with his railroad engineer father and family in the early 1870s. At age 16 he worked in a railroad engineering office, and then apprenticed to architect Wesley Clark Dodson in 1882. The next year he moved to Washington, D.C., to work for the architect of treasury.

Gordon returned to San Antonio in 1887, initially supervising the construction of a massive new Romanesque Revival Post Office and Federal Building on Alamo Plaza. The Texas courthouse law of 1881–allowing counties to sell bonds for new courthouses–had created a healthy but competitive climate for architects in the state, and Gordon joined the bandwagon by 1890.

Italiante and Second Empire temples had been early favorites among county commissioners, but Gordon introduced massive Romanesque models. His standard design replaced the dainty pressed-metal cupola with a bearing-wall masonry tower, signaling drastic changes in the spatial plan beneath. Gordon's plan spun around the tower's hollow core, which acted as a circulation chimney and stair well.

Gordon designed the award-winning Texas Pavilion at the 1893 Chicago World's Fair, and the 1900 Arizona Territorial Capitol at Phoenix. He moved his practice to New York in 1904.

ATLEE B. AYRES, 1874-1969
ROBERT M. AYRES, 1898-1977

Atlee B. Ayres arrived in San Antonio with his parents in 1880, and was to have lasting impact upon the architecture of the city for the first half of the 20th century. After attending courses at the Art Students League and the Metropolitan School of Art in New York City, Ayres returned to San Antonio and entered into a partnership with C.A. Coughlin that lasted until Coughlin's death in 1905. In the next 15 years, the elder Ayres designed numerous residences, including those for Alex Halff and the now-demolished villa for Col. George W. Brackenridge. Large-scale commissions from this period include First Presbyterian Church and the Heimann Building.

The 1920s brought two major changes: the establishment in 1922 of the firm of Atlee B. & Robert M. Ayres, Architects, and the adoption of the Spanish Colonial Revival style by Atlee as his favorite method of Architectural expression. The superb residences for Thomas Hogg, Carl Newton, and Dr. Donald Atkinson captured the romantic image of the city's Spanish Colonial past. Robert M. Ayres, fresh from the architecture program at the University of Pennsylvania, was soon given major design responsibility, the most noted design being the octagonal Smith-Young Tower of 1929, which was to house the firm's offices on its 30th floor. Robert was also responsible for the design of the city's grandest private home, "Oak Court," for H. Lutcher Brown in 1935.

The Firm's range of work was enormous, encompassing such diverse products as the former Federal Reserve Bank and the spectacular Administration Building at Randolph Field.

GEORGE WILLIS, 1879-1960

Born in Chicago, George Willis arrived in San Antonio in 1910 with one of the best architectural educations obtainable at that time. He had studied at the Armour Institute, and from 1898 to 1902 was a member of Frank Lloyd Wright's studio, the latter training showing clearly in his early San Antonio commissions. The houses he designed for L.T. Wright at 342 Wilkins Avenue and Dr. Lemma Young at 828 Cambridge Oval are some of the finest Wrightian works in Texas. The Wright house, built in 1917, was Willis' first work upon leaving the office of Atlee B. Ayres. In the 1920s, Willis obtained other significant commissions, including the Milam Building and the San Antonio Country Club, the latter no longer standing. He was associated with Emmett T. Jackson on the design of the Builder's Exchange. Willis was also an associate along with Jackson and Atlee B. Ayres and Robert M. Ayres on the design of the San Antonio Municipal Auditorium of 1926. Willis maintained an office in the Smith-Young Tower until the time of his death in 1960, but his architectural output seems to have diminished significantly following the Second World War.

RALPH CAMERON, 1892-1970

A native San Antonian, Ralph H. Cameron received at least part of his architectural training in Paris before he returned to San Antonio in 1912. He worked for the firm of Adams & Adams for two years before setting up his own practice. Within two years of opening his own office, Cameron had achieved considerable success, serving as associate architect with Herbert Green on the design of the Scottish Rite Temple. Two years later Cameron received his most noted commission, that for the Medical Arts Building, now the Emily Morgan Motel, famed for its ornate terra-cotta ornament in the Gothic Style. He was also adept in residential design, as the delightful residence, as the delightful residence of F. E. Hornaday at 101 East Kings Highway clearly attests. Cameron was very active in the American Institute of Architects, and played a key role in the holding of the organization's 1932 national convention in San Antonio. He was also a founding member of the Texas Society of Architects.

O'NEIL FORD, FAIA 1905-1982

Otha Neil Ford personified the proverbial poor-boy-to-success-story. From an humble birth in north-central Texas, he aspired to higher education and studied architecture by correspondence course. In 1926 he went to work for David R. Williams in Dallas, designing residences with a composite of regional characteristics. He and Williams drove hither and yon to supervise their work and observe historic Texas architecture *in situ*.

During the 1930s Williams helped Ford secure the 1939 federal commission for the La Villita restoration in San Antonio.

After wartime service, Ford resumed practice in San Antonio and begun work on Trinity University with Bartlett Cocke and Harvey Smith in 1949. He designed a series of innovative facilities for the burgeoning Texas Instruments Company beginning in 1954. In the meantime he became a flamboyant lecturer on architecture and life, and achieved Fellowship in the AIA by 1960.

Ford formed a partnership with Boone Powell and Chris Carson in 1967, and together they designed numerous facilities at HemisFair '68. In the intervening years, the firm's work reflected Ford's penchant for regionally sensitive design. He died one year after the establishment of the O'Neil Ford Chair in Architecture at the University of Texas at Austin.

BARTLETT COCKE, FAIA (1901-1992)

Bartlett Cocke, FAIA, exemplified the consummate architectural professional in his practice and personal life. A product of both the University of Texas and the School of Architecture at MIT, he partnered with Marvin Eickenroht in 1927 and began his own firm in 1931.

Cocke's work with the Kelwood Company and the Historic American Buildings Survey during the Depression provided a foundation for a thriving prewar residential practice, with houses in San Antonio attracting national notice. His first breakout commission came in 1938 to design a distinctive expansion for Joske's of Texas in downtown San Antonio, creating at the time "the largest store in the largest state".

With Trinity University, Cocke established a long association with O'Neil Ford. Joint-ventured, they produced the master plan and all buildings for the campus of Trinity University from 1950-1981, and buildings for the University of Texas at San Antonio during the 1970s. It was said that though neither he nor O'Neil would admit it, they were a perfect team, combining Cocke's wonderful stability, mental toughness and business acumen with O'Neil's personality, creativity, bravado and courage.

He served as president of the San Antonio chapter AIA in 1940, the Texas Society of Architects in 1944, and the Texas Board of Architectural Examiners in 1950. He received numerous honors, from his election to the AIA College of Fellows in 1961, the Llewelyn W. Pitts Award in 1981, and was the first alumnus honored with an architecture professorship in his name at UT-Austin. He retired from practice in 1981.

DAVID LAKE, FAIA 1951 –
TED FLATO, FAIA 1955 –

David Lake and Ted Flato, both native Texans, established their practice in 1984 after working together at Ford, Powell & Carson. Lake was born in Austin and graduated from the University of Texas there in 1976. Flato, born in Corpus Christi, received his architecture degree from Stanford University in 1977. Since its founding, Lake/Flato has gained national recognition for architecture that is rooted to

its place and successfully merged with the landscape. Lake honed his commitment to sustainable design principles while building modern solar sodbuster houses in the Texas Panhandle. As a student, Flato worked summers for O'Neil Ford's former partner Richard Colley, known for innovative structural solutions and site- and climate-sensitive designs. Lake's work merges regional and environmental design aesthetics in site-sensitive architecture that acknowledges historic precedent and incorporates innovative technologies. Complementing this is Flato's appreciation of the pragmatism of vernacular architecture, honesty of modernism and context of the rich and varied landscape. His straightforward regional designs incorporate indigenous building forms and materials that are sensitive to the climate. These approaches are reflected in the firm's design process, guided by six principles based on land, light, craft, community, spaces between and sustainability. Both have been made Fellows of the AIA, Lake in 1995 and Flato in 1997. The firm's regional and national architecture awards include AIA Honor Awards in 1992, 1997, 1999 and 2007 and the national AIA Firm of the Year Award in 2004.

SELECTED BIBLIOGRAPHY

Barna, Joel Warren. *The See-Through Years: Creation and Destruction in Texas Architecture and Real Estate, 1981–1991.* Houston: Rice University Press, 1992.

Bexar County Historical Commission. *A Guide to the Historical Markers of Bexar County.* San Antonio: Bexar County Historical Commission, 2001.

Cagle, Eldon. *Fort Sam: The Story of Fort Sam Houston, Texas.* San Antonio: Maverick Publishing Co., 2003.

Carson, Chris, and William McDonald, eds. *A Guide to San Antonio Architecture.* San Antonio: The San Antonio Chapter of the American Institute of Architects, 1986.

Coote, Robert James. *The Eclectic Odyssey of Atlee B. Ayres, Architect.* College Station: Texas A&M University Press, 2001.

Dillon, David. *The Architecture of O'Neil Ford: Celebrating Place.* Austin: University of Texas Press, 1999.

Everett, Donald E. *San Antonio's Monte Vista: Architecture and Society in a Gilded Age.* San Antonio: Maverick Publishing Co., 1999.

Fisher, Lewis F. *River Walk: The Epic Story of San Antonio's River.* San Antonio: Maverick Publishing Co., 2007.

______. *Saving San Antonio: The Precarious Preservation of a Heritage.* Lubbock: Texas Tech University Press, 1996.

______. *The Spanish Missions of San Antonio.* San Antonio: Maverick Publishing Co., 1998.

George, Mary Carolyn Hollers. *The Architectural Legacy of Alfred Giles: Selected Restorations.* San Antonio: Trinity University Press, 2006.

______. *O'Neil Ford, Architect.* College Station: Texas A&M University Press, 1992.

Henry, Jay C. *Architecture in Texas, 1895–1945.* Austin: University of Texas Press, 1993.

Heusinger, Edward W. *A Chronology of Events in San Antonio.* San Antonio: Standard Printing Co., 1951.

Jutson, Mary Carolyn Hollers. *Alfred Giles: An English Architect in Texas and Mexico.* San Antonio: Trinity University Press, 1972.

Mullen, Robert J. *Architecture and Its Sculpture in Viceregal Mexico.* Austin: University of Texas Press, 1997.

Steinfeldt, Cecelia. *San Antonio Was: Seen Through a Magic Lantern.* San Antonio: San Antonio Museum Association, 1978.

Quirarte, Jacinto. *The Art and Architecture of the Texas Missions.* Austin: University of Texas Press, 2002.

Tyler, Ron. *The New Handbook of Texas.* 6 vols. Austin: Texas State Historical Association, 1996.

SELECTED WEB SITES

Bexar County Historical Commission, Historical Markers, www.co.bexar.tx.us/historic/

National Register of Historic Places–San Antonio, www.nationalregisterofhistoricplaces.com/tx/Bexar/state.html

Texas Historical Commission, Historical Designations, www.thc.state.tx.us/markerdesigs/maddes.html

Texas State Historical Association, The Handbook of Texas Online, www.tsha.utexas.edu/handbook/online/index.html

PROFESSIONAL PHOTOGRAPHY CREDITS

Other than Craig D. Blackmon, FAIA, photography in this book was by:

Peter Aaron/Esto—Northrup Hall.

Architect-provided—Acacia House, Geibel House, Holy Trinity Catholic Church, 100 West Olmos Drive, St. Francis of Assisi Catholic Church.

Brent Bates—Harris Corporation Employee Breakroom

Paul Bardagjy—Clear Channel Communications Headquarters, Promontory Pointe Pool Pavilion.

Leigh Christian—Hill Country Jacal.

Chris Cooper Photography—AT&T Center, Casa 218, Friends Meeting House, Government Canyon Visitor's Center, SBC Center, Triple-S Steel, 222 Austin Highway.

D. Clarke Evans—Wolff Municipal Stadium, St. Philip's College.

Julius Gribou—Alamo Stadium, Arsenal House, Aurora Apartments, Avance Headquarters, Bath Houses, Bennett Building, Bexar County Justice Center, Brackenridge Colored School Annex, Brady Building, Brooks Field Hangar 9, Castillo Home, Christ Episcopal Church, Dignowity House, Ed Friedrich House, Edward H. White II Museum, Emil Elmendorf House, Empire Theater, *Express-News* Building, First National Bank, Frank Murchison Tower, Frost Motor Bank, Galleria Nord, Gardendale Elementary School, Guenther House (p. 99), Heimann Building, HemisFair Plaza, Hertzberg Clock, I&GN Depot, I&GN Hotel, International Center, Brackenridge Park Iron Bridge, Japanese Tea Garden (p. 226), Smith Elementary School, Joske Pavilion, Woods Community Complex, Magazine Building, Main Library, Margarite B. Parker Chapel, Mission Espada Dam and Aqueduct, Mission San José, City Federal Credit Union, Nix Professional Building, O. Henry House, Old Ursuline Academy, Pedestrian Bridge, Pioneer Hall, Public School No. 15, Ruth Taylor Theater, Central Library, San Antonio Loan and Trust Building, San Pedro Branch Library, San Pedro Playhouse, 700 Block of North Olive Street, Slimp House/Lodge, Southwest School of Art & Craft, St. Gerard's Parish Complex, St. John's Lutheran Church, St. Mark's Episcopal Church, St. Paul Methodist Episcopal Church, St. Philip's College, Stable Building, Stevens Building, Stinson Municipal Airport, Sunken Garden, The Spire, Voss Metal Works, Woman's Club.

Robert G. Hanley—Brooks House, Center for Foods of the Americas, Engleman–Muench House, Ernst Homestead, La Quinta Apartments, Paragon Cable Headquarters, Pearl Stable, Ruble Center, Schulze-Schilo House, Thiele House, Time Warner Cable, Willow Way.

Sue Anne Pemberton-Haugh—Arsenal Commander's House, Band Barracks, Brooke General Hospital, Fort Sam Captains' Quarters, Fort Sam Commander's House, Dorothy Pickett Academy, Eisenhower House, Fort Sam Field Officers' Quarters, Fort Sam Housing Units, Fort Sam Long Barracks, Fort Sam Theatre, Gift Chapel, Fannin Elementary School, Pershing House, Stillwell House, Quadrangle.

Hester + **Hardaway—**Blue Star Lofts, Carver Academy, Churchill Baptist Church, Dog Team Too Loft & Studio, Great Northwest Library, H-E-B Science Treehouse, Henry Guerra Branch Library, Holt Corporate Headquarters, International Center, Kel-Lac Transit Center, Kich House, Methodist Healthcare Ministries Headquarters, Pace House, Portal San Fernando, Rangel Housing, Witte Memorial Museum.

Lars Hundere—Jump Start Performance Company, Presidio Plaza.

R. Greg Hursley—Alamo Heights Pool Shade Structure, Alamodome, Alice P. McDermott Building, Cancer Therapy and Research Institute, City of Alamo Heights Swimming Pool, Coates University Center, Cornerstone Church, Incarnate Word Long-Term Care Facility, Southern Pacific Railroad Depot, St. Pius X Catholic Church Family Center, Sunset Depot, Sunset Ridge Shopping Center.

Owner-provided—Lucifer Lighting, UTSA.

Chuck Williams—National Bank of Commerce Boerne.

Patrick Y. Wong, Associate AIA—South Texas Blood and Tissue Center.

INDEX OF ARCHITECTURE

INDEX OF ARCHITECTS

FIELD NOTES